Please return / renew by date shown.
You can renew at: **norlink.norfolk.gov.uk**
or by telephone: **0344 800 8006**
Please have your library card & PIN ready.

Teac 25/1/22

NORFOLK LIBRARY
AND INFORMATION SERVICE

NORFOLK ITEM

30129 070 061 016

D1354505

Teaching Music Through Composition

A CURRICULUM USING TECHNOLOGY

Barbara Freedman

OXFORD
UNIVERSITY PRESS

Oxford University Press is a department of the University of Oxford. It furthers the University's objective of excellence in research, scholarship, and education by publishing worldwide. Oxford is a registered trade mark of Oxford University Press in the UK and in certain other countries

Published in the United States of America by
Oxford University Press
198 Madison Avenue, New York, NY 10016, United States of America

Library of Congress Cataloging-in-Publication Data

Freedman, Barbara.
Teaching music through composition: a curriculum using technology / Barbara Freedman.
    p.   cm.
Includes bibliographical references and index.
ISBN 978-0-19-984061-8 (alk. paper) — ISBN 978-0-19-984062-5 (alk. paper) 1. Music—Instruction and study—Technological innovations. 2. Music—Computer-assisted instruction. 3. Composition (Music)—21st century. 4. Music and technology.   I. Title.
MT1.F76 2013
780.71—dc23   2012011009

1   3   5   7   9   8   4   6   2

Printed in the United States of America on acid free paper

To my students, who have inspired me every day to learn more to be
a better teacher, a better musician, and a better human being.

To the brave music teachers who dedicate themselves to "the other 80 percent"
and pave the way for their students to learn nontraditional music in a nontraditional
environment. Someday soon, ours will be the norm.

Preface

In today's world of music education, old-fashioned, lecture-based music appreciation and general music classes lack relevance for students and, frankly, just don't cut it anymore. Music history classes certainly have their place, especially at the college level. However, college students would clamor to register for music classes that offered them an opportunity to create their own music. Regardless of prior music education, or lack of thereof, students have access to sophisticated music software, which is either free or inexpensive, and they are already composing their own music. All students can have meaningful hands-on applied learning experiences that will impact not only their music experience and learning but also their understanding and comfort with twenty-first-century technology. Technology allows a musical experience for all skill levels—an opportunity, never before available, to compose, manipulate, save, instantly listen to music electronically, and even print standard Western music notation for others to play without having to know much about traditional music theory or notation. We are now faced with a new challenge in music education: how to reprioritize what skills need to be taught in order to foster music composition, given the available music technology. As music educators, we understand that there is and always will be a need to teach students the basic elements of music and music composition if our students are to create sophisticated music. The question is what are the *necessary* skills and how do we best deliver them, given the technology available? This text focuses on teaching students basic music concepts and compositional techniques and has students demonstrate those skills through creating music. Whether the primary focus of your class is to use technology to create music or to explore using technology as a unit or two, this book will show you how it can be done with practical, tried-and-true lesson plans, student assignments, projects, worksheets, and exercises.

This book is the culmination of 11 years of teaching high school music technology, electronic music, and audio engineering. Although the book is organized into several parts that generally follow a sequence, you should feel free to apply these materials to the needs and preferences of your classroom. The lesson plans are organized in units of study and are geared toward understanding specific elements of music or compositional techniques. The projects stretch students to demonstrate a culmination of learning and engage them in new challenges while giving them the freedom to express and create. The intention is to teach students about music through composition, and the focus is on more contemporary music styles, as that is what most young people are interested in. The idea here is to grab them with what they like and enjoy and then slip in what they need! Melody is melody, and harmony is harmony. The principles of music theory, structure, and form are the same whether you are using an electric guitar, synthesizer, trumpet, violin, or voice and applying it to music of living composers or the dead ones. As Howard Goodall says in the 2006 documentary *How Music Works*,

> Whatever type of music you are into, it may surprise you to learn that the things that sound very different to each other on the surface are, in fact, using the same basic musi-

cal tools and techniques. Looking at the mechanics of a beautiful tune, a sweet chord or a hot driving rhythm is a gratifyingly democratic process. When you analyze the nuts and bolts of music you find that the apparent differences between musical cultures, between Eastern and Western, between folk and jazz, or between classical and pop, start to melt away. The underlying techniques and tricks of good music can be and are applied to virtually any and every style. (Opening statement; part 1 of the documentary series *Melody*)

In addition to creating musicians and composers, music teachers create critical listeners, critical thinkers, and critical evaluators of music by conveying an understanding of the elements of music (melody, harmony, rhythm, form, and expression) and teaching students how to speak about these distinctions. In the end, we help to create more sophisticated human beings.

According to research collected by Nathan Edwards and the work of Rick Dammers and Dave Williams, reported on the website http://musiccreativity.org, fewer than 20 percent of secondary students participate in traditional performance-based ensembles—band, orchestra, or chorus—in secondary schools in the United States. A strong movement is afoot in the nation and around the world to serve the "other 80 percent" with meaningful, applied music learning using technology. Rick Dammers comments on the website that "developments in music technology offer the opportunity to establish a new strand of music classes in middle and high schools to stand alongside existing bands, orchestras, and choirs. This new branch of music classes is needed to bolster efforts to reach the 'other 80%' of students who do not participate in performance-based classes."

Music technology is not a wave of the future. It's here. It's in almost everything we do. Listen around you. If you hear something via a speaker or headphones, anything that was produced or re-created using electricity, someone had to study what we teach in music technology class for it to be produced. Using technology to teach music is fun, engaging, and cutting edge, it teaches twenty-first-century and critical listening skills, and it's been around for a long time. My school has had music technology classes continually since 1969! Again, it's here. It's here to stay, and schools around the world, elementary through university, use technology to teach music more than ever before. Are you ready to jump on board?

If we retain our present monolithic concentration on bands, orchestras, and choruses as the major ways to offer special musical opportunities, and if we continue to concentrate on performance-focused methodologies as the major way to provide general music education, then we may find ourselves left in history's dust. (Bennett Reimer, "Music Education as Aesthetic Education: Toward the Future," *Music Education Journal,* March 1989, p. 28)

Acknowledgments

I am forever grateful to my partner, Yelena, my parents and family, and the entire "gantze mishpochah" for your support and encouragement and for understanding when I just couldn't attend!

No words can adequately thank my editor at Oxford University Press, Norm Hirschy, for believing in me and in what so many of us do for our students through music technology and for his vision to have us share it with the world.

Thank you Oxford University Press for elevating and legitimizing our passion for teaching music with technology by producing a series of books for the educator and musician.

Many thanks go to my colleagues, including Scott Watson and Jim Frankel, for their expertise, support, and encouragement. Without these and many other dedicated and brave colleagues who had the vision and spent countless hours learning and fixing (!) technology and then enthusiastically sharing their knowledge with the rest of us, we would not be able to integrate it into so many aspects of music education. Thanks to all of you for the many frustrating days and sleepless nights.

Thank you to my friend Edith "Ish" Bicknell for your unique expertise and perspective as a musician, composer, educator, and professional editor. This book would not have been possible without your early and ongoing advice and guidance.

I am deeply grateful to music teacher Ann Modugno and the Greenwich Public Schools for having the vision to establish one of the first music technology classes in the country in 1969. It was years of continuous support and enthusiasm from students, parents, teachers, and administrators that brought us to today's music technology programs in the Greenwich Public Schools.

The graphics for the Piano Supplemental Material, on pages 285–291, were created by Phillip Lohmeyer. All other graphics were created by Barbara Freedman except where otherwise noted.

Contents

About the Companion Website

A companion website has been created for this book and can be accessed at

www.oup.com/us/teachingmusicthroughcomposition

The website contains all of the student assignment sheets, handouts, worksheets, overhead sheets, and other resource materials referenced in the lessons, including video, audio, and MIDI files. It also contains all the piano supplemental material, including the fingering charts and piano video demonstrations. All are marked in the text by the icons 🎵 and 💻.

Teachers can download these resources, distribute them to students, and project them for classroom viewing and use.

Access the website using username Music5 and password Book1745.

Introduction

Teach Music; The Technology Will Follow

No matter what your skill level in technology, you already have the most important skills to teach composition. You are a musician and probably a highly skilled one. Remember, we are music educators, and we teach, first and foremost, music. In my first few years of teaching, especially working with a new and very advanced piece of software, Apple's Logic Studio, students would ask me how to do some of the craziest, most complicated things that the software could do. (Regardless of what it could sound like, they wanted to turn it upside down, backward, inside out and, oh yeah, make it stand on it's head!) I had no idea. But you know the saying: "If you want to know something about technology, ask a 10-year-old." I showed my students the manual and told them, "You learn it, teach it to me, and I'll buy you a High School Special" (a lunch special offered by a local food establishment—deep-fried chicken nuggets with French fries and a soda, a $5 "power" lunch for the teenager). I went through a lot of Specials those first two years! I learned the intricacies of the software, some of which we never used again; they learned that often simple is better; and they also learned valuable research and self-teaching skills. Kids love showing up their teachers, too. I took many courses, went to conferences, read books, asked questions of colleagues in my personal learning network, used online video tutorials free and paid, and of course, asked a student. Today, if you want to learn something about a piece of software, take a course, read a book, look it up on the Internet, or ask a kid!

The curriculum objective of this book is to teach basic musical concepts through the creative process of music composition. The lessons and projects presented here are resources through which learning music can be accomplished. The tool with which students create, edit, save, and reproduce music is the technology. The tool must not hinder the learning or creative process but must enhance it. Understanding how to use the tool and the ease with which one does so helps the creative process. This book will not teach you how to use a specific piece of software. It is intended to teach musical and technical concepts that can be applied to any software. If you need to learn a piece of software, do the student assignments using that software and refer to any number of available resources to learn the tasks necessary to complete the assignments. Check your software manufacturer's website for free tutorials and forums. Paid video tutorials for many music software titles can be found at www.macprovideo.com and www.lynda.com.

Fortunately, the entry-level software programs that can be used for many of the exercises and projects in this book are either free or inexpensive and can be learned in just a few hours. If you keep your focus on teaching music and learn what you need about the technology to teach and convey a musical concept, then learning the technology will not be overwhelming. Teach music. The technology will follow.

How to Use This Book

The material in this book is presented in an order designed to give students cumulative knowledge to complete compositions and projects and to give them musical tools to create increasingly more sophisticated music. However, teachers should feel free to use whatever material in whatever order they wish, modifying content as needed to suit their students' needs, their teaching style, and the genre focus of the class or unit.

Each chapter represents a teaching unit. Units contain related lesson plans, student assignment sheets, worksheets, handouts, and overhead sheets. Overhead sheets are digital files to be viewed by the entire class while the teacher refers to the file. This can be done with an old-fashioned transparency and overhead projector or via the teacher's computer or iPad using a projector or network management software such as Remote Desktop (Mac) or an interactive whiteboard (IWB) such as a Smartboard or Promethean. Overhead sheets, student assignment sheets, MIDI and audio files, and other digital files are located on the companion website. Some of the digital files are in a format that teachers can edit to accommodate their students' needs or teaching styles. Worksheets are provided as a tool for engaging students. Given that the materials in this book are to be used in a digital environment, it is recommended that teachers explore using as many resources as they can. Online video instruction about using the specific software is available through the manufacturer, third-party user sites, or YouTube. Materials for learning technical concepts unique to music in a digital environment, for example the use of plug-ins in mixing and mastering, can also be obtained online. Teachers should also consider using additional resources for teaching music, including computer-assisted instructional (CAI) software for music theory, appropriate to the students' level, for example Practica Musica by Ars Nova, Essentials of Music Theory by Alfred Music Publishing, and Musician and Auralia by Sibelius/Avid. Online sites that are free or fee based include:

> www.musictheory.net
> www.dolmetsch.com/theoryintro.htm
> www.aboutmusictheory.com
> www.teoria.com, http://music-theory.com
> www.emusictheory.com

An excellent resource for younger learners or those with special needs that require functional age-appropriate learning differentiation include Music Ace and the free website of Alabama music teacher Karen Garrett, www.musictechteacher.com. These resources can be used in the classroom and for supplemental materials at home.

This book has several lessons that focus on basic music concepts and music theory. The purpose of the multitude of exercises and drills presented in these lessons is to provide a means for students to "practice" their craft of music composition on their "instrument" of technology much as any musician would practice his or her instrument. There must be a balance of time in each class to present new material, to practice newly learned material, and to create with the skills obtained. The use of technology is only as fun and engaging as the teacher allows it to be. Boring lessons and material will always be boring even with the most sophisticated technology. Know what material is going to be somewhat dry but necessary and gauge your students' tolerance. Practicing a little each day over time will be more beneficial in the long run than long assignments completed in one or two days. Warn your students that the material may be tedious and remind them that the exercises are meant to teach them a very necessary skill that they can apply to their own music. Kids' tolerance for "boring" increases if they know the purpose and have an end in sight!

When one is practicing an instrument, a practice session will have several components, including a warmup, playing scales and arpeggios, learning and practicing new techniques via technical studies, and work on larger pieces for musical expression and growth. A typical class session should have many of these elements, with some days focusing more on one or the other, depending on the students' learning needs. It is suggested that the teacher not spend entire class sessions teaching and reviewing music theory if at all possible. Students do best when engaged with the composition and creative process as much as possible. A typical 50-minute class session for students, past the introductory material, can be structured as follows:

5–7 minutes: piano practice.
5–7 minutes: dictations, theory work, or other warmup, or 15–20 minutes of lesson or review.
20–40 minutes: student work.

This book has a great deal of material—far too much for any teacher to cover in one or even two semesters. However, it is not exhaustive. There are many more things teachers can do and many different ways to present the musical, compositional, and technological concepts addressed here. This book is just one way. It is a place for many teachers to begin or, for some, a resource for new material in their already established classrooms. You are encouraged to use the lessons that work for you and your students, change lessons, and jump around the book to suite your needs. The book is intended to help those new to teaching music with computers and to be a springboard for creating new lessons and projects specific to your students' needs. College professors can use this book as a method for teaching music to nonmusic majors, for teaching basic composition to music majors, or as a text for music education majors demonstrating a curriculum for teaching music with technology.

Suggested Uses of This Book for Various Courses

BASIC INTRODUCTION TO MUSIC FOR SECONDARY AND COLLEGE STUDENTS
Units 1–8 (approximately 25 50-minute class sessions)

LEVEL 2 FOR STUDENTS WITH NO PREVIOUS KNOWLEDGE OF MUSIC
Units 9–21

SONGWRITING COURSE
Units 1–8: Basic Introduction
Unit 10: Basic Music Theory (3–4 class sessions)
Unit 12 (optional): More Rhythms (1–2 class sessions)

Unit 13 (optional): Dictations
Unit 14–18 (10–12 class sessions)
Unit 19–21 (14–15 class sessions)

Projects in Music Technology
Units 1–8: Basic Introduction
Unit 9: The Sound FX Piece (3–5 class sessions)
Unit 11: MIDI Remix (3–5 class sessions)
Unit 17: The Ringtone Project (2–3 class sessions)
Unit 24: The Art Project (3–5 class sessions)
Unit 25: The Speech Project (3–5 class sessions each)
Unit 26: The Radio Commercial Project and The Podcast (3–5 class sessions each)
Unit 27: Aural Reporting

Resources for Elementary and Early Childhood Education with Technology

This book is intended to offer materials to teach students in grades 6 through college. Of course, many of the concepts can be taught to younger students. Any teacher should feel free to re-write and rearrange lessons and student assignment sheets in this book for their students' needs. Some great lessons designed specifically for elementary education are also in Scott Watson's *Using Technology to Unlock Musical Creativity* (Oxford University Press; for more information: www.enter.net/~ascott). Music teacher and music technology integration specialist Amy Burns also has a book created specifically for elementary music teachers, *Technology Integration for the Elementary Classroom* (Hal Leonard; for more information: www.amymburns.com).

Software

Technology for music has undergone many changes in the past ten years. An understanding of this evolution can go a long way toward understanding some of the terminology used and the basic functions available in hardware and software today.

In its earliest incarnation, software for music was created to perform a specific function with regard to music and was limited to that function. There was a time when there were three distinct kinds of music software each with its own use: to create music on the printed page with standard notation, to record sound/audio, or to create music to be played back through a computer using MIDI. The generic terms for these software programs based on functionality was notation, audio recording, and sequencing. It used to be that if you wanted to create or re-create music with the intention of printing out parts for musicians to read and perform from, you needed to use notation software. The most popular music notation software pro-grams are Finale and Sibelius. If you wanted to record a live performance or performers in a recording studio, you needed to use audio software. The most popular audio software was ProTools. In the late 1980s, computer musicians and electronic instrument manufacturers created a standard language for creating, saving, manipulating, and transmitting music information digitally. This standard is called Musical Instrument Digital Interface (MIDI). It is what was used in older cell phones for ringtones and for early synthesizers. Computer software that used MIDI was called sequencing software, and its main purpose was to create, manipulate, save, and instantly listen to music electronically. At that time, the only thing ProTools could do was record music in an audio format. Today, ProTools has more advanced MIDI functions and extremely good notation functions, given that its parent company, Avid, also owns and produces Sibelius. Sibelius, once limited to music notation, now has a very powerful music playback engine. Logic, by Apple, was originally conceived as a specific kind of sequencing software that can be described as digital graphic linear sequencing. Today, Logic has a very powerful audio recording and notation capabilities and is widely used not just for creating music with software instruments and MIDI but also for recording and manipulating audio.

Today, the lines have blurred, and most computer software, from entry-level programs such as GarageBand and Mixcraft to professional-level software such as Cubase, ProTools, or Logic, includes some aspect of at least two of these functions—notation, audio recording, or sequencing. Even apps for the iPad such as MusicStudio and the iPad version of GarageBand, include software instruments (MIDI) and audio recording functions. (In this book, software is referred to as "software for music creation.")

Although most high-end software will include the ability to do notation, audio recording, and sequencing, when choosing software, keep in mind its primary use. Logic Studio is a powerful tool that contains good music notation functions. However, if you are going to use software to create music for an ensemble to perform and you'll need to print scores and parts, you would be better served working in a program such as Sibelius or Finale. Some free software, for example Noteflight and MuseScore, can be excellent alternatives for notation functions. Alternately, for those who do not read standard music notation and want to create music using software instruments and MIDI, a program such as GarageBand, Mixcraft, Logic, Digital Performer, Cubase, and any number of other programs originally created as "sequencing" software will be good choices. It all depends on what your needs are and whether the software can suit them. Given that this book is a curriculum for teaching music to students who may not know notation or need to know notation, the use of software traditionally labeled "sequencing software" is suggested. The examples in this book are screenshots from sequencing software for Mac OS, Windows PC, and the iPad.

Twenty-First-Century Tools

There are many ways to engage students with using technology in music education. This book focuses on the use of digital linear graphic software for music creation, such as GarageBand, Mixcraft, Logic, Digital Performer, ProTools, Cubase, the linear portions of Ableton Live and Reason, or any of the many quality software programs available online for free, such as Soundation and JamStudio. This book can also be used with nonlinear digital software for creation, like the nonlinear areas of Ableton Live, Reason, and AudioMulch. The entire book can even be taught on Apple's iPad or iPod Touch.

In addition to commercially available computer software or traditional software available online, there are some other options for creativity with electronics and electronic music. VJ

Manzo, the creator of Electro-Acoustic Musically Interactive Room (EAMIR), says that "EAMIR is an open-source music technology project involving alternate controllers, sensors, and adaptive instruments to facilitate music composition, performance, and instruction through a collection of interactive music systems. The EAMIR software apps have been implemented in classrooms, including special needs and disabilities populations, research projects, and composition/performance environments" (www.vjmanzo.com). At www.eamir.net, you can download and use EAMIR and see other projects VJ is working on, including his Modal Object Library and books and projects using Max/MSP/Jitter. At Manzo's website (www .vjmanzo.com), you can view and download a variety of other interactive music system software programs he has created.

There are many ways to create music electronically beyond the desktop computer. Students can make music in an ensemble using handheld devices, for example the Korg Kaossilator and the Alesis Sr-16 drum machine. A few years ago, my students created a small ensemble they called Total Kaoss using these instruments. (The companion website has a video of them performing one of their pieces.)

One of the hottest trends in music education is creating live performance ensembles using the iPad and its various apps. Many fabulous instruments, synthesizers, and sound-effect processors are available for the iPad, and more are being created every day. Once a student chooses a favorite instrument from among these options, that student will likely to spend time learning and practicing it. For this purpose, an area of the classroom can be set up with one or more stations equipped with iPads or other handheld devices, including iPod Touches or smartphones. All of these can then be cabled into a JamHub (www.jamhub.com/), where students can listen on headphones and silently rehearse while the rest of the class works on computers. The JamHub can also be used as it was probably originally intended, with more traditional electronic instruments such as electric guitars, electric basses, and electronic drum sets. Some models of the JamHub also allow an output to a computer for recording or allow recording directly onto the device. This kind of creativity, improvisation, jamming with friends, and collaborative composition is a valuable experience for all musicians. The skills learned in ensemble playing can't be duplicated in formal composition lessons and assignments. Participating in an ensemble using handheld devices has proven to be so valuable that I make it mandatory in my advanced classes. A collection of tutorials and demonstration videos for the JamHub can be found at www.youtube.com/user/hubhed?feature=results_main. (For a picture of students using handheld music devices and a JamHub, see the companion website.)

Notation

Notation was created as a means for re-creation. If someone can write down signs and symbols to represent certain musical sounds, and you can understand the signs and symbols that person used, you can then re-create those sounds. The Catholic Church discovered this in the fifth century as a means by which they could make all music in Christendom uniform. The greatest musical minds of the Middle Ages created a method of writing down music so that others could re-create it anywhere in the world. Modern notation was born.

Standard music notation is an important skill and is an essential one for anyone who wants to pursue music as a profession, even as a producer or engineer. Music notation is a language skill, and like any other language, it requires constant use to retain. If people do not use this skill frequently, they forget it. This is why many students who may have learned music notation in elementary school may forget it by the time they get to middle or high school. If they do not play an instrument or sing in a chorus or have continual exposure to music notation, they simply forget it.

Language teachers know that students can speak a language more efficiently than they can read or write it. Students' reading and writing skills often lag behind their spoken skills. Patricia White, a music educator in upstate New York, puts it best: "Ask a class of second-graders to create a story and have them tell you the story. What wonderful stories they create! Now, tell your class of second-graders that they are to write down their story but only use words that they know how to write down. Imagine how limited they now become. Isn't that exactly what we do as music educators when we limit our students' creativity to only using standard music notation?"[1]

Bennett Reimer pointed out in 1989 that given today's technology, notation could now become a secondary skill, not a primary one, for student composers. It is no longer necessary to first learn an elaborate notation system to be able to create, save, edit, listen to music creations instantly, or produce notation for others to play from. Students can be creators of sophisticated music and need not be limited by their sparse knowledge of standard notation. Furthermore, and possibly more important, teaching music through composition might provide a new paradigm in which people experience music and could potentially transform music education. As Reimer put it:

> Increasingly the potential to compose with few if any of the traditional obstacles [to learn an elaborate notation system and to master complex technical information about musical instruments and the voice, what they can and cannot do, and how to combine them] will become as realizable, if not more realizable, as the potential to perform. Electronic technologies now allow students to accomplish all the essentials of genuine composition: to produce and retain a musical idea by recording it directly; to review it and make whatever refinements they choose; to extend it, enrich it, and develop it while keeping it available for further refinements. When it is finished, it exists immediately and permanently for others to experience by listening to it, and an accurate notation of it can be produced by pushing a button. . . . The effects on young people's musical understandings through composing involvements may be so dramatic as to change forever our present notions of what quality of musical experiences are possible for the nonprofessional populace. And that, in turn, would change the standards of music education dramatically.[2]

Lessons, Assignments, and Projects

Teaching the same format of lesson every day can be, to say the least, less than engaging for students and the teacher. Standard lesson plans are included here, as they are not only, well, "standard," but often required by school districts. The lesson plans provided are as detailed as possible, but they all can be adjusted to suit your particular teaching style or the needs of your students. The lesson plans do not specify grade levels. All the lessons can be used for middle school through college, depending on the teacher's use of the included extensions or modifications.

Some of the lessons don't have formal assignments for assessment. Sure, you can make an assignment out of almost anything you show them, but do you really need to? Sometimes it's important to just allow students time to explore. In class, they can explore the software or practice recording a drum beat and experiment with changing sounds by adding plug-ins or by layering instruments. When we teach the flute, violin, or piano, we call this practicing. Practicing is important, and students need time to practice independently. They need to try things out, make mistakes and learn from practice sessions. They gain confidence and knowledge this way that they might not gain through a typical lesson-and-assignment format. If students are not expected to have the equipment at home so they can practice outside of class, they need time during the class period to practice, explore, and experiment with skills and concepts they have learned.

In many schools, music is not required. It is an elective. Students are taking music not because they have to but because they want to. They are kids. Kids will thrive in an environment where they have an opportunity to learn playfully.

The projects are often the culmination of several concepts learned or a way to extend an assignment so as to provide students with a larger project to work on over time. This kind of assignment requires different skills from students. A project needs to be completed within a certain time frame, so they need to stay focused on the specific requirements of the project over a longer period of time than for a standard lesson-and-assignment. They need to be organized and conscientious about time management. Projects, whether done individually, in pairs, or in groups, provide a different learning experience that makes the class more interesting and fulfilling in the long run.

Creating Distinctions Through Listening

Many students will immediately know whether or not they like a piece of music; however, they may not be able to discuss the specific reasons why. The same can be said about listening to their own music. A student may think something is "wrong" and not know just what, or how to fix it. These are the distinctions in music that we teach students to listen for when critically listening to music. There are two aspects to listen for. One is the musical elements, including melody, harmony, rhythm, and overall form and structure. The ability to hear these clearly is influenced by the other aspect to listen for: the overall mix and balance of these elements in the piece. As we listen to music, it is important to address both of these areas, so students can learn to distinguish details. As a result, they begin to hear things they didn't know existed or didn't know they should be listening for.

When you were a kid and it was your family's "Pizza Night" or you went to a pizza party, you probably didn't care where the pizza came from. It was just pizza! But over time as you grew older and your experience broadened, you came to prefer certain pizza sources. Likewise, when students are asked what their favorite pizza is, they will tell you exactly which store they love to get their pizza from and why. They know every nuance of the pizza and what their likes and dislikes are. Basic pizza is made up of only three elements: dough/crust, sauce, and cheese. The variations and quality are innumerable, but with time and experience they begin to understand the distinctions of pizza: thick crust, thin crust, spicy sauce, sweet sauce, salty cheese, not salty cheese, lots of cheese, a little cheese, and the lists go on. When we understand distinctions in versions of a food or beverage, we are said to have a sophisticated palate. We can develop students' aural palates and create sophisticated listeners by teaching the various elements of music and sound and how to listen for them.

Evaluation and Assessment

Since music is an aesthetic art, and you don't devise a rubric for an aesthetic, you devise a rubric for the assignment. On major assignments, for example the final one for my most advanced class, there is a very specific rubric, and points are deducted for any aspect missing from the assignment. For the most part, my grading sheet is pretty simple. (The companion website has a .pdf version.)

Regarding item 1: First and foremost, did the student complete the basic requirements of the project? That's a yes or a no. If the assignment was to create an eight-measure melody and the student came up with seven measures, you can take off points. Deduct points for each missing piece. How many points is up to the teacher and should be consistent.

Regarding item 2: Working diligently during class time is a big one for me. Occasionally, students have a bad day. They don't feel well, they are tired, they had a fight with their parents, boyfriend/girlfriend, or best friend, or they just have general teenage angst. Let those days go. Students can make up the work if needed. However, if a student is on the Internet, playing a game, or just not focusing, and this occurs more often than not, then they are wasting valuable time, or they have a serious learning issue and may need more help than you can give them in the classroom.

Regarding items 3 and 4: Working with partners can be a very engaging experience. It can also be a major distraction or problem. These two questions on the grading sheet help keep everyone on their toes.

A rubric for the assignment can be based on the elements required for the specific assignment. For instance, in lesson 2c, the assignment is to create a piece, using the two previously created loops melodies in AB song form, that is at least 40 measures long and contains four instrument tracks. A rubric for this assignment can be as follows.

1. Student completed the basic requirements of the assignment: 80 points
   a. Include both of your previously created loops melodies: 10 points for each melody: 20 points
   b. AB song form: 30 points
   c. At least 40 measures: 10 points
   d. Four tracks: 5 points for each track: 20 points
2. Student worked diligently on the assignment during class time: 20 points
   a. Tardy to class: minus 2 points for each instance
   b. Unexcused absence from class: minus 10 points for each instance
   c. Worked on something other than the project during class (on the Internet without permission, worked on another music project, did something other than the assignment): minus 5 points for each infraction

STUDENT EVALUATION SHEET

Name: ....

Class: ....

Assignment: ....

1. Did you complete the basic requirements of the assignment or project? ❏ Yes ❏ No

2. Did you work diligently during class time? ❏ Yes ❏ No

3. Did you work well with your partner? ❏ Yes ❏ No ❏ NA

4. Did you contribute equally to the project? ❏ Yes ❏ No ❏ NA

Grade ....

Comments: ....

....

....

....

....

....

....

....

....

....

....

....

....

....

....

....

Teachers don't give grades as arbitrary decrees; they report on what a student has earned. (That's why it's called a report card.) This means that students are in control of their grades. For secondary students, coming to class and coming on time is crucial to their learning experience and the experiences of others. This is also true in university, but infractions are at the discretion of the university and instructor. A student's grade should be based on the rubric for each assignment. Use a grading system consistent with your school's policy: A+, A, A–, B+, or 100, 95, 90, 85, and so on.

Comments get the most space. Aside from stating what may not have been completed in the assignment, comments are basically an assessment of an aesthetic. This is a great opportunity to discuss some distinctions in music that will help the student clarify his or her musical intentions or the mix and balance of the piece. It's a good idea to discuss why you thought a piece or section was particularly engaging or not, especially if your comments point to a specific element in music or how the technology was used to help convey the music. Be very careful to not let your personal taste enter into an evaluation or assessment of a student's composition. You may never want to listen to the piece again, but that shouldn't enter into a student's grade. Adhere to your rubric.

Try to comment, on paper or in the classroom, in a "praise sandwich." Start with what you thought worked in the piece, especially something that impresses. Proceed with your comments in the order in which the piece proceeded, for example: "The intro was very engaging, and the first section really caught my attention with a great melody underlined by a really fabulously funky drum beat. That was a great choice and combination of instruments for the B section, and it was a wonderful contrast to the A section"; and so on. Include things that you thought were not working as well as they might, and why you think they weren't. Include thoughts you might have for the student's consideration regarding how to make anything work better, for example: "The guitar countermelody in the second section was the same instrument and in the same range as the synthesizer melody. It seemed to cover up the melody. Consider changing the instrument or the range of one of them to allow the melody to be heard more clearly." Always end with some praise so as to leave a good taste in the student's mouth.

Although teachers have a great deal more experience with music than students do, our opinions are no more valuable than those of anyone else in the room. The comments of teachers, students, guest teachers, or composers are their opinions, and students should listen to opinions and weigh them for themselves. Students should ask themselves if they agree with the commentator. Is there something they might want to try? Does it lead them to other ideas for their piece? The most important opinion is the composer's. In the end, students need to be happy with the choices they make in their compositions and not merely make changes just to please the teacher.

Peer Feedback and Evaluation: Listening

When it comes right down to it, listening is the skill on which all music teachers focus. We listen to how we sound when we play our instruments. We listen to the ensemble and our balance when we play together. We listen to recordings to learn from how others perform or how we performed. We listen to distinguish one note or chord from the other. We listen to analyze, evaluate, and understand. We do a lot of listening to music. When students listen to each others' compositions, there's nothing wrong with listening to decide whether they like them or not. However, active listening requires focusing on details and listening for what works and for what might be missing. Encourage students to listen for why they might be bored with a piece. In the process of listening for something, students need to adjust their focus to what their aesthetic reaction to music is and begin to think critically in a nonjudgmental way. They begin to listen to their opinions as filtered through specific questions intended to focus their listening and expand their ability to talk about music intelligently. They begin to think about what they are saying about music instead of merely casting judgment. They become more thoughtful about how they listen to music and to each other. They begin to think and speak about music constructively and use musical terms to express their own thoughts and ideas about what they are listening to. Students become critical listeners not just to music but also to just about everything around them.

Let's talk about ice cream. You may not like a specific flavor, but in general, ice cream is a good thing. My friend likes coffee ice cream. I am a vanilla fan myself, and I really don't care for coffee ice cream. Sometimes she thinks a particular brand of coffee-flavored ice cream is just so special. She thinks it's particularly sweet or extra creamy or something that just makes this brand stand out from the rest of the coffee-flavored ice creams. She offers me a taste. I try it. Why? Do I really think this brand is going to convert me to become a coffee ice cream lover? Probably not, but I try it so as to understand the distinctions that make this specific version special to her, to try to taste what she tastes. I don't like coffee ice cream any more than I used to, but in tasting it, I learn. I appreciate. I understand. Music is like ice cream. Students do not have to like any specific style or type of music. When we listen to student compositions, I remind them that it's like tasting ice cream. They just need to take a taste. They will learn and discover what their peers think and feel. Who knows, maybe they will like it.

I can always listen to a composition on my own and grade it. The reason for playing music in class and eliciting responses from other students is because of what students—the composer and the listener—learn from this exercise. As they practice listening attentively, they learn to hear more of what is there, and as they learn vocabulary to describe what they are learning to hear, that tool in turn helps them grasp what they hear with even greater understanding. Students who are new to discussing music beyond saying that they like or dislike something rarely have the vocabulary to discuss details of a composition. Keeping a list of questions posted in the classroom is helpful.

> What, specifically, did you like about this piece?
> What worked?
>> The Sound or Use of an Instrument
>> The combination of instruments
>> A melody
>> Accompaniments
>> A specific section
>> Transitions between sections
>> Tempo

Did the piece bring any images to mind?

What do you think might improve the piece?

What was your overall impression of the piece?

During a class listening session, try to make sure that all the students give comments on the music. Written feedback, using the student evaluation sheet shown here or in another format, might be something to consider. It's a good way for the students who might be shy to express their ideas and can be used to formally assess the listener. (The companion website has a .pdf version.)

You can use the evaluation sheet when listening to any piece of music. Completing all the questions on the sheet may take more than one listening and might be a good assessment for a final or midterm exam. If you are going around the room and listening to pieces once through for quick feedback, evaluation, and assessment, it might be a good idea to ask students to answer only a certain number of questions about the piece.

Listening can also be done online posted in a blog, wiki, or other site that is only open to your students. If you can load student music onto a website, students can listen to and make comments on their peers' work. If you have a large class, this is a lot of work for both students and the teacher, so limiting the number of pieces students are required to review and write comments on may be helpful. For instance, as part of a midterm or final evaluation, students could upload their music and be required to make comments on a minimum of three of their peers' pieces. They can use the evaluation sheet; they can be asked to limit their comments' word count, say to 300–500 words; they can be given a few specifics to comment on, like form and structure, orchestration, use of effects, use of volume, and so on. College students can comment on music and then comment on others' comments, a common practice in online courses. No matter who is doing the commenting, all students will need to understand how to practice good manners and communication skills in making comments.

Homework

The first question to ask here is "Why give homework in the first place?" Practice, repetition, and reinforcement of a skill are important, but does it have to be in the form of homework or out-of-class assignments? Teachers are encouraged to consider the number of times they see students in a week and the effect that giving homework has on their students. The culture of each school and community will have different demands on their students with regard to after-school activities and homework. Also consider the impact your homework assignments have on how students perceive your class. This will have an effect on how students feel about the class and future enrollment requests if you teach an elective subject. The best music advocacy is making your class the most requested in the building. These decisions are up to the individual teacher.

If the district gives every student in your school a computing device and you know each student has the technology and software, all students will have the capability to complete homework assignments. If the district does not give students the technology and software, homework can be tricky. Many websites offer free access to software that can be used for a variety of assignments, including composition and music theory. However, not all students have access to a computer at home, and teachers should be cautioned about expectations for student assignments. Of course, handouts and written assignments are always an option. Teachers may also consider reading assignments. Printed (yes, actual paper!) magazines specific to music classes are available for students of all ages. They include *Music Express* (www.musicexpressmagazine.com) for grades K–6, *InTune Monthly* (www.intunemonthly.com) for grades 7–12, and *Electronic Musician* (www.emusician.com) for grades 9 to college. Reading assignments can be given prior to discussions in class.

Tips for Working in a Lab

It doesn't really matter if you have a permanently installed lab with desktop computers, laptops, iPads, iPods, or other configurations. There are a few practices that will work in all these situations.

Setting up a Lab or Classroom Configurations

There are so many ways to set up a classroom—with seats or stations in rows, clusters, around the periphery, and so on. Many factors come into play when deciding how to configure student stations in the classroom, including the number of student stations, the available space, established electrical and other wiring, local building and fire codes, and the possible uses of the room for classes or activities other than music.

If you have a permanently installed lab, consider the furniture for the student stations. Unfortunately, the currently available furniture for music labs does not put the piano/MIDI keyboard at a proper playing height. One solution is to have the furniture custom made. In the long run, it might even be less expensive! A countertop with a drawer underneath for the piano/MIDI keyboard is an excellent solution. Make sure the drawer slides are heavy duty, so they won't break with usage. (The companion website has photos of my lab.)

If possible, have computers networked. This can be through a server or creating a local area network (LAN) of several computers. Have the network manager create a "Hand Out" folder where you can place files for students to pick up and a "Hand In" folder where they can deposit their work for you. Distribute student assignment sheets and other instructions as .pdf files. This prevents students from accidentally making changes on a shared computer if you're not on a managed system.

On a networked computer, it is important how you start and end your session. If another class, especially a music or art class, has used the computers before your class, the computers should be restarted before new students log in. This clears the cache and gives students clean memory to work with. Students can do this, or you can initiate this for all computers using network software. At the end of a session, for files to be properly saved, you must save the file and quit out of the software before logging out or shutting down the computer. Often students will just log out or shut down and let the computer quit out of the software. Simply logging out

Listener's Name .... Date ....

Composer .... Title of Piece ....

1. What, specifically, did you like about this piece?

2. For 4 out of the 10 areas below, comment on what worked or didn't work. (Answer in complete sentences.)

   a. Tempo (Why did it work or not?)

   b. The sound or use of an instrument (Which instrument? Be specific by naming the instrument or describing its sound and section of the piece.)

   c. The combination of instruments (Which instruments? Be specific by naming the instruments or describing their sound and section of the piece.)

   d. A melody (Which one? In what section? What instrument played it?)

   e. Accompaniments (Which one? In what section? What instrument played it?)

   f. A specific section (Why did it work or not?)

   g. Transitions between sections, if any (Why did it work or not?)

   h. Did the piece bring any images to mind? Describe them in detail. (This must be "Disney Rated G." Don't get funny!)

   i. What do you think might improve the piece?

   j. What was your overall impression of the piece?

of the network may also close the software, but files can become corrupt or lost if you do not properly quit out of the software before logging off. Instruct students not only to save their work often during a class session but also at the end of the class to save and quit out of the software before they log out or shut down the computer.

Audio splitters and adapters of various configurations, audio cable clips, cable ties, wire cutters, and hooks for headphones are other things to consider keeping handy in a lab.

Cleaning Supplies

Keep disinfectant wipes such as Clorox or Seventh Generation for the computer keyboards, mice, piano keyboards, headphones, and other equipment. Check with your administration and custodians to see if there are restrictions on certain chemical items for classroom use. Disinfectant wipes are great for keeping the areas around computers clean and work great on nonelectronic whiteboards, too. I make them available for students by placing them in a central location in the classroom. On occasion, I hand them out to students as they walk into the classroom and ask them to clean up their stations, especially when it's "cold season." While they do this, I go around and clean any stations where a student might be absent. This way, I know I have cleaned the whole classroom. You need to be careful that the wipes aren't too wet when used on computer keyboards.

I do not have issues about asking students to clean their stations. It's not a punishment but a way to protect them from illness. There is just no way the custodial staff can come in between classes to clean. It is in the students' best interest to be at a clean station. If they were interns in a recording studio, they would be making coffee and cleaning! If a student objects, I would not force the issue, but I have never had a student object.

Hand sanitizer is another must in almost every classroom but especially in a computer lab. I make a couple of bottles available in different places around the room. If you ask, your school may be willing to have a dispenser attached to the wall near the entry door and have the custodial staff keep it properly supplied.

Getting the Class's Attention

Whenever I ask for a student's attention, I ask the student to save his or her work and put his or her headphones on the table. Headphones dangling around the neck just don't work. The pull is too strong for students to put one ear to a headphone and doodle on their keyboard. This is a statement I might as well record and simply play back, but I always say it anyway: "May I have your attention please. Please save your work, put your headphones on the table, and hands off the mouse and keyboards." Repeat this a few times until all students have complied.

One-on-One Coaching

Even if you have a classroom management system like the Korg GEC4 or the Yamaha LC3, it is really good to go over a student's work sitting right next to the student. You get a chance to have a little time to look the kid in the eye and see how he or she is doing musically and personally. I always ask how they are doing. Things are good in other classes? Home? School is going well?

It bears repeating here that when I am listening to a student's work, the very first thing I say is something positive. Students can be nervous about letting you listen, and they want to know if they are doing the assignment correctly and if you like it. There is always something positive to say about a student's work.

When I sit next to and work with a student individually on his or her music, the very first thing I do is save the student's work. If I think I'll be needing to make many changes to the file, as when making suggestions on specific parts or helping the student quantize a passage, I will save a new copy of the file. I may use "save as" and rename the file, with either my initials or by adding the number 2 to the file name, or I may create a new copy of the file and make my changes to the copy. This way the original material is saved as a reference, or if I make mistakes, we can go back to the student's original material. It is important to make sure that I don't change or obliterate the student's original work!

Recording Audio

Recording sound is a course and life study unto itself. It is beyond the scope of this book to fully cover the options and techniques for recording sound. There are many ways to record sound, and students should be encouraged to use as many of these techniques as is practical. They will learn many things by using different devices in different situations. The most important thing is for them to listen critically to the sound that is coming from the sound source and the sound that comes out of their devices. Are the two sounds similar? Is the recorded sound clear? Is there a lot of background noise that interferes with the main sound? Did the recording overload and is there now distortion on the recording?

Below are a few things to keep in mind when recording. A few products are suggested, as these are well known, and some are considered "industry standard." Listing them is not an endorsement of the product, and research on the "best" product for your school's price range and application will be needed.

The closer the mic is to the sound source, the less background noise will be captured.

Sometimes, recording the ambient sound—the sound in the room, as opposed to what is coming directly from the source—is desired. Recording a band or chorus concert with a mic or two closer to the middle of the room will capture more of what the audience hears instead of what comes directly out of the instruments or singers close up.

Record the best sound possible. If it isn't good going into the device, it isn't going to be good coming out. Avoid thinking that you can fix it electronically later.

Record with the best equipment available. Most schools will not need to purchase a $3,000 microphone. However, it is a good idea to spend a little more money on quality equipment than to go with the least expensive equipment. Save your money and buy one decent microphone rather than several of lesser quality.

Know what will work in various situations. A good dynamic microphone such as the Shure SM58, the Sennheiser E835, or the Rode M1 will work great for students' recording of the Commercial Project and the Podcast voice-overs. Another alternative is a large condenser microphone, like the AKG C3000B, the Audio Technica AT4040, or the Rode NT1000. When you use either one of these depends on the circumstance and purpose. In my classroom, I have a tabletop recording booth that sits in an alcove and has plenty of sound insulation from the rest of the noise in the room. Here, I like to use two AKG C3000 mics. When students are doing recording right at their desks, we use Shure Beta58s with a Blue Icicle USB interface. A dynamic mic like the Shure requires students to get very close to it, and because it is not as sensitive as a condenser mic, it won't pick up as much background classroom noise. With a foam pop filter on the mic ball and the kids' coats or a blanket over their heads, several students could record in the room at once! For field recording, a good handheld audio or video recorder will work. These do not need to cost more that a couple of hundred dollars, and many are available on the market for less. Sometimes the microphone on a cellphone or iPad will be sufficient to capture sounds as a field recording device.

For vocals close to the microphone, use a pop filter. Spoken or sung words contain consonants called plosives: P, K, T, and D. The sounds made by speaking these consonants create a burst of air afterward that "explodes" into the microphone, creating a "popping" effect. Hold your hand close to your lips and say the word "plosive." Feel the air hit your hand on the *p*. This is what goes into a microphone. A simple pop filter, either a foam windscreen or mesh filter, will work. A quick search on the web will bring you to many sites that will give you instructions on how to build your own pop filter. This could be a great class project!

If you are recording directly into the computer, you'll need an audio interface. This can be as simple as a USB microphone such as the Blue Snowball, Snowflake or Yeti, or Samson Meteor Mic. You can also plug most microphones into a USB microphone converter such as the Blue Icicle, Alesis MicLink, Shure X2U, or MXL MicMate Pro. A multichannel audio interface may be needed to use more than one microphone at a time. These can be a simple two-channel interface such as the Apogee Duet, the Presonus Audio Box or FireStudio, and the M-Audio Fast Track Pro.

When adding a USB microphone or audio interface to your computer, check the settings in your system preferences and in the software to make sure that the device is engaged. Most of these settings are under "sound" or "audio" preferences in the system settings and the software preferences. Check your user manual for more details.

Check the input levels before you record. As with any type of track, you want to make sure that the recording does not overload in the track, creating distortion. Once you have a recording with distortion, you can't get it out. Set the input volume levels to avoid the loudest sound overloading along the signal chain, from the mic, down the cable, to the audio interface to the computer, into the software, and so on. One way to help avoid overloading is to use a compressor. This device or software plug-in will help keep the signal within a certain range. More on compression can be found in the books and articles listed in the bibliography.

Recording and processing audio uses a great deal of your computer's memory. Before you record, process audio, or bounce tracks ("Send Song to iTunes" or turn the file into a file that can be burned onto a CD or put on an iPod), restart your computer by selecting "Restart" from your computer's menu options. This clears the RAM (random access memory or what is now referred to as *memory*) and gives you a clean slate to work on. Most computers today have 2–4 gigabytes (GB) of memory. If you are going to process a lot of audio, get as much computer memory as possible. With today's processors, 2 GB might work, but 4–8 GB is not expensive and is a good thing. Ask your school's IT experts for help and advice before purchasing memory.

Back up your work and make copies. Most of today's software processes audio in what is known as "nondestructive" manner. In other words, when you drag in the end of an audio region or cut a region, you don't actually destroy the recording. The material is still there but hidden. However, there are some functions that are destructive, so it's a good idea to work on a copy of your original audio files so that you have a backup of the original, just in case. Once you are done with your piece, back it up as well.

Food for Thought

The curriculum in this book is presented sequentially as the materials lend themselves to this format. However, the lesson plans, exercises, and assignments are aimed at giving students a guided experience in understanding and creating music. The students' experience with and knowledge of music can inform the teacher as to the appropriate delivery sequence for content knowledge. Teachers need to be aware of their students' needs every step of the way and make changes and adjustments accordingly.

Music is not always logical and sequential. Music can be an expression of pure emotion outside any formal structure or "rules." Quite often, I let my students create any music they like in any style they like. Students should be encouraged to have their music be pure expressions of themselves. Let them create and explore on as many tools and instruments as you possibly can. Some students will like composing on the computer; others will prefer to do it on an iPad. Some students will enjoy recording, editing, and processing audio; others would rather be recorded singing or playing a guitar. Technology is a tool for creation, just like any instrument. Let students explore and discover which instrument they like to create with. Envision your students as artists in front of a blank canvas ready to paint. Some come to the class with experience of painting and understand different brush techniques, use of other painting tools, and color combinations. Others may never have held a paintbrush in their hands and have no or little experience of painting. It is our job, as educators, to give our students tools and techniques so they can freely express themselves through their creations. I hope the materials in this book help you and your students fulfill this vision.

1 Patricia White, "A Dozen Ways to Use Technology to Improve Music Instruction," presentation at the New York State School Music Association Conference, Albany, New York, August 2009.
2 Bennett Reimer, "Music Education as Aesthetic Education: Toward the Future," *Music Education Journal*, March 1989, pp. 27 and 28.

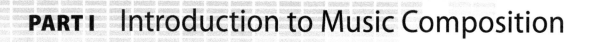

PART I Introduction to Music Composition

Creating Software Instrument Tracks

It is important to get students on the computers the first day of classes. Give a very quick overview of the software program; then give an assignment to explore the software instruments and try out recording if they like. Remember, the idea is to get them on the computers and let them explore. They will have questions. This gives you a chance to go around the room and interact with the students individually.

> **TIP**
>
> I don't need to give students a formal assignment the first day or two. I will show them how to add, access, play, and change software instruments on a track and then give them the task to explore the software instruments. I'll just tell them to explore the software and to ask me if they have a question or need help. I'll leave them alone exploring the software for several minutes or work individually with students I know need differentiated instruction or individual help. Then I walk around the room and ask if anyone has a question or needs help. Usually, I just ask, "Is everyone happy"? The next day, I show them the loops and ask them to explore the loops and manage the classroom as the day before. I have found that students are very excited and thrilled to have a chance to explore and try the software out by themselves. Some students will ask questions and ask for help, while others will only do it when you walk near them. The actual assignments can be given a day or two later if time permits.

Skills Required:

Basic computer and mouse skills.

National Standards:

• Standard 4, Composing and arranging music within specified guidelines.

Objectives:

Students will demonstrate their ability to add software instrument tracks by creating a file with three software instrument tracks.

Materials:

Software sequencing program with built-in Loops Library.
Creating Software Instrument Tracks student assignment sheet.
Anatomy of the Software handout.

Procedure:

1. Describe the anatomy of the software by showing students different parts of the software's main screen.
2. Review the student assignment sheet.
3. Give students time to explore the different software instruments.
4. Circulate in the room and answer students' questions.

Extensions:

1. Demonstrate how students can customize a software instrument track by using plug-ins and track editing tools. Have students create customized tracks.
2. Have students record anything they like on each of the three tracks.

Modification:

Provide a file with instruments preloaded for students to explore specific instrument sounds.

Anatomy of the Software

There are many different brands of software for music creation for both Mac OS and Windows personal computers. Below are the basic elements found in software for music creation. For the most part, all software contains the same elements, although each brand may have an overall different look and locates these elements in slightly different areas of the screen.

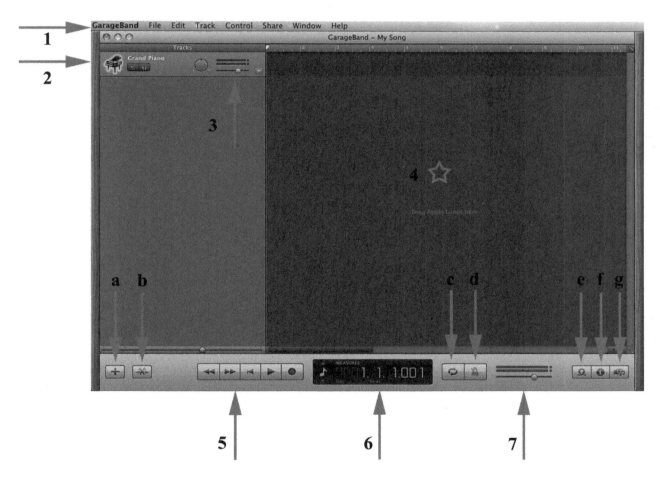

1. Pull-down menus
2. Tracks
3. Track mixer
4. Arrange window
5. Transport controls
6 LCD
7. Master volume control

a. Add a track
b. Edit
c. Cycle region
d. Metronome on/off
e. Loop library
f. Track information
g. Media

6

Creating Software Instrument Tracks

A software instrument track is a track that uses instrument sounds that are stored in the software. These instruments are selected on each track and can be changed and edited.

Assignment:

Create three software instrument tracks with three different instruments in the software.

Procedure:

1. Open a new file by choosing File > New.
2. Save your file as "Tracks __" (your two initials).
3. Add a new track to the file.
4. Select an instrument for the track.
5. Add a second track.
6. Select a different instrument from the first one.
7. Add a third track.
8. Select a third instrument.

Tour of the Loops Library

This lesson gives students time to explore the Loops Library and gain an understanding of some of the basic functions in the software.

Most software for music creation organizes music on the screen in tracks. This visual organization in linear tracks has become a standard practice in much of the software for music creation and recording. Each track represents a performer, and all the musical information for that performer is stored on a designated track. Software for music creation has tracks that come in two basic varieties, software instrument tracks and audio tracks.

When recording or adding music to a track, the encapsulated area of music that appears in the Arrange window is called a region. Regions come as two basic varieties, MIDI and audio. In addition to being able to create MIDI and audio, most software for music creation contains a library of prerecorded music. These short segments of music can be dragged and dropped in the main Arrange window for manipulation and appear and function as any MIDI or audio region.

There is a direct correlation between tracks and regions. Software instrument tracks allow recording and playback of MIDI regions. Audio tracks allow recording and playback of audio regions.

MIDI is a standardized format for digital music created in the early 1980s. Its purpose is to serve as a common "language" for electronic music instruments. MIDI information can define many musical parameters, including pitch and volume. MIDI information does not, however, have sound. Sound is in the playback engine, in this case the computer software's MIDI instrument tracks. A MIDI region will take on the characteristics of the software instrument track the region is played on. Change the software track instrument, and the MIDI region will sound like the new instrument. Recording onto a software instrument track via a MIDI controller (keyboard, drum pad, or other interface) creates a MIDI region.

Audio loops are little bits of prerecorded audio. Someone sat in a room, played an instrument or sang, and recorded what was performed; or MIDI regions were converted to audio regions. Audio loops are like listening to little pieces off a CD. These little snippets of audio can be manipulated in the software in many ways, including changing pitch and adding effects, but because they are sound recordings, you cannot change the basic instrument sound. You can record onto an audio instrument track using the computer's built-in microphone, or an external microphone plugged in via USB, or an audio interface, to create your own audio regions and use them as loops if you wish.

MIDI and audio regions can be automatically copied and pasted consecutively multiple times by simply clicking and holding a corner of the region with the mouse and dragging to the right along the track. This creates a series of "loops" of the region. The term "loop" comes from an early electronic music technique. Prerecorded music was once captured on tape. Cassette tapes were one-eighth inch wide. Studio tape is anywhere from one-quarter to two inches wide and is stored on reels. Composers would take an actual piece of tape, anywhere from one foot to several feet long, and splice the ends together. This spliced piece of tape would create what looked like a big circle or a loop. When you mounted the loop on a reel-to-reel tape machine and played it back, the sound on the tape would repeat automatically over and over until the composer or performer stopped the tape. In many software packages, the library of pre-recorded music is also referred to as the "Loops Library."

Skills Required:
Basic computer and mouse skills.

National Standards:
• Standard 4, Composing and arranging music within specified guidelines.

Objectives:
Students will demonstrate their ability to add prerecorded loops from the software's Loops Library by creating three tracks with loops.

Materials:
Software sequencing program with built in Loops Library
Tour of the Loops Library student assignment sheet

Procedure:
1. Have students open the previously created file "Tracks _ _" (their two initials) or a new file.
2. Show how to access the Loops Library in the software.
3. Describe the Loops Library.
4. Define a "region": an encapsulated piece of MIDI or audio music information that can be edited.
5. Define and demonstrate MIDI regions.
6. Define and demonstrate audio regions.
7. Demonstrate how the sound of MIDI regions can be affected by changing the sound on the software instrument track. For instance, record on a software instrument track or drag and drop a MIDI region from the software's Loops Library. Play the region back, demonstrating the sound of the music being played through the instrument chosen. Then choose a different instrument for that track and play back the region, so students hear the same music but played through a different instrument.
8. Review the student assignment sheet.
9. Give students time to explore the different loops.
10. Circulate in the room and answer students' questions.

Extensions:
Demonstrate how students can change the sound of MIDI regions by changing the instrument on the software instrument track. Have students change software instrument tracks for

MIDI regions. Point out how changing the tempo and the instrument has a significant influence on style and genre.

Modification:

Distribute a file with a few tracks and some loops preloaded into the tracks.

STUDENT ASSIGNMENT SHEET

Adding Loops

The software contains a library of prerecorded music. These short segments of music can be dragged and dropped in the main Arrange window for manipulation. When you drop them into the Arrange window, they appear as an encapsulated area of music called a "region." Regions come in two basic varieties: MIDI and audio. A MIDI region will take on the characteristics of the software instrument track the region is played on. Change the software track instrument, and the MIDI region will sound like the new instrument. Audio regions are little bits of prerecorded audio. These little snippets of audio can be manipulated in the software in many ways, including changing pitch; but because they are sound recordings, you cannot change the basic instrument sound.

Assignment:
Create three tracks by adding loops from the software's Loops Library.

Procedure:
1. Open the previously created file "Tracks _ _" (your two initials).
2. Open the Loops Library in the software.
3. Explore the Loops Library.
4. Choose a loop that you like.
5. Select the Favorite box to store the loop in your favorite file if the software provides this option.
6. Drag and drop the loop into the Arrange window. Notice that a new track is created.
7. Find a different loop with a different instrument sound.
8. Select the Favorite box to store the loop in your favorite file if the software provides this option.
9. Drag and drop the loop into an empty space in the Arrange window. Notice that a new track is created.
10. Find a third loop with different instrument sound from your first two loops.
11. Select the Favorite box to store the loop in your favorite file if the software provides this option.
12. Drag and drop the loop into an empty space in the Arrange window. Notice that a new track is created.

Be prepared to answer the following questions:

1. Did you use MIDI or audio loops? How can you tell?
2. For each loop added, was a MIDI software instrument track or an audio track created? How can you tell?
3. Can you change the instrument sound of a track by changing the software instrument for the track?

Creating Melodies with Loops

Regardless of their musical experience, student composers have difficulty composing a melody. If students aren't listening to, playing, or singing melodies, they have very little experience with melodies and probably will have difficulty creating them.

This lesson introduces students to editing prerecorded loops and creating melodic material and is part of a series on loops culminating in the Loops Project.

Looping is when a short segment of music is repeated over and over again. It comes from a technique used in earlier electronic music when composers took an actual physical piece of prerecorded tape and spliced it together creating a big circle of the tape. When this circle of tape was placed on the open-reel tape deck and played back, the segment "looped" over and over across the play head. Software allows you to automatically copy and paste a region continuously across a track, simulating the looping of a tape.

Around 1998, a piece of software called Fruity Loops became very popular (Fruity Loops has evolved into the current FL Studio). One of the appeals of this software was that you didn't need to know anything about music to create music because it came with an array of prerecorded, short segments of copyright-free MIDI music. All you needed to do was choose which segments you wanted to use, place them into the file, and decide how long you wanted the software to continuously and automatically copy and paste, or "loop," the segments. The prerecorded segments were known as "loops" because of how they were used in the software, just like the old circle of tape on the open-reel tape machine repeating over and over again. The collection of prerecorded "loops" stored in the software is commonly called the Loops Library.

The example below is a screenshot of a portion of a Loops Library. It shows how these loops are labeled. There are five House Warm Fuzzy Pad loops and five Mini Mono Synths. These loops are related to one another, as they share the same instrument characteristics and name but have different musical material and are differentiated by number. They could be considered to be in the same "family" of loops.

In Figure 2a1, the second track has an example of an 8-measure melody created using 3 related loops, Latin El

	House Warm Fuzzy Pad 01	128	D	16
House Warm Fuzzy Pad 02	128	D	16
House Warm Fuzzy Pad 03	128	D	16
House Warm Fuzzy Pad 04	128	D	16
House Warm Fuzzy Pad 05	128	D	16
Mini Mono Synth 01	95	C	4
Mini Mono Synth 02	95	C	4
Mini Mono Synth 03	120	C	4
Mini Mono Synth 04	120	C	8
Mini Mono Synth 05	120	C	4

FIGURE 2a1

Clan numbers 7, 12, and 15. The three tracks below the melody are the loops in their original four-measure form. Loops created using MIDI will take on the attributes of any software instrument chosen. To demonstrate this, the last track is the eight-measure loop melody placed in a new track with a new software instrument. Also note the original playback tempo indicated in the Loops Library (right column) is 100. The loops will play back at whatever tempo the students choose in the Transport window. In this case, it is 116.

FIGURE 2a2

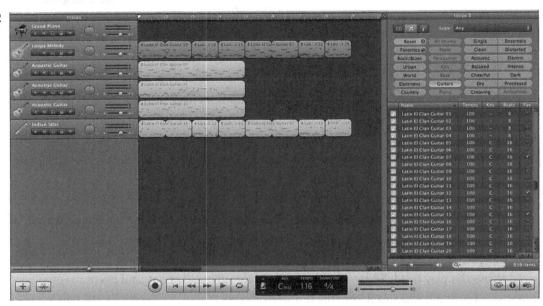

The assignment for this lesson is to create two eight-measure melodies using loops. Students will choose a minimum of three but no more than four related loops and edit them to one measure each. They will then use these three or four loops to create an eight-measure melody. Students will need to copy and paste their chosen, edited loops. This process demonstrates how melodies are created using music motives that are repeated. If a modification of the assignment is used and the melody is limited to a total of four measures, have students use only three one-measure loops, so they, too, will need to edit the loops and repeat a loop.

TIP

Students will need to understand what constitutes melodic material. First and foremost is to distinguish Western musical pitch from pitch of any sound. Shaking of house keys creates a high-pitched sound, and stomping on the floor creates a lower pitched sound. These sounds can be used musically but are not considered Western musical pitch. The pitches you want to use for this assignment are like the notes of the piano. I will demonstrate musical pitch by playing some individual notes on the piano melodically, one note at a time. To demonstrate harmony, I will play two pitches together. A chord can be played melodically, as an arpeggio, and harmonically, all notes played simultaneously. I then introduce the topic of the Loops Library and play a few examples of guitar-like instruments that play music material one note at a time. Bass lines are also good examples of music that is melodic in nature. I contrast this with strumming gui-

TIP *continued*

tars. I play and give examples and check for understanding by asking students "Is this music material melodic or harmonic in nature"? I also play drum beats and percussion loops. Of course drums can be played melodically, and some drum loops will only have one note at a time, but remind students that the assignment is to use loops with musical pitch. Frame it as something someone could add lyrics to and sing in a tune. No matter how many times I describe melodic material as containing musical pitch and tell students "No drums or percussion," inevitably students will use drums. Go around the room and check students' work.

Some piano and guitar loops will contain both melodic and harmonic material. That's the nature of these types of instruments and their appeal. I ask my students to focus on one note at a time for this assignment. Of course, you will need to be somewhat flexible, to allow students to be creative, as there are many piano and guitar loops that have good melodic material with harmony.

I will also tell students that they will eventually use these melodies to create a piece that has two main parts. I compare it to the music they listen to and say that one melody will be like the verse and the other will be like the chorus of a song. This helps them consider their choices of instruments and musical material for future use.

Skills Required:
Navigating the Loops Library.
Basic editing.

National Standards:
• Standard 4, Composing and arranging music within specified guidelines.

Objectives:
Students will demonstrate their ability to create melodies from prerecorded material by selecting and editing loops.

Materials:
Software sequencing program with built in Loops Library.
Creating Melodies with Loops student assignment sheet.

Procedure:
1. Define "melody": a combination of pitches and rhythms that forms a musical idea; the tune; usually one note at a time.
2. Describe some aspects of melody writing (i.e. repetition of ideas, rhythmic continuity, etc).
3. Review how to access and review prerecorded loops in the software's Loops Library.
4. Review how to add loops to the Arrange window.
5. Review how to edit loops.

6. Review how to automatically copy and paste ("loop") loops.

7. Review the student assignment sheet.

8. Give students time to explore the Loops Library.

9. Circulate in the room and answer students' questions.

Extensions:

1. Have students create two contrasting melodies.

2. Have students combine unrelated MIDI loops on the same track, for example La Marca Flamenco with Dusty Road Dobro. Then try changing the software instrument for that track to something completely different, for example Pop Horns.

Modification:

Have students create one or two 4-measure melodies.

Creating Melodies with Loops

A "region" is an encapsulated area of music in the Arrangement window. Regions can be created by recording your own music or by using the prerecorded music provided in the software. These prerecorded segments of music are known as loops.

Choose a loop from the Loops Library. Drag and drop it in the Arrange window to see the region. Regions can be automatically copied and pasted in the software by "looping" them, grabbing the upper right corner of the region by clicking and holding with your mouse, and dragging across the track to the right. Regions can also be edited to make them shorter by splitting them into sections or grabbing the lower right or lower left corner of the region by clicking and holding with your mouse and dragging the region inward to make it smaller.

Definition of "melody": a combination of pitches and rhythms that forms a musical idea. The tune, usually one note at a time. Melodies have repetition of ideas. Melodies have a beginning, middle, and end.

Assignment:

Create two separate melodies using the prerecorded music in the software's library. Use a minimum of three but no more than four of the prerecorded "loops" found in the software's Loops Library. However, each "loop" must be limited to a one-measure region. You can edit longer, multiple-measure loops to create one-measure regions. Use these three or four one-measure regions to create a melody that is a total of eight measures long, by copying and pasting or looping the region.

Procedure:

1. Create a new file: File > New.
2. Name the file "Loops Melody _ _ " (your two initials).

3. In the software's Loops Library, choose at least three but no more than four related loops. A related loop is one that shares the same name but has a different number. For instance, in Figure 2aSA1 Latin Heart Guitar has six related loops and Latin Jam Guitar has six related loops.

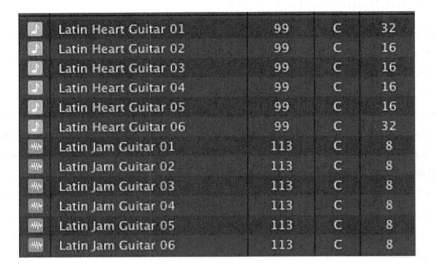

♪	Latin Heart Guitar 01	99	C	32
♪	Latin Heart Guitar 02	99	C	16
♪	Latin Heart Guitar 03	99	C	16
♪	Latin Heart Guitar 04	99	C	16
♪	Latin Heart Guitar 05	99	C	16
♪	Latin Heart Guitar 06	99	C	32
⩊	Latin Jam Guitar 01	113	C	8
⩊	Latin Jam Guitar 02	113	C	8
⩊	Latin Jam Guitar 03	113	C	8
⩊	Latin Jam Guitar 04	113	C	8
⩊	Latin Jam Guitar 05	113	C	8
⩊	Latin Jam Guitar 06	113	C	8

4. Drag the loops into the Arrange window of the software. You will now see the loop as a region in the Arrange window.

5. Each of your three or four regions can only be one measure long. If the loop that you chose is more than one measure long, you must edit down the region to one measure.
6. Check to make sure you now have at least three but no more than four one-measure regions.

7. Use these three or four one-measure regions to create your eight-measure melody. You will need to repeat your regions by copying and pasting or looping them.

8. Repeat steps 3–7 above to create a second melody on a separate track. These melodies need not sound good being played together, as they are meant to be played individually.

LESSON 2b

Understanding Song (AB) Form

Most students have a good idea that music is organized in sections, especially as it relates to contemporary song form. Two-part or AB song form is as simple as verse/chorus and is especially accessible, with examples from contemporary popular music or classic popular songs.

TIP

You can use any classic song or folk tune, but I like to pick one of the latest hits, the Grammy Song of the Year or possibly something many of them are listening to, as long as it is a good example for the lesson and appropriate for the classroom. This helps me to establish a certain "cool" factor with students in the class and anyone else who might hear it walking through the halls or in another classroom nearby. "Cool" helps establish your reputation and rapport with students. Students will be more inclined to listen to you during class and trust that the assignments you give them, even the boring ones, will make them better at their craft. Students will also choose an elective class based on the subject, the content, and most definitely the teacher. The best music advocacy is making your class the most requested in the building. Consider establishing a "cool" factor as a kind of job security. Of course, music content, pedagogy, and professional decorum should always dominate what goes on in your classroom. I will caution teachers that establishing a certain "cool" factor with your students may open a new area of social and emotional learning for everyone. Teachers must, at all times, maintain respect and professional distance with students. I noticed that some students started to call me by my first name. In my school culture, this is not normally done. When this happens, I immediately correct them and remind them that until they are 21, they need to address me properly. Over the years, students have come up with several acceptable nicknames for me, and I am perfectly happy and honored that my students now call me "Freeds" as a way of showing their affinity for me while maintaining respect.

Whatever music you choose, or if you ask students to bring in their own examples of songs to share with the class, make sure you prescreen them and understand any slang or idiomatic expressions fully! It's also a good idea to use audio recording and not video. Audio helps focus their listening skill, and you just never know what's on those videos!

Skills Required:
No technical skills required.

National Standards:
- Standard 5, Reading and notating music.
- Standard 6, Listening to, analyzing, and describing music.

- Standard 7, Evaluating music and music performances.
- Standard 8, Understanding relationships between music, the other arts, and disciplines outside the arts.
- Standard 9, Understanding music in relation to history and culture.

Objectives:

Students will demonstrate their understanding of AB Form by analyzing and mapping a contemporary music piece on the Song Analysis worksheet.

Materials:

A prerecorded contemporary music piece.
Song Analysis worksheet.

Procedure:

1. Define "melody": a combination of pitches and rhythms that forms a musical idea. The tune. Usually one note at a time.
2. Explain that music has form and structure.
3. Define the different sections of a song (verse or A, chorus or B, bridge or C).
4. Explain how AB form can be compared to verse and chorus in contemporary songs.
5. Explain how we listen for the changes in melodies that define different sections.
6. Listen to a contemporary song. (Make sure you prescreen the lyrics and the intention of the lyrics as rated "G" for the classroom!)
7. Listen for melodic phrases. Count as the bars go by.
8. Map out the melodic phrases, that is, the A section (verse), the B section (chorus), and so on.
9. Point out how instruments or vocal harmonies highlight these sections and help distinguish them from other sections.
10. Notice how sections repeat.
11. Highlight any changes that may occur in the repetitions.

Extensions:

1. Have students dictate the melody for the A section and the B Section.
2. Have students map a song of their choice. (Rated "G"!)
3. Have students add chord symbols to the Song Map.

Modifications:

Distribute a completed Song Map for listening and discussion.

WORKSHEET | Song Analysis

Name: ....

Date: ....

Song title: ....

Composer: ....

Date composed: ....

Performers for this version: ....

Year recorded: ....

1. Comment on each section defined in your form analysis in terms of (a) orchestration/instruments, (b) melody, (c) harmony (chord progressions), and (d) lyrics.

Intro:

   a. Orchestration/instruments: ....

   ....

   b. Melody: ....

   ....

   c. Harmony (chord progressions): ....

   ....

   d. Lyrics: ....

   ....

A section:

   a. Orchestration/instruments: ....

   ....

   b. Melody: ....

   ....

   c. Harmony (chord progressions) : ....

   ....

   d. Lyrics: ....

   ....

B section:

   a. Orchestration/instruments: ....

   ....

20

b. Melody:...

....

c. Harmony (chord progressions) :...

....

d. Lyrics: ....

....

Other section (C, bridge, or other name):

a. Orchestration/instruments:..

....

b. Melody:...

....

c. Harmony (chord progressions):...

....

d. Lyrics: ....

....

Other notes:..

....

2. The "hook" in a piece is a portion of the piece, usually in the melody, that grabs the listener's attention. It is repeated often. Where's the "hook" in the piece?

....

....

....

....

....

....

....

3. Map out the structure of the song (form analysis) on the back of this sheet, as in the example below.

Intro	A (verse)	A1 (verse)	B (chorus)	
4 bars	8 bars	8 bars	8 bars	etc...
		Adds Solo guitar for variation	A new instrument is added; organ	

LESSON/PROJECT 2c

Loops Piece in AB Song Form

In this lesson and assignment, students will create their first piece using the melodies they created in lesson 2a and other loops from the Loops Library following AB song form.

As students create their music, they will want to make adjustments to the volume of their tracks. This is their first venture into mixing. Mixing music is as much an art form as a science, the study and mastery of which can take a lifetime. The essence of mixing is using technology to manipulate timbre, volume, and placement of instruments in the ensemble. For the teacher who may find this topic daunting, think of it as re-creating what you know as a musician and conductor on the computing device. Many of your students may not have developed advanced listening and hearing skills. They will know that what they are hearing is not what they want, but they may not know exactly what the problems are and how to fix them. When we teach mixing, we are really teaching listening and hearing skills and how to use the technology to manipulate the music to get what you want.

Various elements of mixing, including volume, panning, and equalization (EQ), are addressed at different points in this book. It is up to each teacher to decide when it is best to address these topics with his or her students. It is likely that a little of each will be discussed throughout the course as student music dictates the need for each new technique. The more they learn and the more experience they have, the better they will be at mixing.

The first step is to teach students how to manage volume across tracks and in the master track/output. A track or master track/output is said to be "overloading" when the volume units (VU) meter or maxes out and goes in the red. Many times, you can hear this overloading as a cracking or crunching sound when listening to the track. This is distortion. If a student likes this effect, it might be best to use a plug-in to create distortion electronically, much as a guitarist uses a distortion pedal to engage a distortion sound when desired. There may be many other reasons why you hear distortion on a track that may not be apparent from the VU meters, but they are beyond the scope of this book to address. Here are a few very guidelines for volume management:

1. No single track or the master/output track should overload or go beyond the limitations of the software or monitoring device (go in the red zone of the VU meter).
2. The track that you want to be loudest at the loudest part of the piece should not overload or go in the red.
3. If the track that you want to be loudest at the loudest part of the piece is not loud enough unless you turn up the volume to overload or go in the red, turn all the other tracks down. Less is more.

Managing the overall output volume of each track is the very first step in volume adjustments. Students should listen and watch the VU meters of the tracks and master/output track at the loudest part of the piece to make adjustments to the overall output of the track and the master/output track. In figure 2c, notice how the master volume in the lower right corner has been lowered and the track output volumes for the other tracks have been adjusted for balance.

When checking different, softer sections, students may find that the volume levels need to be adjusted. In the figure 2c, the desired outcome is to have the vocals in track 6 be soft at first and then louder the second time. Sometimes it is best to create a duplicate tracks and place the music into the new track and adjust the overall output volumes of each track. Track 6 was duplicated in track 7, and the second repetition of the vocal was added at measure 3. Notice how the output volume for each track was adjusted to achieve the desired effect, first soft, then louder, simply by using two tracks, track 6 softer than track 7.

Sometimes, students may want tracks to gradually get louder or softer. This will require automating the track. In most software, it is as simple as revealing the volume automation window for a track and creating a few dots or nodes along the volume automation line and dragging the node up or down. In the figure 2c below, this was done on tracks 3 and 4. This technique can also be used on the master/output track to create an effect across the entire piece, for example ending the piece by fading out. It is not recommended that students choose a parameter where the program creates an automatic fade-out for them. Students have spent a lot of time and effort creating their pieces. It is not recommended that they allow algorithms to decide how their pieces will end. Encourage students to make their own choices about when to begin and end a fade-out.

It should be stressed that track automation is the very last thing to be done in mixing. If a track is automated, changing volumes needs to be done manually by adjusting the levels of the nodes. This can be a tedious prospect if many tracks contain automation. First and foremost, create a rough mix by mixing tracks for overall level output and create new tracks when needed. Finally, automate individual or master/output track after a good rough mix is achieved.

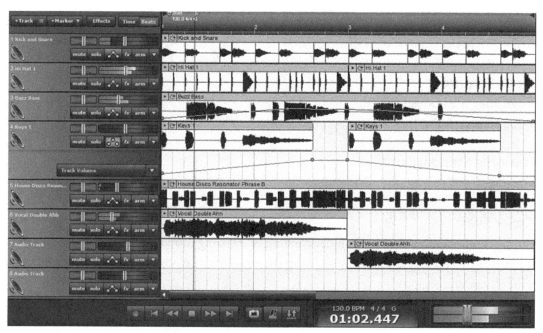

FIGURE 2c

> **TIP**
>
> Since this is the first full piece that students will be creating and playing in class, they will have a certain amount of anxiety about their grade or what their peers and teacher will think about their music. To deal with this issue, one or two class sessions before we begin a formal listening session where everyone listens to music over the classroom speakers, I have students listen to each other's music at their stations. I let them come into class and work on their pieces. About 15–20 minutes before the end of the class, I stop them all and say, "Save your work and leave your piece up on the screen. I am going to have you get up out of your seats and go listen to at least three of your classmates' pieces. Do not worry if your piece is not finished. You will still have time to work on your piece. The purpose of this exercise is for you to listen and see what other people are doing and get ideas. Do not judge your music against theirs or their music against yours. Some people have more experience playing an instrument or creating music than others. For some people this comes easier than for others. I do not judge your music against anyone's, so please don't do that to yourself. Honestly, do you really care what the kid across the room's piece sounds like? You just want it to be great. Why do you think that he or she listens to your piece any other way? No one is judging you. Everyone wants your piece to be great. So, now, look around the room, notice where there are three people you do not know. Get up, go to those stations, put on the headphones and listen to their pieces. Listen to what works about their piece. Do not go to your friends' stations."
>
> When they are done, I have them go back to their seats, and I ask them what they have noticed. I take responses or ask questions: "How many of you learned something new that you can do in your piece? How many of you feel better about your music? How many of you see you need to work more on your piece? If you are feeling completely stuck, you need to let me know so I can help you."

I use this technique before every major listening session at every level of my classes. It helps relieve performance anxiety.

Skills Required:

Navigating the Loops Library.
Basic editing skills.

National Standards:

• Standard 4, Composing and arranging music within specified guidelines.

Objectives:

Students will demonstrate their understanding of AB song form and the elements learned in lesson 2b by creating a composition using the two loop melodies created in lesson 2a and other loops and regions.

Materials:

Software program with built-in Loops Library.

Loops Piece student assignment sheet.

Procedure:

1. Review AB Song Form.

2. Explain that students are to create a piece of music using the two melodies from the "Loops Melody _ _" (their two initials) file in AB song form. Each melody defines a section of music. One melody is going to be section A (verse or chorus), and the other melody is going to be section B (verse or chorus).

3. Explain and demonstrate how the melodies are to be arranged/orchestrated by adding other loops under each melody such as bass, drums, guitars, or other melodic instruments.

4. In some software packages, when a key is designated in the settings of a file, all the available loops will automatically be transposed and available in the key of that file, regardless of what key they were originally recorded in. You will need to know if your software package does this. If it does not, then you will need to explain that while looking for loops that have pitch or harmony, it is best to stay within the same key of the melody. If the melody is in C, then it's a good idea to limit your search of bass loops to the key of C. Students do not need to know anything about music theory. However, if students like something that is in a different key and they like how it sounds, they can use it.

5. Explain and demonstrate how changes in the accompaniment can highlight changes in the sections defined by the melodies. In other words, the accompaniment can change slightly from one section to the next.

6. The assignment is to create sections and then decide on the repetition and order for the arrangement. Many software packages allow you to designate specific measures as a section, label that section, and easily copy and paste that section into different parts of the file. Check your software for this capability.

7. Review the Loops Piece student assignment sheet.

8. As students work individually, go around the room and help students with any problem spots.

9. Incorporate time for the class to listen to and comment on students' work.

Extensions:

1. Have students create an introduction (intro) and a coda, often referred to in popular music styles as an "outro."

2. Have students create a new bridge, section C.

Modifications:

1. If students created only one melody in lesson 2a, have them work in pairs and combine their two melodies to create one Loops Piece.

2. Limit students' choices of loops.

3. Provide students with two Loops Melodies to work with.

Loops Piece

Looping is the process of continuously copying and pasting regions across a track. The software allows you to this do automatically. The software contains a library of prerecorded regions, also known as loops.

Assignment:

Create a piece of music using your previously created Loops Melodies and the software's prerecorded loops that is at least 40 measures long.

Procedure:

1. Open your previously created file "Loops Melody _ _ " (your initials).
2. Save this file with a new name by choosing File > Save As > and name the piece "LoopsPiece _ _ " (your initials). This will create a copy of your "Loops Melody _ _ " file with the new name "LoopsPiece _ _ ."
3. One of your Loops Melodies will be the A section of your piece, and the other will be the B section.
4. Arrange the loops so they play separately. For instance, one melody will be in measures 1–8, and the second melody will be in measures 9–16.
5. Choose loops from the Loops Library and place them in the Arrange window as accompaniments for each of your melodies, creating sections A and B. Add whatever loops you would like to accompany your melodies. You do not need to edit these loops to one measure each, as you did in the Loops Melody. You can use them in their entirety. If you like a loop, try it in the Arrange window under the melody to see if you like it in the context of the piece.
6. Use at least four different instrument tracks, with different music on each track. Two tracks can contain your melody and any other material when the melody is not playing. All four tracks do not have to be playing at the same time.
7. Use any and as many of the loops as you like. However, you cannot just use drums or percussion. You must use other instruments such as guitars, keyboards, strings, vocals, or other instruments.
8. Avoid using loops that are 32 or 64 measures long.
9. You can, but do not have to, record your own regions on new tracks using the software instruments.
10. Once you have accompaniments for each of the two sections, A and B, arrange your sections to make a piece. Try A, A, B, A. How about A, B, A, A, B? Would you want to change anything in the repeated A section? Maybe add an instrument or change the drum part? What will happen if you overlap sections, in other words, A on top of B? What if you use the A melody with the B accompaniment, or vice versa? What if you use some of the

B accompaniment with the A section? What if you only use part of section A (four bars) and then a part of section B? Can you create a C section?

11. Check to make sure that you used both of your Loops Melodies and that your piece is a minimum of 40 measures long.

Understanding Rhythmic Notation with Rhythm States

Software for music creation allows you to edit MIDI information. One of the functions is to have the computer automatically align notes to a rhythmic grid based on rhythm values (quarter notes, eighth notes, sixteenth notes, etc.) This process of aligning to the grid is called *quantization*. In order for students to quantize, they will need to know the basics of rhythmic notation. Many students have not learned standard notation. And if a student's experience with reading standard notation was limited to an old-fashioned "general music" classroom, the student probably won't remember much about notation. If they don't use it, they lose it!

Introducing Rhythmic Notation with Rhythm States

Rhythm States is a method of teaching standard rhythm notation using words and phrases students already know to simulate the articulations of the rhythms. I derived this from something I heard many years ago from an elementary school teacher. She demonstrated the sound of 4 sixteenths followed by 2 eighths as "Pea-nut-But-ter Sand-wich." She then used various other phrases for other combinations of rhythms. Since I didn't start learning music until I was in middle school, I never had the aid of these "shortcuts." This technique eliminates having to teach rhythms in a two-step process. Using traditional methods, the first step is showing students standard rhythmic notation. They are confronted with a "visual" that they don't understand. Lines, dots, and slashes amounts to hieroglyphics to students. The second step is teaching traditional counting methods, how to count this "visual." Methods include the Kodály and French Rhythm syllable use of "ta," "ti," "ka," the Gordon method use of "du," "da," "ta," or a more standard method using "1 +, 2 e + a." In this method, a new language that students don't understand is being introduced to explain a visual image they also don't understand. They have a two-step process and have to learn each step. It's like teaching students how to speak Latin in order to read Greek. Using words they already understand eliminates one step. They are just left with the Greek!

Rhythm States is a standardized formula. The rhythmic notation and the corresponding states' names are shown below.

FIGURE 3a

Maine   U - tah   Mi - ssi - ssi - ppi   Ar - kan - sas

Each note (sound or event) is represented by a syllable. Syllables are interchangeable. For instance, U-tah represents two consecutive eighth notes. Mi-ssi-ssi-ppi represents four consecutive sixteenth notes. You can replace the second eighth of a beat with two sixteenths, so the new "word" is U-ssi-ppi. Two sixteenths followed by one eighth is Mi-ssi-tah. Students will perform complex rhythms more quickly using Rhythm States. For high school students, once they get the hang of it, you can start using standard "1 +, 2 e + a" as you please, and they will pick up on it quickly. A video example of a class using Rhythm States can be found on the companion website.

Note: Avoid issues with English teachers! Please point out to students that "Mississippi" is not hyphenated correctly according to English word division rules. The correct hyphenation would be "Mis-sis-sip-pi." For rhythm teaching purposes, words are hyphenated according to how the syllables sound when said out load.

Everyone has his or her own style of teaching students how to read notation. If you like to use a particular method, or if your district has a method they want you to use, then use it. Keep in mind that students won't remember what they learned in "general music" a year or two ago if they don't read music notation on a regular basis.

This lesson helps students understand how basic rhythms relate to one another. It can also be used as a warm-up/review at the beginning of any class. Refer to the Reading Rhythms overheads in the appendix throughout the course, and use as a separate lesson to teach eighth and sixteenth combinations and as another lesson to teach triplets.

Skills Required:

No prior skills required.

National Standards:

- Standard 1, Singing alone and with others, a varied repertoire of music.
- Standard 2, Performing on instruments, alone and with others, a varied repertoire of music.

Objectives:

Students will demonstrate an understanding of reading basic rhythms by singing, clapping, or playing the rhythms on the Reading Rhythms overhead.

Materials:

Reading Rhythms overheads 1, 2, and 3 in the appendix.

Procedure:

1. Display the Reading Rhythms overhead either with an overhead projector, whiteboard, computer projector, or Apple Remote Desktop. Any variation of displays can be used as long as the teacher can freely point to the rhythms.
2. Explain basic rhythm notation of quarter, eighth, and sixteenth notes and their relations to each other.

3. Have half the room say quarter notes ("Maine") to a click track or prerecorded drum groove while the other half says eighth notes ("U-tah"). Make sure they listen to each other to hear how the rhythms line up. Switch rhythms with groups.

4. Repeat the same exercise using quarters and sixteenths.

5. Switch rhythms with groups.

6. Repeat the same exercise using eighths and sixteenths.

7. Switch rhythms with groups.

8. On the Reading Rhythms overhead, set a metronome to 80–90, depending on your students' experience and skill level.

9. Point to a rhythm and vary the rhythms at random, combining quarters, eighths, and sixteenths.

10. Have the students speak, play, or clap the rhythm in time to the metronome. Be sure to point to the rhythm just before the click (on the upbeat, at the second eighths of the beat) so students have time to read the rhythm and be able to perform it correctly on the beat.

11. Show how the rhythms, quarters, eighth, and sixteenths, align to the beats and subdivision boxes in the software's Piano Roll/Matrix Editing window.

12. Demonstrate quantizing in the software.

Extension:

Have one group of students clap steady quarters or eighths as the other group performs the random rhythms in steps 8 and 9. Switch groups.

Modification:

Teach only quarter and eighth notes.

Reading Graphic Rhythms with Rhythm States

This lesson will reinforce students' understanding of basic rhythms in the context of the Piano Roll/Matrix Editing window. The lesson can be used again later in the course with Reading Rhythms handout 2, which uses more sophisticated eighth-sixteenth combinations.

This is a great opportunity to teach quantizing. Quantizing is the ability to automatically align MIDI notes to a rhythmic grid in the software. For instance, if you wanted to record a series of eighth notes but did not perform them perfectly, you can select notes and click a button to have the software place the notes perfectly in the eighth-note grid. Students will need to choose the rhythmic value that they want to quantize to, so they need to know what this looks like in the Piano Roll/Matrix Editing window. It really is just a matter of counting boxes. If there are eight boxes in a measure, each box represents an eighth note. It might be helpful to give students the Quantizing Chart from the appendix.

Some software allows you to choose your quantizing parameters before you record, so that when you are done recording, all the notes are perfectly aligned to the rhythmic value you chose. I do not show my students this option because I would rather they paid very close attention to their performance, recording as close to the metronome click as possible, and then choose the proper rhythmic value to correct the recording. Since music need not always be computer perfect, at a certain point I let them make their own decision whether to quantize or not. Not quantizing lends a more human feel to electronic music.

Skills Required:
None.

National Standards:
• Standard 1, Singing alone and with others, a varied repertoire of music.
• Standard 2, Performing on instruments, alone and with others, a varied repertoire of music.

Objectives:
Students will demonstrate their ability to read basic rhythms from a Piano Roll/Matrix Editing window by performing or recording Reading Rhythms handout 1.

Materials:
Reading Rhythms handout 1 (or 2, as appropriate)

Procedure:
1. Distribute the Reading Rhythms handout.
2. Have students write the beat numbers over each beat.

3. Have the students write the words ("Maine," "U-tah," "Mi-ssi-ssi-ppi") or other syllables used by the teacher ("1 +, 2 e + a") over each rhythm and rest.

4. Set a metronome, click track, or prerecorded drum groove to 80–90, depending on your students' experience or skill level.

5. Have students perform (say the words or syllables out loud) each two-measure example.

6. Have students perform (say the words or syllables out loud) *and* clap simultaneously each two-measure example.

7. Review how the rhythms, quarter notes, eighths and sixteenths, align to the beats and subdivision boxes in the software's Piano Roll/Matrix Editing window.

8. Demonstrate how to quantize the rhythms in the software's Piano Roll/Matrix Editing window.

9. Demonstrate how to record the two-measure examples.

10. Have students record each two-measure example.

11. As students work individually, go around the room and help students with any problem spots.

Extensions:

Later in the course, use Reading Rhythms handout 2, which uses eighth-sixteenth combinations.

Modification:

Distribute the Reading Rhythms handout with the beats, words, or syllables written in.

Reading Rhythms

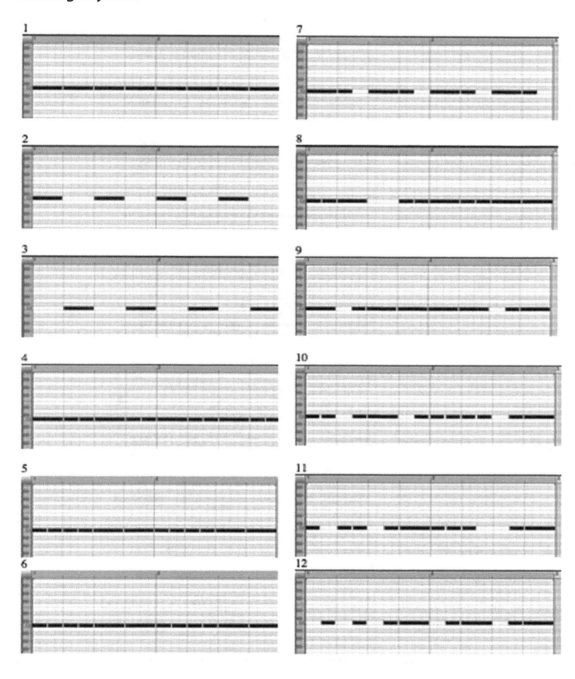

34

Reading Rhythms

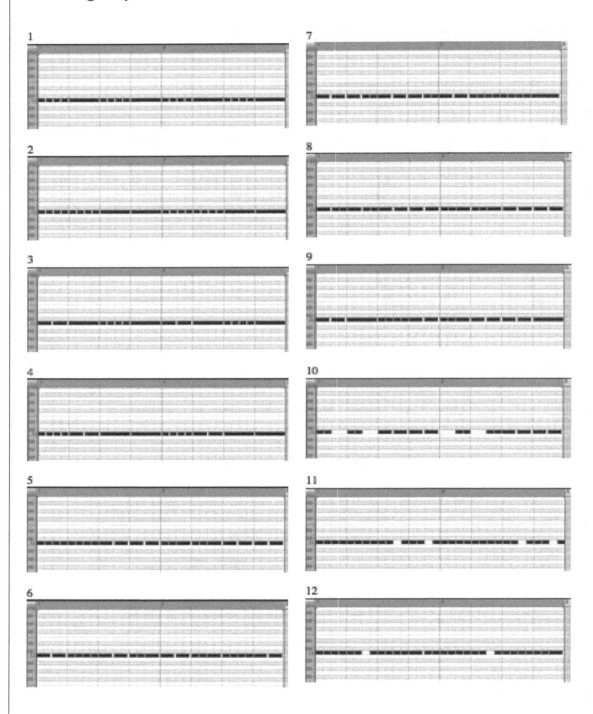

Rhythm Dictations

There's nothing like imitation. Students learn so much through doing dictations. They learn important basics like how to play to a metronome, rhythms, rhythmic subdivisions, and idiomatic musical phrases. Most important, dictations are the first steps to listening critically. Dictations require focus. This can be difficult for students, and it can take time to develop the skill of being able to focus for longer and longer periods of time. Listening in a focused manner can also be tiring to the ear, so do dictations in small bites but frequently. The most advanced student should only do about 10 minutes of challenging dictations a day and even less for beginning students. Remember, doing even the simplest dictations for the beginning student is hard! The better they get, the more advanced the dictations, so in a way, dictations are always going to be a challenge. If they are not, then they aren't worth the time and effort. However, you don't want students so frustrated that they give up and feel discouraged. Go around the room and help them out. Give them a few beats or part of a phrase. They will see and hear you perform it on their keyboards and learn to imitate your live performance and then be able to go back to the recording with more and more success. Success is more important than perfection.

There are three Rhythm Dictation audio files on the companion website. Each file contains six 2-measure examples. The examples get progressively more difficult and add different combinations of instruments from a standard drum set. This helps students prepare for the drum patterns in the next unit. Have students do one to three or four dictations a day as a warm-up for the class. College students can complete all the dictations as assignments for a week or series of class sessions.

> **TIP**
>
> Some students will find it difficult to record the dictations from an audio file. Visual learners will do well with a video of the rhythms being performed. Sometimes I will go to the students and play the first few beats or first measure and ask them to repeat it after me. I will keep showing them until they get it. Two or three times will usually suffice. They can then record what they learned by visual imitation. On a rare occasion, I have a student who has difficulty with even that, so I show the student and we play together. Playing together seems to work even for the student who finds this extremely challenging.

Since this is the first time students will be recording using MIDI software instruments, some understanding of MIDI parameters, such as quantizing and velocity and how they affect music, is important.

Some software for music creation allows you to select quantizing parameters before you record. For example, selecting eighth notes as a quantizing parameter before you record will automatically quantize your recording, even if you record sixteenth notes, to the nearest eighth note. Assuming you know the shortest rhythm that you will be performing, this can save time for advanced musicians. I do not recommend this for beginning students. Students should record as close to the metronome click and perform subdivisions of a beat as accurately as possible, and then open the Piano Roll/Matrix Editing window and quantize by selecting the proper rhythm. This reinforces critical thinking skills, as students need to make editing decisions and demonstrate a clear understanding of rhythm, rhythmic notation, and how rhythms appear in the software.

Velocity is another MIDI parameter, and it affects volume. I explain to my students that the velocity is the speed with which you send the signal to the computer. The harder you press the keys on the MIDI keyboard, the faster the signal is sent, making the notes louder.

Playing softly by not pressing hard on the piano keyboard, or any MIDI input device, will result in very low velocity. Some students "tickle" the piano keyboard because they are inexperienced or afraid to hit the keys. Students will need to be sure that the velocity is high enough to send a strong signal (loud enough) out each track. When you play your track and the track volume meter is barely showing a signal, you need to increase the signal. Sound has to come out of the computer! Slamming the volume slider up to +6 is not always the best solution.

Of course, as with many acoustic instruments, the volume of your playing may affect the tone quality (timbre) of the instrument. If you pluck an acoustic string instrument hard enough, you'll hear the strings slapping against the fingerboard. Many software instruments simulate this effect in the velocity parameters; the higher the velocity number, the louder the sound, and the timbre changes. If you increase the velocity of MIDI notes to make them louder, you may also increase the velocity to a point that changes the timbre to an undesirable sound.

In both these situations, I tell the students, you can set the velocity as high as is possible without creating an undesirable timbre and then turn the track volume slider up or down to the desired mixing level. If you are still not getting enough volume, if your track is not loud enough in the mix, double the track. Have two tracks with the same instrument play the same material!

Keyboard Skills Required:

Locating drum sounds.
Basic recording.

National Standards:

• Standard 5, Reading and notating music.

Objectives:

Students will demonstrate their understanding of rhythmic notation by accurately completing the Rhythm Dictations student assignment.

Materials:

Rhythm Dictations student assignment sheet.
Rhythm Dictations audio files 1–3.

Procedure:

1. Explain that the students will hear a brief two-measure rhythmic pattern. They are to re-create what they hear by recording it in the software.

2. Demonstrate how students can listen to Rhythm Dictation audio files 1–3 either in play-back software such as iTunes or Real Player or directly from the operating system on a Macintosh computer (highlight the file and press the space bar), or demonstrate how to import the audio file onto a track in the software.

3. Demonstrate how to add a drum track in the software.

4. Play example 1 from Rhythm Dictations audio file 1 and demonstrate how to imitate and record into the software. Use the chart below to locate common drum sounds:

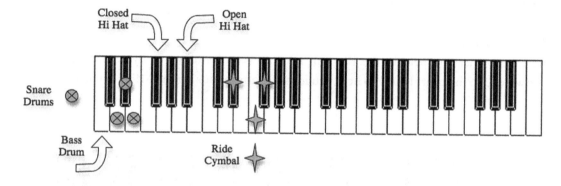

5. Review how the rhythm's quarter, eighth, and sixteenth notes align to the beats and sub-division boxes in the software's Piano Roll/Matrix Editing window.

6. Review how to quantize the rhythms in the software's Piano Roll/Matrix Editing window.

7. As students work individually, go around the room and help students with any problem spots.

Extension:

Either distribute or have students locate a simple snare drum part or drum groove on the Internet, either in audio or video, for them to re-create (dictate) in the software.

Modifications:

1. Require fewer dictations per class session.

2. Supply students with a video of the teacher or another student performing each dictation on the keyboard or a drum.

STUDENT ASSIGNMENT SHEET

Rhythm Dictations

Dictation is when you write down what you hear. In this case, you will re-create what you hear by recording it in the software. Below is a chart of where to locate standard drum sounds on the keyboard. Each sound will be slightly different, depending on which drum set you choose in the instrument track. For instance, the bass drum in a Rock Kit will sound different from the bass drum in a Techno Kit.

Assignment:

Re-create what you hear in the Rhythm Dictations audio files 1–3 by recording it in the software. Use the chart below to help you locate drum sounds on the MIDI keyboard.

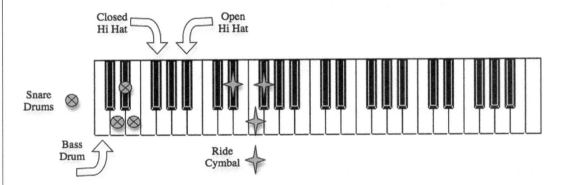

Procedure:

1. Open Rhythm Dictations audio file 1 in a playback software (iTunes, Real Player, etc.) or import the audio track into a track in the software.
2. Open a new file in the software: File > New.
3. Save the new file as "Rhythm _ _" (your initials).
4. Add a new instrument track and choose a drum sound such as a Rock Kit.
5. Set the metronome to 85.
6. Listen to the first example in Rhythm Dictations audio file 1.
7. Record the two-measure pattern on the drum track you created in the software.
8. Record as close to the click as possible.
9. Record only the drum sounds, not the click in the background.
10. Quantize your recording.
11. Skip one measure.
12. Listen to the second example in Rhythm Dictations audio file 1.
13. Record the two-measure pattern on the drum track you created as close to the click as possible.
14. Quantize your recording.

15. Proceed through all six examples in Rhythm Dictations audio file 1.

16. When you are finished with Rhythm Dictations audio file 1, proceed to Rhythm Dictations audio file 2 .

17. Create a second track to record each of the six 2-measure examples in Rhythm Dictations audio file 2.

18. When you are finished with Rhythm Dictations audio file 2, proceed to Rhythm Dictations audio file 3.

19. Create a third track to record each of the six 2-measure examples in Rhythm Dictations audio file 3.

LESSON 3d

Drum Beats

> "Miss, I just wanna make phat beats!"
> —ANY NUMBER OF STUDENTS, AROUND 2002

Phat beats! For those of us that do not watch music video television, "phat" means something that is cool or excellent. Let's face it, that's what all kids want to create, something very cool and something they and their peers think is excellent. No better place to start than drums. It's the basis of many genres of music, from traditional African music to contemporary urban sounds, and it's the foundation of contemporary popular music. People are making millions of dollars from them, and kids know it. Go ahead! Let them make "phat" beats. A lot can be taught with just a drum beat. Not only will you hook them in to composition but also they'll learn how to record to the metronome, how to quantize (align their music to the grid in the software), how to create layers of rhythmic elements, and how to combine sounds. They can also get a taste of mixing, editing, processing, and producing the first product they can be proud of. And when they listen to each other's music, they can begin the process of listening with an open mind and an open ear.

This is a great time for students to watch a drummer. You can have a student who plays drums explain the different parts of the drum set and demonstrate various drum beats. You can also find demos of drums and drum patterns on websites like VicFirth.com or YouTube. Let them learn through example. If you have a drum set, you can have several students play at the same time. For instance, have one student keep steady eighth notes on the ride cymbal. Have another student play a bass drum pattern of steady quarter notes. Make sure they are lining up! Have a third student play the snare drum on beats 2 and 4. Is it all lining up? Can they keep the beat to a metronome? Switch! If you don't have a drum set, they can play in small ensembles on their computers.

The collection of drum beats in this lesson is too much for most students to accomplish in a single day. The material is provided either for the teacher to refer to in future lessons or for extension of the lesson for those students who read standard music notation well. Students who have a thorough understanding and experience with rhythmic notation may be bored with a lesson or review of reading quarter and eighth notes. Give them the assignment sheet and let them work at their own pace. You might only need to review sixteenth combinations in the last few examples.

It is important that students understand how to locate and re-create basic standard drum sounds and how those sounds interact with one another in the beats given. Students should use the sounds located on the piano keyboard diagram before they use variations. The project in unit 4 will give them plenty of opportunity to create on their own drum rhythms/grooves with whatever sounds they want to use.

You will need to review quantizing rhythms and the different rhthyms, how long a note is held. A Quantizing Chart with examples of drum rhythms is in the appendix and on the companion website.

Videos of demonstrations of quantizing, duration of sound, and rhythm lengths to a class are on the companion website.

> **TIP**
>
> Some students will have trouble reading rhythms. This is another good time to play one of the lines of a pattern for them; let them imitate you, and then they can record. They can also record while you play with them, depending on their needs. Aim for success for each student, according to his or her own needs.

Keyboard Skills Required:

Locating drum sounds.
Basic recording.

National Standards:

- Standard 1, Singing, alone and with others, a varied repertoire of music.
- Standard 5, Reading and notating music.

Objectives:

Students will demonstrate their understanding of rhythmic notation by accurately completing the Drum Beats student assignment sheet.

Materials:

Drum Beats student assignment sheet.

Procedure:

1. Review reading basic rhythm notation of quarter, eighth, and sixteenth notes as appropriate for the drum beats assigned for the class session
2. Review the Drum Beats student assignment sheet for basic understanding of the assignment.
3. Explain which drum beats students will be recording.
4. Each student should record the Basic Techno Beat.
5. Review each line of the beat and have students clap or sing the rhythm to check for understanding.
6. Demonstrate how to add a drum track in the software.

7. Demonstrate how to record each line of the drum beat onto separate drum tracks.

8. Use the chart below to locate common drum sounds.

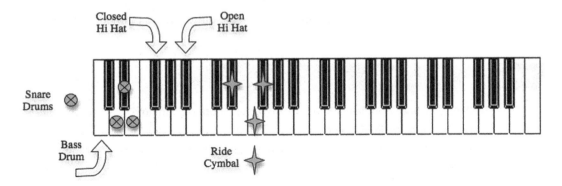

Extensions:

1. Provide students with different drum beats to re-create, either from any standard drum book or from printed music available on the Internet.

2. Provide students with drum beats that also incorporate drum fills.

Modifications:

1. Provide students with a video of the teacher or another student playing the beats at the keyboard.

2. Play each line of the beat and have students record what they hear by imitation.

43

Drum Beats

The following is a diagram of where to locate specific sounds on the MIDI keyboard for each drum beat.

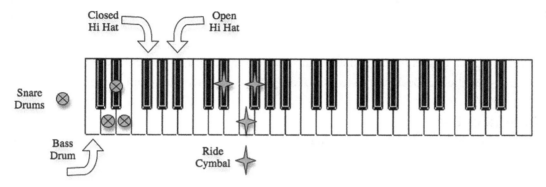

Assignment:

Record the drum beats below into the software, one track at a time. If possible, record all four measures of each track without stopping. Do not copy and paste or loop. If you have to stop, just start the recording where you left off.

Procedure:

1. Open a new file by choosing File > New.
2. Save the file as "Drum Beats _ _" (your two initials).

Do the following procedure in the same file for each of the drum beats given below.

3. Add three software instrument tracks and choose drum sounds appropriate for the style you will be re-creating (techno, rock, hip-hop, etc.).
4. Set the metronome to what is comfortable to record as close to the click as possible between 80–95.
5. Record each part on a separate drum track.
6. Record as close to the metronome click as possible.
7. Record four measures at a time without stopping.
8. Do not copy and paste or loop measures.
9. Quantize each track before recording the next track. If you play quarter notes, quantize to the 1/4 note. If you play eighth notes, quantize to the 1/8 note. If you play sixteenth notes, quantize to the 1/16 note.

Basic Techno Beat:

This is a very basic drum beat utilizing quarters and eighths. The variation in the hi-hat, using an open sound or "splash" (B♭) on the upbeats, adds a nice color to the groove. Record each part at 80–95 to be as close to the metronome click as possible, but play back the drum set pattern/style at a techno tempo of 126–144.

If your original drums sounded like techno (electronic) drums, change the drum set to a rock kit and slow the playback tempo to 116. Now you have a disco beat from the 1970s!

Basic Rock Beat:

Choose three accoustic drum kits like a rock kit. Record at 80–90 but play back the beat at 104–116.

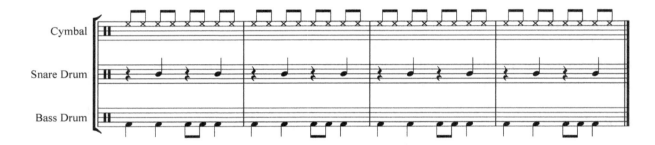

Rock Beat Variation:

If you leave out the cymbal pattern, this is the basic beat to the Queen song "We Will Rock You." You may want to set the metronome to 70–80 to record the cymbals. Playback tempo is 72–92.

Basic Hip-Hop:

Choose hip-hop, 808 or 809 drums, if you have them. Record the cymbal part first. When you record the bass drum, aim for the eighths in the cymbal. Playback tempo is 88–98.

Slow Hip-Hop:

This is the same as the Rock Beat variation, except the first beat introduces sixteenth notes in the bass drum. Record the cymbal part first at a tempo of 70–80. When you record the bass drum, listen to the sixteenth notes in the hi-hat. The first two measures of the bass drum part are written with sixteenth notes and rests, so you can see each of the four sixteenth notes of the beat. The second two measures show the traditional way to notate this figure. Playback tempo is 76–92.

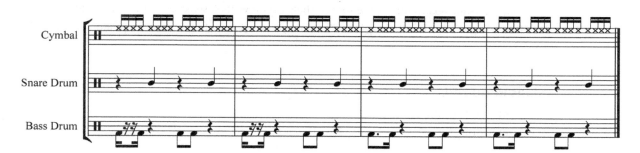

Advanced Hip-Hop:

This is pretty sophisticated stuff. Set the metronome to 70–80 to record the cymbal part first. Playback tempo is 88–98.

Drum Beats Project

Now that students have some understanding of the locations of typical drum sounds used to create standard drum beats and how to record them, they have a solid foundation from which to create and record their own.

> **TIP**
>
> It's a lot easier to create one perfect measure and then copy and paste that measure as many times as you need it. However, this is also an exercise in recording and recording to the metronome. Explain to students that this is also an exercise in recording to the metronome over time. Playing to and recording to a metronome helps improve their sense of and accuracy with time. Recording in what is called "real time" is when you keep recording without stopping.

Skills Required:

Locating drum sounds.
Basic recording.

National Standards:

• Standard 4, Composing and arranging music within specified guidelines.

Objectives:

Students will demonstrate their understanding of how to perform and record basic rhythms and how to create simple drum beats by composing their own 8-bar drum pattern.

Materials:

Drum Beats Project student assignment sheet.

Procedure:

1. Demonstrate how to record a simple drum pattern such as steady eighth notes on a hi-hat or alternating quarter notes on the bass drum and snare drum.
2. Demonstrate how to add a track and how to select a different drum sound.
3. Record a simple pattern in "real time."

4. Review the Drum Beats Project student assignment sheet.

5. As students work individually, go around the room and help students with their individual concerns.

6. Incorporate time for the class to listen to and comment on students' work.

Extensions:

1. Have the students record 16 measures.

2. Have students work in pairs and record two tracks at the same time.

3. When listening to student beats, ask:

   What influence does the selection of a particular sound have on the style of the beat?

   What if you keep the recording the same but change the instrument, i.e. change the drum set from hip-hop to rock?

   What happens to the style if you speed up or slow down the tempo?

   What influence does the tempo have on the style?

Modifications:

1. Have students to work in pairs.

2. Demonstrate a drum beat and let students imitate it.

3. Allow students to record one or two measures and copy and paste.

4. Allow students to add prerecorded loops.

Drum Beats Project

Assignment:

Create an eight-measure drum beat using at least three separate drum tracks. Follow these guidelines:

Record in "real time."

You do not need to record in one pass.

You can record in sections.

If you make a mistake, stop, edit out the mistake, and continue where you left off.

You cannot record a few measures and then cut and paste.

You cannot loop measures.

Two tracks must be playing simultaneously for all eight measures, but they don't have to be the same two tracks.

Procedure:

1. Create a new file: File > New and name the file "My Beat _ _" (your initials).
2. Create three new software instrument tracks.
3. Choose any drum sounds you would like for your three tracks.
4. Set the metronome to 80–95.
5. You *must* record as close to the click as possible. You can speed up the tempo to play back your piece.
6. Record one part per track.
7. Quantize before you record anything else.
8. Go back and record a second part on the second, separate track.
9. Quantize before you record anything else.
10. Go back and add other percussion instruments or other drums, as you like, on a third, separate track.
11. Quantize.

Understanding the Piano Keyboard

There are thousands of resources, including free online ones, available to introduce and teach the layout and notes of the piano keyboard. In addition to reviewing the note name and the given worksheet, it is recommended that you use other resources over a period of a few days as reinforcement. These reviews can be done as review or warm-ups in class.

Skills Required:

None.

National Standards:

- Standard 6, Listening to, analyzing, and describing music.
- Standard 7, Evaluating music and music performances.

Objectives:

Students will come to understand the basic layout and note names of the piano keyboard by completing the Understanding the Piano Keyboard worksheet.

Materials:

Understanding the Piano Keyboard worksheet.

Procedure:

1. Describe the basic layout of white and black keys and note how the black keys are arranged in groups of 2 and 3.
2. Explain that notes are assigned names according to the English alphabet (Latin letters) A–G, which then repeat.
3. Explain that these are the names of the white keys on the piano keyboard.
4. Explain that the black keys are slight variations of A–G called sharps and flats.
5. Explain how when a sharp is added to a note, it raises (up is to the right) the note to the next nearest key, black or white. For instance, to find an F#, first locate an F and then move to the nearest higher (to the right) key. In this case, it is the black key between F and G. Show the key on the keyboard.

6. Explain how when a flat is added to a note, it lowers (down is to the left) the note to the next nearest key, black or white. For instance, to find a B♭, first find the B and then locate the nearest lower key. In this case, it is the black key between B and A.

7. Explain that there are two instances where there is no black key between white keys: between B and C and between E and F.

8. Review the Understanding the Piano Keyboard worksheet.

9. Circulate through the classroom as students complete the worksheet.

Extension:

Use computer-assisted software or free online games to reinforce the lesson before the students complete the worksheet.

Modification:

Only demonstrate and expect students to understand the white keys.

Understanding the Piano Keyboard WORKSHEET

Name...

Date...

Assignment:

On the keyboards in the example below, place an *X* on the notes given.

Example:

Example: ___E___

1) ___C___

2) ___G___

3) ___B___

4) ___F#___

5) ___Eb___

6) ___D___

7) ___A___

8) ___C#___

9) ___Gb___

10) ___Bb___

11) ___F___

12) ___Db___

LESSON 5b

Melodic Dictations

Once again, we use imitation. This time, students learn how melodies are shaped. Students will understand movement by step and small intervals, different kinds of motive repetition, rhythmic continuity and other aspects of melody writing as it relates visually to the piano keyboard and by ear.

Students can play the Melodic Dictations file 1 in a playback program such as iTunes or Real Player or through the operating system on a Macintosh, or they can load the file into one track of the software and record their piano parts onto a second track. This may pose a problem, as the audio track may not line up exactly with the beats in the MIDI track. Students may want to record lining up the MIDI track with the audio track (transients) as opposed to recording to the click and editing in the Piano Roll or Score Editor.

> **TIP**
>
> Some students will be able to do all four melodies in ten minutes, and others will struggle with the first two melodies. Most students will have difficulty with one or more spots. After a little time struggling with the problem spots, students may become frustrated. There is a point of struggle for each student that yields a negative return. Before this is reached, it's best to play the problem spot for the student and let the student imitate you. They will see and hear the intervals and will learn from this. Most students will progress at their own pace after a few demonstrations. Allow those students who can only do two melodies in the time permitted to do just those two. This is one of those times that it is necessary to differentiate the approach for students due to the differences in their musical experiences as well as learning concerns. Assessment should focus on students' diligence and attention to their work during class time, not on how quickly or easily they accomplish the task in whole or in part.

Skills Required:
Basic understanding of the piano keyboard.

National Standards:
• Standard 2, Performing on instruments, alone and with others, a varied repertoire of music.

Objectives:
Students will demonstrate their understanding of recording melodies by accurately re-creating and recording the melodies given into the software.

Materials:

Melodic Dictations student assignment sheet.
Melodic Dictations file.

Procedure:

1. Explain that they will listen to a recording of tunes with which they may be familiar and that they are going to record these melodies into the software:

    "Mary Had a Little Lamb"

    "Twinkle, Twinkle"

    "Frère Jacques"/"Brother John"

    "Yankee Doodle"

2. Explain that "Mary Had a Little Lamb" begins on the note E and ask students to locate an E on the keyboard.

3. Check to see that all students have located an E.

4. Explain that students need to listen to each note and decide if successive notes are higher, lower, or repeated.

5. Demonstrate the first two notes of "Mary Had a Little Lamb" and show that the second note is lower than the first note.

6. Play the first piece, "Mary Had a Little Lamb," on the Melodic Dictation file/audio track and demonstrate how the students are to record the melody. It is not necessary to figure out the entire melody, memorize it, and then record it. Students can work in small phrases, recording and then going back and doing the next phrase.

7. As students work individually, go around the room and help students with each problem spot.

Extension:

Have "Yankee Doodle" be extra credit.

Modifications:

1. Require fewer dictations per class session.

2. Play portions of the melodies for students to imitate and then record.

3. Supply students with a video of the teacher or another student performing each dictation on the keyboard.

Melodic Dictations

Assignment:

Re-create what you hear in Melody Dictations files 1–4 by recording it in the software.

1. "Mary Had a Little Lamb" (start on E).
2. "Twinkle, Twinkle" (start on C).
3. "Brother John" ("Frère Jacques") (start on C).
4. "Yankee Doodle" (start on C).

Procedure:

1. Open the Melodic Dictations audio file 1 in a playback software program (iTunes, Real Player, etc.) or the operating system, or import the audio track into the software.
2. Open a new file: File > New.
3. Name the file "Melodies _ _" (your initials).
4. Add a software instrument track and choose a flute or violin as the instrument. Set the metronome to 85.
5. Listen to the first piece and figure out how to play it on the piano keyboard.
6. You do not need to memorize the entire melody. You can play a measure or two at a time and then record more.
7. You *must* record as close to the click as possible.
8. Do not cut and paste. Record in "real time."
9. Quantize before you record anything else.
10. When you are finished recording the first melody, either skip a measure and record the second melody or add a track and record the second melody on a new track.
11. Quantize each melody.
12. Record all four melodies.

Evaluating Melodies

If there were a formula for writing great melodies, every composer would be a millionaire. The good news is that there are some things to keep in mind when composing melodies, and these can be gleaned from evaluating the timeless melodies students recorded in the previous lesson. The Evaluating Melodies lesson leads right into Composing a Melody.

> **TIP**
>
> You'll need to explain a little bit about generic intervals, at least the root or tonic note and the dominant, or five up from the root. Check for understanding by asking what the dominant (5th above) from a given note is. Give the students several notes to figure out, and make sure they all understand that if the tonic is D, the dominant is A, and they can find these on the keyboard. At this point, write the names of the notes on the white keys of the keyboard for those students who require modifications.

Skills Required:

None.

National Standards:

- Standard 6, Listening to, analyzing, and describing music.
- Standard 7, Evaluating music and music performances.

Objectives:

Students will understand the elements that go into traditional melodies by evaluating and describing these elements.

Materials:

Melodic Dictations MIDI file.

Procedure:

1. Open the four melodies from the Melodic Dictations MIDI file in a sequencing program.
2. Review the melodies with the students to understand what they have in common that makes them "timeless" melodies that endure for generations. Ask questions:
   a. How long are they? All are eight measures, except for "Twinkle, Twinkle," which is eight plus four (ABA).
   b. Are there a lot of different notes?
   c. How many notes are there per beat?

d. How do the notes move? Explain stepwise motion. In a sequencer's matrix editing window, it really looks like steps!

e. If there are leaps or jumps, are they big?

f. How do the leaps or jumps resolve? What's the next note after the leap or jump?

g. Is there repetition? There are a few kinds of repetition to be noted in these melodies. "Frère Jacques"/"Brother John" has four basic ideas that get repeated immediately after being stated. "Mary Had a Little Lamb" has the repetition at measure 5. "Twinkle, Twinkle" has the exact repetition at measure 9. "Yankee Doodle" has repetition in measures 1, 3, and 5, with different measures in between.

h. Describe the structure of four bars plus four bars in most of the melodies. Measure 5 can start on the tonic or on the dominant. "Twinkle, Twinkle" is a great example to use for this demonstration.

Extensions:

1. Have students work in pairs or groups to evaluate and describe one of the melodies to the class.

2. Have students work in pairs or groups to compare two melodies.

Modification:

Evaluate one or two melodies a day.

Composing a Melody in D Dorian

This will be students' first attempt at melodic composition. This can be challenging for any student. D Dorian is chosen because students will use this melody in their first piece, and this key allows them to use only the white keys and have the advantage of not having to know too much about music theory. Students need not be concerned with advanced music theory when combining or overlapping melodies in Dorian mode. For the most part, any combination of notes in Dorian mode will sound good when played harmonically.

The use of a flute or violin as the instrument will encourage students to make conscientious choices in rhythm. A flute or violin will sustain the sound when the note is pressed and held, as opposed to the quick decay of plucked or struck instruments, so students will need to choose rhythms, that is, the lengths of the notes, deliberately. Students should be encouraged to use sustained sounds and full-length half, quarter, and eighth notes, as it will make it easier for them to make the necessary rhythmic alterations in the following lessons.

TIP

Some students are timid about pressing and holding the keys on the keyboard. There will be those who play short and very light notes. Encourage them to make sure their notes last until the next note is played. Of course, short and soft notes are allowed in music! However, this is an exercise, and long notes with a solid velocity will be very helpful for the lessons and assignments that follow. Work with each student and show the student how to lengthen the notes by hand and how to increase the velocity for each note recorded. Some programs will let you do these actions across several selected notes. Making changes to note length and velocity in this assignment will save a lot of editing in the next few lessons. When working with students on their music, don't forget, to make a copy of the file or the region you are working in and then work in the copy to preserve the student's original file. Not all of our suggestions or changes work or work for the student. I obliterated more than one student's work before I got into this habit!

Skills Required:
Knowledge of the layout of the piano keyboard.

National Standards:
- Standard 3, Improvising melodies, variations, and accompaniments.
- Standard 6, Listening to, analyzing, and describing music.
- Standard 7, Evaluating music and music performances.

Objectives:

Students will demonstrate their knowledge of the elements of traditional melody writing by composing their own eight-bar melody in D Dorian.

Materials:

Composing a Melody in D Dorian student assignment sheet.

Procedure:

1. Review the elements of traditional melody writing, as discussed in lesson 5c, Evaluating Melodies.
    a. Record one note at a time.
    b. Use simple rhythms, one or two notes per beat.
    c. Use stepwise motion.
    d. After a leap (skipping of a few notes), continue in stepwise motion.
    e. The fifth measure (halfway point or B section) can start on D or the higher A.
    f. Repeat one- or two-measure small ideas.
2. Review the Composing a Melody in D Dorian student assignment sheet.
3. Allow students time to work through ideas.
4. Go around the room and review melodies with each student. The teacher may need to make suggestions, edit, help students adjust note lengths and quantize.

Composing a Melody in D Dorian

Assignment:

Write a simple melody like a folk tune or lullaby. The melody is to be eight measures long in 4/4 time, and will begin and end on the same middle D. You are to use only the *white* keys (D Dorian mode).

Procedure:

1. Open a new file: File > New.
2. Name the file "D Melody __ __" (your initials).
3. Add a software instrument track.
4. Choose a standard flute or violin instrument.
5. Set the metronome at 85–95.
6. The melody is to be eight complete measures long. You can record in short 1- or 2-measure segments.
7. You *must* record as close to the click as possible.
8. Begin and end on the same middle D.
9. Use only the white keys.
10. Keep it simple and follow these guidelines:
    a. Record one note at a time. Do not press two keys together.
    b. Use only one or two notes per beat (quarter notes and eighth notes).
    c. Use stepwise motion, one note next to the other.
    d. After a leap (skipping of a few notes), continue in stepwise motion.
    e. The fifth measure (halfway point or B section) can start on D (root or home tone) or the higher A (5th above).
    f. Repeat one- or two-measure small ideas. You can copy and paste after you have quantized the measure or measures.
    g. Quantize after you record and before you record anything else.

Melodic Fragments, Rhythmic Augmentation, and Rhythmic Diminution

All three Melody Variations assignments can be given all at once; or if time and the class size permit, have the students do each one of these assignments after you as you explain it. It might stretch to encompass two or three classes, but you can check students' work individually as they progress.

Repeating the same melody over and over can be boring. Remember, we are not writing songs. Since there are no lyrics to add variation and interest to repeated melodies, we need to create interest in an instrumental piece with very little knowledge of composition or music theory. The easiest way to create melodic variations is to create short segments of the original melody (melodic fragments) and then alter the rhythm of those segments (rhythmic augmentation and rhythmic diminution). This also reinforces previous learning of rhythmic notation.

TIP

I show my students all three basic variations in the assignment sheet, fragment, augmentation, and diminution at once before I send them to work on the student assignment sheet. Most seem to get it, and then I have time to help those who might struggle a bit with these concepts or execution of the assignment. Either way, it's a good idea to give an overview of what the final product will be, your D melody with three tracks:

Track 1 has the D melody.
Track 2 has the fragments.
Track 3 has the rhythmic augmentation of the fragments.
Track 4 has the rhythmic diminution of the fragments.

Skills Required:

Basic understanding of how to copy and paste in the software.
Basic understanding of how to edit note length in the software.

National Standards:

• Standard 4, Composing and arranging music within specified guidelines.

Objectives:

Students will understand melodic variations by creating melodic fragments and altering their rhythms to form variations from their original D Dorian melody composed in the "D Melody _ _" file.

Materials:

Melody Variations student assignment sheet.
"D Melody _ _" file.

Procedure:

1. Explain that each student will be using his or her D Dorian melody as a foundation to create an entire piece.
2. Explain the concept of melodic variations and their importance.
4. Explain all three variations at once—fragment, augmentation, and diminution—demonstrating the process and showing examples of each.
5. Review the Melody Variations student assignment sheet.
6. As students work individually, go around the room and help students with each problem spot.

Melody Variations

Assignment 1: Melodic Fragments

A fragment is a portion of a melody. Melodic fragments can vary in length. Composers use melodic fragments to add interest to melodies.

You will create two melodic fragments from your D Melody. Each fragment must contain different musical material.

Procedure:

1. Open your "D Melody" file.
2. Save this file with a new name: File > Save As "D Variations _ _" (your two initials).
3. Select a two-measure section of your eight-bar melody.
4. Add a new software instrument track and choose a flute or violin sound.
5. Copy and paste this two-measure segment into the new track (track 2).
6. Select a different two-measure segment of your eight-bar melody.
7. Copy and paste this two-measure segment into the new track. (track 2) at measure 6.

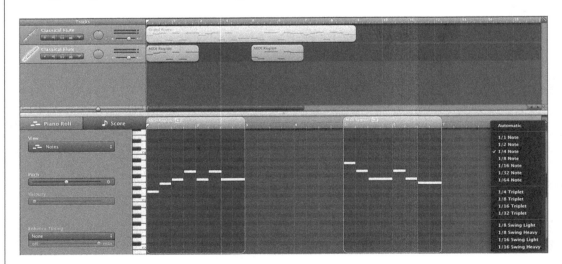

Assignment 2: Rhythmic Augmentation

Augmentation means to make larger. In music, you can make melodies or parts of melodies (fragments) longer by increasing the duration of each note. For instance, if you have a pitch that lasts for one beat, change it to last for two beats. This lengthens the melody or fragment.

You will create augmentations of your fragments on a separate track.

Procedure:

1. Open your "D Variations" file.
2. Add a new software instrument track (track 3) and choose a flute or violin sound.
3. Select both two-measure fragments in track 2 and paste them into the new track (track 3).
4. Expand each of the two regions in track 3 to make each region last for four measures (see A on the illustration below).
5. Double click on the region to view the notes in the Piano Roll/Matrix Editing window.
6. You will now need to manually make each note twice as long.
7. Don't forget to make rests (spaces where there are no notes) twice as long, too.

> **TIP**
>
> It might be easier to select all the notes and move them over to the right to make room for the longer notes. Make the first note twice as long, select the second note and move it into place over to the left then make it twice as long. Move the remaining notes into place on the left and make them twice as long, one by one (see B on the illustration below).

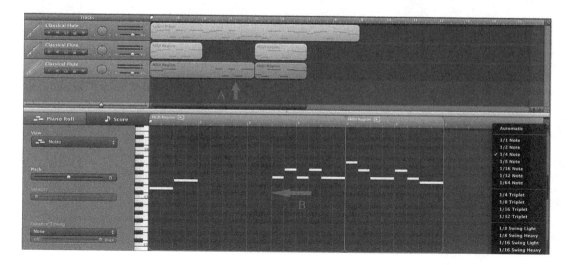

Assignment 3: Rhythmic Diminution

Diminution means to diminish or to make smaller. In music you can make melodies or fragments shorter by decreasing the duration of each note. For instance, if you have a note that lasts for one beat, you can make it twice as short and have it last for half a beat. Or if you have a note that lasts for two beats, you can make it shorter to last for one beat. This shortens the length of the melody or fragment.

You will create diminutions of your fragments on a separate track.

Procedure:

1. Open your "D Variations" file.
2. Add a new software instrument track (track 4) and choose a flute or violin sound.

3. Select both original two-measure fragments in track 2 and paste them into the new track (track 4).

4. Double click on the region to view the notes in the Piano Roll/Matrix Editing window.

5. You will now need to manually make each note twice as short. Don't forget to make rests (spaces where there are no notes) twice as short, too.

6. Manually move the shortened notes to the left to maintain the spacing between notes as in the original fragment.

7. When you have finished making each note twice as short and moving it over, make the region smaller in the Arrange window (see A on the illustration below).

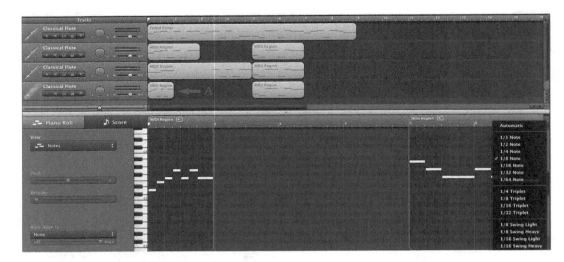

Manually Changing the Pitch Level of a Region

It's a simple and effective task to move a melody, fragment, or variation up or down an octave to create yet more variations. Since students have a general idea of intervals, they can try creating variations at the 3rd or 6th to create instant parallel motion and harmonies. Many software programs have a way to automatically transpose the pitch of regions by half step when adjusting a parameter. However, the notes that appear in the Piano Editor do not move up or down. Selecting notes in the Piano Editor and manually moving the notes up or down reinforces students' understanding of the piano keyboard.

The augmentation an octave or two lower makes a great bass line. The diminutions an octave higher make great melodic variations. Students can even use fragments of the augmentation or diminutions at different intervals for more variety.

> **TIP**
>
> For beginning students, I try to avoid using the software to make adjustments to music such as transposition, inversion of melodic material, retrograde (playing backward), and arpeggiation. I prefer to have my students make adjustments manually, as it reinforces their understanding of these music elements. However, there is a lot to be said for these very powerful software tools and the speed and freedom they provide for the composer and beginning student. The choice is yours.

Skills Required:
Basic understanding of how to copy and paste in the software.
Basic understanding of how to move notes in the software.

National Standards:
• Standard 4, Composing and arranging music within specified guidelines.

Objectives:
Students will understand melodic variations and simple intervals by creating variations of their fragments.

Materials:
Manually Changing the Pitch Level of a Region student assignment sheet.
"D Variations" file.

Procedure:
1. Explain to the students that they will create a few more variations by changing the pitch level (notes) of their fragments.
2. Review the basic concept of intervals. Check for understanding by asking some questions, such as:
   a. If D is the home tone or tonic, then count D as 1 and count up (E is 2, etc.).
   b. What is the 3rd above D?
   c. What is a 3rd below D?
   d. What is the 6th above D?
   e. What is a 6th below D?
   f. What is the 8th (octave) above D?
3. Explain to the students that they will continue working in their "D Variations" files.
4. Explain and demonstrate how they can add two additional tracks to their "D Variations" files. If you like, have the students do this after you explain and demonstrate.
5. Explain to the students that they will copy and paste some of the existing regions into new tracks and simply drag the notes up or down a certain distance—an octave, a 3rd, a 6th.
6. Review the Changing the Pitch Levels of Regions student assignment sheet.
7. As students work individually, go around the room and help students with each problem spot.

Extension:
Have students create variations at the 3rd or 6th.

Modification:
Have students move only one or two variations an octave up and/or down.

Manually Changing the Pitch Level of a Region

Assignment:

Create more melodic variations by copying and pasting your regions into different tracks and changing the notes and ranges.

Procedure:

1. Open your "D Variations" file.
2. Create a new software instrument track (track 5).
3. Change the instrument to be any bass instrument of your choice.
4. Select both Rhythmic Augmentation regions in track 3 and paste them into track 5.
5. Double click on the first region in track 5 to view the notes in the Piano Roll/Matrix Editing window.
6. Select all the notes in the region and drag the notes down one octave. Check the piano keyboard along the left side of the window to verify the new octave.
7. Repeat steps 5 and 6 for the second region in track 5 to create a second bass line in the second region.
8. Create a new track (track 6).
9. Change the instrument to any treble instrument of your choice.
10. Select both Rhythmic Diminution regions in track 4 and paste them into track 6.
11. Double click on the first region in track 6 to view the notes in the Piano Roll/Matrix Editing window.
12. Select all the notes in the first region and drag the notes up one octave. Check the piano keyboard along the left side of the window to verify the new octave.
13. Repeat steps 11 and 12 for the second region in track 6.

The image below shows the new tracks and where to drag the notes up or down an octave.

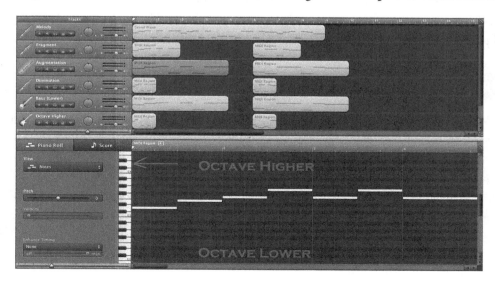

D Melody Piece in Modified Sonata Allegro Form

With all the elements in place in the "D Variations" file, students can create a piece using a modified Sonata Allegro form. It is modified because students will not use modulations to change keys in sections, nor will they use two contrasting melodies, as is customary in classic Sonata Allegro form.

Comparing Sonata Allegro form to the form and structure of a simple expository essay makes it easy for students to relate to and conceptualize the form. Most students will know the five-paragraph structure of basic essay writing, and administrators will love how you integrate writing concepts into your music classroom! The first paragraph is the "thesis statement," sometimes called the "expository" statement. This paragraph clearly states the main idea of the essay. The central three paragraphs of the essay go on to make supporting points about the main idea, backing them up with facts and documents. The final paragraph, called the "conclusion," wraps up the essay. Most students will tell you that to create the conclusion they simply take the first paragraph and restate it, bringing in some additions from the body paragraphs.

Students may want to burn their pieces onto CDs or export their files to play back on a music device. They will need to export only the music section of the file and not the workspace with the fragments, augmentations, diminutions, and other elements. Some software will let you select just the measures to export. Others will only allow the entire file to be exported. If this is the case, a new file will need to be created and the workspace material deleted. Copy the completed file by going to File > Save As > and choosing a name for the piece. Then select the workspace material and delete it. Select all of the remaining music, the piece, and drag the first measure of the music to the first measure of the file. Go to the end of the piece and pull in the end marker. Save the piece again and export.

> **TIP**
>
> Most software for music creation will allow you to label and name regions. It will be easier for students to keep track of the elements they are using by labeling regions before they begin to work on this piece. Please refer to the software manual or "help" menu for more information on how to label and name individual regions.
>
> Remind students that this is an exercise in understanding melody and melodic development using simple melodic variations. This piece will not be in a form they are familiar with. This

TIP *continued*

is not an exercise in creating a piece that they might want to share with their friends. It's great if they like the piece in the end, but the purpose is to gain understanding of melodic development and to practice working in a modified Sonata Allegro form.

Skills Required:

Basic understanding of how to copy and paste in the sequencer.

National Standards:

• Standard 4, Composing and arranging music within specified guidelines.

Objectives:

Students will demonstrate their understanding of Sonata Allegro form by creating a piece in this form using their own loops.

Materials:

D Melody Piece student assignment sheet.
"D Variations" file.

Procedure:

1. Explain to the students that they will be using their own loops to create a piece in any style they choose. This will include choosing an appropriate tempo.
2. Explain the basic elements of Sonata Allegro form, exposition, development, and recapitulation.
3. Explain the need for the statement of the original melody twice in the exposition.
4. Demonstrate some possible orchestrations of the second statement of the melody in the exposition to add interest, for example doubling the melody at the octave or adding augmentation.
5. Demonstrate some possible combinations they could use in the development section.
6. Explain how they should try many combinations and test them to see if they like them.
7. Explain how dynamics can be used to create interest.
8. Explain how the recapitulation is the return to the original melody.
9. Demonstrate how students can add fragments and melodic variations around the original melody in the recapitulation without obliterating the melody.
10. Explain that most pieces do not end on the fourth beat of a measure.

Demonstrate how to end a piece by fading out (see lesson/project 2c) or looping the last regions to the downbeat of the next measure so the piece ends on the first beat of the last measure. As stated in lesson/project 2c, it is not recommended that students choose a parameter where the program creates an automatic fade-out for them. They have spent a lot of time and effort creating their pieces. It is not recommended that they allow an algorithm to decide how their pieces will end. Encourage students to make their own choices about when to begin and end a fade-out.

1. Review the D Melody Piece student assignment sheet
2. Incorporate time for the class to listen to and comment on students' work.

Extension:

Use key changes. Move from the tonic to the dominant in the exposition and from the dominant to the tonic in the development.

Modifications:

1. Provide students with specific material to use in the development section.
2. Provide students with a list of specific techniques to use and the steps to take to accomplish those techniques in the development section.

D Melody Piece

Assignment:

Create a piece of music using your original D Melody, the melodic variations from the Melodic Treatments assignment, and, if you choose to use a drum beat, the drum beat you created this semester in the "My Beat" file. The piece will be a minimum of 48 measures long. You can use any instruments you like and mix and match them any way you like.

Procedure:

1. Open your "D Variations" file.
2. Save this file with a new name: File > Save As "My D Piece _ _" (your initials).
3. If you want to use drums, add three software instrument tracks, choose any drum sounds, and save this file again.
4. Open your "My Beat" file and copy the contents of the file.
5. Open your "My D Piece" file again and paste the contents of your "My Beat" file into your drum tracks.
6. Now you will have all the elements that you need for your "My D Piece": your original eight-bar D Melody (track 1), the fragments (track 2), augmentations (track 3), diminutions (track 4), bass line (track 5), and higher elements (track 6) and your drum beat (tracks 7–9) all in one file.
7. Save this file again. It will look something like this:

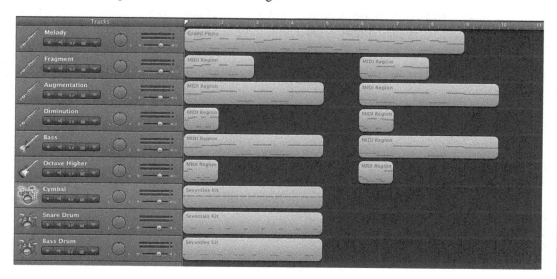

8. The first 10 or so measures will be workspace to save all the elements you now have in this file. Basically, this workspace serves as your Loops Library in the file.
9. Your piece will start at measure 11. You will be selecting an element from the workspace (measures 1–8) and copying it into the file starting at measure 11. Do not drag and drop from measures 1–10. Always copy and paste to save all your work in the first 10 measures.

10. Copy and paste your fragments and variations into any track. They do not need to stay on the track on which you created them. They can be on different tracks and can be played using different instruments.

11. You will use a modified Sonata Allegro Form. It has three sections, Exposition, Development, and Recapitulation.

12. You can create any style piece at any tempo using any combination of instruments. Feel free to change instruments in tracks or add tracks.

13. You can add an Introduction of up to four measures, using material from measures 1–10 if you like, but you do not have to.

14. The Exposition: You must have your entire 8-measure D Dorian Melody twice at the beginning of the piece (16 measures). Consider making some addition or changes in the second statement of the melody to add interest for the listener, such as adding the melody to another instrument, moving the melody up or down an octave, or adding a bass line. Make sure the melody can be heard clearly.

15. The Development: This is the section where you will use the melodic fragments and the variations located in the first 10 measures of this file. The Development section should be between 24 and 36 measures long. You do not have to use all of the materials in the workspace area (measures 1–10), but you will need to use several of them. You use these materials to create a conversation between instruments. Here are some ideas for creating this conversation section (Development):

    • Use a melodic variation or fragment in one instrument track and then repeat it in another (call and response).
    • Layer one fragment or melodic variation on top of another in different instrument tracks and offset them so one enters while the other is playing (stretto). You can separate them at any length: two, four, or more beats.
    • Use a melodic variation or fragment and in another track loop a fragment or melodic variation so they play simultaneously (melodic ostinato).

    This example shows these techniques:

16. You can record new elements into your piece if you like, but you do not have to.

17. You cannot change your original D Dorian Melody.

18. You cannot use anything from the software's prerecorded Loops Library.

19. The Recapitulation: This section is a return to the main idea, you original D Dorian Melody. At this point, because the listener has heard your melody, fragments, and

variations, you can add some of the material you created in the Development section to "color" the melody. This section should be between 8 and 16 measures long.

20. Your piece needs to be a minimum of 48 measures long, starting at measure 11. That will take you minimally to measure 59.

21. End your piece on a beat or fade-out.

22. Once you have completed your piece, mix the piece for volume. Keep in mind that the loudest track at the loudest part of your piece cannot be so loud that it goes into the red (overload), and the Master Volume also cannot go into the red (overload). If an instrument is not loud enough, lower the volume on the other instruments or double the track. Once you have your rough mix, try using volume automation to change the volume levels of your tracks over time. Be careful to not overload each track or the Master Volume.

PART II Developing Basic Musical Skills

How Ideas Evolve over Time

Most software for music creation contains a variety of sound effects as short prerecorded audio regions in the Loops Library and in the software synthesizer modules that can be triggered from a MIDI device (keyboard, pad, etc.). Students can also record and collect their own sounds. In this project, students can explore developing ideas over time without the constraints or concerns of their knowledge of musical elements. This project also provides an excellent vehicle for introducing some of the technical elements needed for mixing tracks. The use of volume, panning, and reverb are the basic elements in mixing that help create sonic space for all the tracks to be balanced well and clearly heard. Given that mixing is a combination of other considerations, including the use of EQ and compression, the teacher may decide to incorporate these ideas, as explored in unit 26.

Students can work in pairs or in small groups as a modification. This is also a great "getting to know you" project for everyone at the beginning of a semester. The entire class can brainstorm some possible scenarios together. Working in pairs, students get to meet one another, they can refresh their memory on how to use the software, and they can work collaboratively.

Depending on the age group you teach, you may choose to give students a variety of scenarios to choose from or limit their choice rather than leaving it to their imagination.

There are three lessons for the Sound FX Project—lessons 9a, 9b, and 9c—but only one student assignment sheet. If the teacher chooses to just do lesson 9a and not delve into panning and reverb, a modification of the student assignment sheet will be necessary. Since this project will take a few class sessions, the first class can set up the project, and subsequent classes can begin with the lessons on panning and reverb as tools for students to consider using in their projects.

TIP

I have some content restrictions for this project. First, it must be what I call "Disney Rated G," or as I say: "If you wouldn't say it or play it sitting next to your grandmother in a house of worship, don't do it here," and "No locker-room talk and no sounds of bodily functions." The other restriction is that no one can be injured, shot, blown up, or killed! For some reason, the most popular scenario treats us to the sounds of a car driving through a storm and then breaking down, steps

> **TIP** *continued*
>
> in the mud, knocking on a door, the door creaking open, screams, gunshots or explosions, and running and screaming. I make the rules known in advance, as they are in the student assignment sheet, and I remind them daily throughout the project.

Skills Required:

Basic understanding of how to record and use loops in the software.

National Standards:

- Standard 2, Performing on instruments, alone and with others, a varied repertoire of music.
- Standard 4, Composing and arranging music within specified guidelines.
- Standard 6, Listening to, analyzing, and describing music.
- Standard 8, Understanding relationships between music, the arts, and disciplines outside the arts.
- Standard 9, Understanding music in relation to history and culture.

Objectives:

Students will demonstrate their understanding of how sounds create imagery by creating a piece using sound effects.

Materials:

Sound FX student assignment sheet.
A library or collection of sound effects or a means to field record audio.

Procedure:

1. Explain and demonstrate some of the sound effects in the software.
2. Explain and demonstrate how the sounds can be placed or recorded together to create a series of images that tell a story.
3. Explain and demonstrate how to create imagery with sound effects over time.
4. Review the student assignment sheet, especially the rules.
5. As students work individually, go around the room and help students with any problem spots, always checking for appropriate content.
6. Incorporate time for the class to listen to and comment on students' work.

Extensions:

1. Let students work independently.
2. Have students brainstorm several scenes and write them on index cards. Either individually, in pairs, or in small groups, have students pick a card and work on that project.
3. If recording devices are available, and they are on most smartphones today, this entire project can be accomplished with students' "found" sounds. Students can work in teams to gather sounds and use them in a single project or individual projects. Students can either be

restricted to use their own found sounds or allowed to augment them with what they can find in the software or obtain from their peers.

Modifications:

1. Create and provide students with stories.
2. Have students work in pairs.
3. Distribute a library of sounds for students to choose from.

STUDENT ASSIGNMENT SHEET

The Sound Effects (FX) Piece

Assignment:
Create a piece using sounds and effects.

Procedure:
1. Open a new file: File > New.
2. Save the file as "Sound FX __" (your two initials).
3. Explore the sound effects in the software, both in the software instruments and the loops.
4. Write a few sentences that describe your story.
5. Create your story. Each sound should bring images to mind. The sounds should combine together and evolve over time to "tell" your story. When we listen to your piece, we should be able to understand the story just by listening.
6. Keep in mind that the listeners do not have any visuals to help them experience your piece. It might take 20–30 seconds for someone to walk out of his or her home, close the door, and walk down the stairs and across the front walkway to get to the car, but the listeners don't need to hear all this in "real time." A few seconds of walking should be sufficient for the listeners to get the idea.
7. Your piece is to be a minimum of 45 seconds long.

Rules:
1. You can use any sound effect or create any imagery, as you like, as long as it is "Disney Rated G."
2. No explosions, gunshots, laser shots, or any other sounds of destruction followed by people screaming and/or running away. Do not have it sound like something is being killed!
3. No sounds of or sounds like bodily functions.
4. No sounds or imagery that might be offensive to any individual or group of people.
5. Use your common sense. If you have a question about using a sound or producing an image in the listeners' minds through that sound, ask the teacher.

Things to Consider:
1. Have you timed one element to the next so the listener is always interested and engaged?
2. Is there so much time spent on one element that the listeners lose their engagement with the piece? (They get bored!)
3. Are the volume levels of each sound element even from one to the next?
4. When one element should be much louder or softer, is it?
5. Have you used panning to separate your sounds or to have the listener's attention going to one side (left or right)?
6. Have you used reverb to make sound elements appear farther away or closer to the listener?

Creating Two-Dimensional Sound Images and Sonic Space

This extension to the project introduces students to the basics of mixing. Mixing is both a science and an art. Professional mixers spend a lifetime perfecting their skill and craft. It is an enormous subject and could consume an entire semester or year of study. For the teacher who has little or no experience mixing, treat this subject much as you would conduct an ensemble. Although each genre of music has some standard mixing practices, panning a track is similar to deciding where each instrument will sit in the ensemble, and the overall volume of an instrument/track is dependent on what part of the piece should be more present, that is, should sound closer to the listener, at any given point in the piece.

The Sound FX project is an excellent time to explore panning and volume. Panning moves sound from left to right. Panning also shifts the volume output of a track to the side to which you are panning it. Panning the track more to the left adds more volume, also referred to as energy, to the left side of a mix. Creating an equal balance of energy along each side, left and right, should be considered when using panning in music. Volume moves sound forward and back. The louder something is, the more present or closer it sounds. The softer something is, the less present or further away it sounds. If a student wants one part of a track louder than another part of the track, the student can simply copy the region to a duplicate track and move the volume slider or knob. Use multiple tracks for the same sound if multiple volumes are desired. Most software allows for many tracks in a single piece.

A good place to start mixing is to determine the loudest section of the piece and mix from there. The loudest track at the loudest part of the piece should never exceed the volume capabilities of the system (i.e., go into the red). This overloading of volume will cause distortion on the track. The overall output volume of all the tracks (the master or output track) should also never overload. Once you have determined the loudest part of the piece and the volume setting for the loudest track, mix tracks down from there. In mixing, less is more.

Because this project uses sound effects, you will not have to worry about the common mistake of the bass drum being the loudest part of the piece. The presence of a bass drum is not just determined by volume but also by timbre and EQ, and that is beyond the scope of this lesson. Students can concentrate on making mixing decisions based on nonmusical elements in their Sound FX piece. Should it sound closer or further away?

Track automation allows the software to make changes in a track automatically. You can automate various parameters, including panning and volume. Panning automation moves sound automatically from one ear to the next. Remember, panning also shifts volume from one side to the other. So watch your track and output volumes. Volume automation changes volume as the track progresses, creating crescendi and decrescendi along a track. You can demonstrate these kinds of track automations. However, it is crucial to impress on students that track automation is the very last step that should be taken when mixing a piece. When you automate the volume of a track, you decide how soft or how loud it will be. How can you decide the maximum volume output of a track before the whole piece is created, including panning and so many other factors? It is difficult to change volume for mixing once a track is automated. The general overall output volume of each track, the balance of volumes in the left and right ear, and which instruments should be more present than others should be determined before any volume automation is used. Volume automation should be the last process in mixing a track and should not be used in the composition process if at all possible.

Skills Required:
Basic understanding of how to record and use loops in the sequencer.

National Standards:
- Standard 2, Performing on instruments, alone and with others, a varied repertoire of music.
- Standard 4, Composing and arranging music within specified guidelines.
- Standard 6, Listening to, analyzing, and describing music.
- Standard 8, Understanding relationships between music, the arts, and disciplines outside the arts.
- Standard 9, Understanding music in relation to history and culture.

Objectives:
Students will demonstrate their understanding of creating two-dimensional space in their Sound FX piece by using panning to separate tracks into various places along the left-right ear aural plane and to make things sound closer or further away using volume.

Materials:
"Sound FX" file.
Sound FX student assignment sheet.

Procedure:
1. Define "stereophonic": reproducing a sound signal using two or more sources. A pair of speakers or a pair of headphones can create a stereo sound "image," specific sounds clearly heard in the left or right ear as opposed to all sounds in both ears.
2. Explain that the default setting of the pan knob/dial (potentiometer or pot) is in the center. This gives the listener the impression that the sound is coming from one source (monophonic), the center. Since we have two ears, we can create an image of sound coming from the left or right ear and combinations of both.
3. Explain and demonstrate how turning the pan knob/dial to the left sends most of the sound signal to the left ear and turning the pan knob to the right sends most of the sound signal to the right ear. The pan knob sends the sound signal as far to the right or left as you turn it. You can vary how far left or right you send a signal, creating sonic space for each track.
4. Explain and demonstrate how volume makes something sound closer or further away. The lower the volume, the further away something sounds. The louder the volume, the closer something sounds.
5. Explain how volume can be manipulated using the track volume slider or knob. Track automation should be demonstrated at this point with caution.

Extensions:

1. Explain how track automation of panning can change the placement of a signal over the course of the track. Have students use track automation for panning when appropriate.
2. Distribute the same file to all students and allow them to add panning and make volume adjustments.

Modification:

Give students specific parameters for panning and notice how the sounds change. For example, pan one track left to 20, pan one track right to 20.

LESSON 9c

Using Reverb to Create Three-Dimensional Space

This is an excellent time to explore the use of reverb to simulate placing sound in a space to create a three-dimensional sound image. Reverberation, or reverb for short, simulates the sound of a room. Is something being played in a small space or a large space? Is the large room a church or a gymnasium? In general, the number of different reverb settings used in a single piece should be limited. Listeners can only be in one place at a time, so they can only listen to a sound being made in a particular room. If we are in a large room and someone is walking and then running in the room, it should sound as though we are in the same room with the same reverb. Change the reverb, and you change the environment.

All software has preset and editable settings for reverb. Ideally, instruments/tracks are grouped and added to reverb by sending the signal to a separate channel, an auxiliary or bus channel on the mixing board. This allows control over the amount of reverb for each track. In some entry-level software, reverb can only be added to each track or the output/master track, and creating an auxiliary or bus channel is not possible.

Skills Required:
Basic understanding of how to record and use loops in the sequencer.

National Standards:
- Standard 2, Performing on instruments, alone and with others, a varied repertoire of music.
- Standard 4, Composing and arranging music within specified guidelines.
- Standard 6, Listening to, analyzing, and describing music.
- Standard 8, Understanding relationships between music, the arts, and disciplines outside the arts.
- Standard 9, Understanding music in relation to history and culture.

Objectives:
Students will demonstrate their understanding of creating three-dimensional space in their Sound FX piece by using reverb to simulate a room or space.

Materials:
"Sound FX" file.
Sound FX student assignment sheet.

Procedure:
1. Define "reverberate" or "reverb": the sound of a specific room or space after the original sound source is removed.
2. Explain that reverberation is adding effects to simulate rooms of various sizes. Compare the sound in a coat closet to that of a gymnasium. Sound bounces off hard surfaces until

it dissipates or fades away. The larger the room and the harder the surfaces, the more reverberation.

3. Demonstrate how to find and load a reverb unit into the track.

4. Demonstrate some of the presets in the reverb unit.

5. Demonstrate what key components of the reverb unit—such as room size and shape, reverb time, and the combination of wet and dry signal—do to affect the quality of the sound.

6. Caution students about overuse of reverb and other plug-ins.

Extensions:

1. Discuss a few important parameters: room size, room shape, predelay, reverb time, wet/dry mix, and balance.

2. Show students how to save their custom settings if available.

3. Have students create three distinct reverb settings for three different tracks.

Modification:

Give students specific preset reverb selections to choose from.

Whole and Half Steps

This section is designed to give an outline of what you might explore in order for students to gain an understanding of the mechanics of music, that is, music theory, as it relates visually to the piano keyboard. Once students can memorize the piano keyboard, envision it in the mind's eye, and understand and describe the relationship of one note to the next, they will be able to comprehend even the most advanced music theory concepts. Understanding whole and half steps, how to build a major scale, basic intervals, and building chords on scale degrees is the foundation for music composition in all styles and genres. There is only a taste here of what you might use to explore these valuable concepts. Hundreds of free resources are available online and in print to help teachers explain and reinforce the basic concepts of music theory.

Skills Required:
Understanding of the piano keyboard.

National Standards:
- Standard 6, Listening to, analyzing, and describing music.
- Standard 7, Evaluating music and music performances.

Objectives:
Students will understand and be able to identify whole and half steps on the piano keyboard by verbal identification to the teacher.

Materials:
A graphic of the piano keyboard projected to the students with an overhead projector, with an interactive whiteboard, or via the networked computers.

Procedure:
1. Define a half step: the shortest distance between any two notes.
2. Show half steps on the keyboard, white key to black key and black key to white key. Make sure to show the two half steps between the white keys: between B and C and between E and F.

3. Check for understanding by asking students to describe half steps up and down from a given key (note). The teacher can elicit answers from the group or go around the room to individuals and have students hold up flash cards with the pitch names. Or if an interactive whiteboard is available, have students come up and play the notes. Students can also play and record the intervals into the software or use a notation program.

4. Define a whole step: two half steps equal one whole step.

5. Show whole steps on the piano keyboard.

6. Make sure students understand how to find half steps up and down from all notes but especially B, C, E, and F. Check for understanding, as shown for the half steps up in procedure 3.

LESSON 10b

Understanding Basic Generic Intervals

Understanding basic, generic intervals is a foundation for understanding scales and scale degrees.

Skills Required:
Knowledge of the piano keyboard.

National Standards:
- Standard 6, Listening to, analyzing, and describing music.
- Standard 7, Evaluating music and music performances.

Objectives:
Students will understand how to identify basic, generic intervals by completing the Basic Intervals worksheet.

Materials:
Basic Intervals worksheet.

Procedure:
1. Define "interval": the distance between any two notes.
2. Explain that the first note is always counted as 1, no matter what note you start on, and that you count every note up to the final note to determine the interval.
3. Check for understanding by asking the students to hold up their fingers to identify these intervals:
   a. C to D (they should hold up two fingers).
   b. E to G (they should hold up three fingers).
   c. A to F (they should hold up six fingers).
4. Hand out the Basic Intervals worksheet and review.

Extensions:
1. Give students intervals on a piano keyboard to identify or draw.
2. Give students intervals in standard notation to identify or draw.
3. More advanced students or college students can identify the quality of intervals, major, minor, diminished, augmented and perfect.

Modification:
Limit the number of intervals (one or two) for students to identify each day.

Name:...

Date:..

The distance between any two notes is called an interval. Basic intervals can be described as prime, 2nd, 3rd, 4th, 5th, 6th, 7th, and octave. You can figure out the basic interval by counting the first note as 1 (prime) and then counting up using only the white keys. For instance, the distance between C and E is a 3rd. C is 1, D is 2 (the second note), and E is 3 (the third note). In other words, E is the third note above C. Remember, always count the first note as 1.

Compound intervals (larger than an octave) also exist. The 9th, 10th, 11th, 12th, and 13th are the most common, but you can create any interval just by counting the first note as 1 and counting up from there.

Assignment:

Put an *X* on the keyboard for each pair of notes given in the illustration below. Name the basic interval below each keyboard.

Example: C to G

Name the notes: **C   G**

Name the interval: **5th**

1) D to F

Name the notes:_____

Name the interval:_____

2) A to B

Name the notes:_____

Name the interval:_____

3) G to C

Name the notes:_____

Name the interval:_____

4) E to E

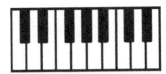

Name the notes:_____

Name the interval:_____

5) B to F

Name the notes:_____

Name the interval:_____

6) C to A

Name the notes:_____

Name the interval:_____

7) C to E

Name the notes:_____

Name the interval:_____

8) F to E

Name the notes:_____

Name the interval:_____

9) A to E

Name the notes:_____

Name the interval:_____

10) E to G

Name the notes:_____

Name the interval:_____

Understanding Major Scales

The foundation of all Western music theory is the major scale. If students can understand how to build a major scale and visualize any major scale on the piano keyboard, they can then understand how to alter the major scale to make any number of scales or modes and understand how those alterations affect intervals and chords built around that scale or alteration. If students can take it a step further and can understand key signatures, the circle of 4ths, and the circle of 5ths, they will have a tremendous vocabulary of music theory.

Dozens of publications are available both in print and online, in the form of books and software, for students to use for practice in building major scales and for teachers to use for assessment. In this lesson, students record major scales in various keys. You can use either real-time or step input, depending on the students' abilities and your preferences. If students are to record in real time, make sure they slow the metronome down to about 80–85 for recording. Record one note per click (quarter notes).

Skills Required:
Knowledge of the piano keyboard.

National Standards:
- Standard 6, Listening to, analyzing, and describing music.
- Standard 7, Evaluating music and music performances.

Objectives:
Students will understand how to build a major scale starting on any key by recording a major scale in the keys given.

Materials:
Understanding Major Scales student assignment sheet.

Procedure:
1. Review the layout of the piano keyboard and how to locate notes.
2. Review half and whole steps.
3. Define "scale": a specific combination of whole and half steps that forms a series of notes.

4. Define "major scale": a specific order of whole and half steps such that all the notes are a whole step apart, except for two half steps: the one between the third and fourth degrees of the scale, and the one between the seventh and eighth degrees.

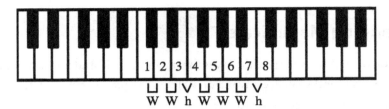

5. Review the student assignment sheet.

Extensions:

1. Have students record in real time (playing to the metronome as time goes by).
2. Have students record two octaves of scales.

Modifications:

1. Let students step-input (draw the notes in).
2. Allow student to drawing the notes on a blank piano keyboard to refer to when recording
3. Allow students to record while following along with the piano supplemental material found on the companion website.

Understanding Major Scales

A major scale is a combination of notes in a specific order of whole and half steps. All the notes are a whole step apart, except for two half steps: the one between the third and fourth degrees of the scale, and the one between the seventh and eighth degrees.

The diagram below shows a major scale beginning on the note C and the placement of whole and half steps in relation to each degree of the scale.

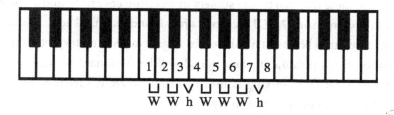

Assignment:

Using the combination of whole and half steps described for a major scale, record one octave of each of the following major scales:

1. C major
2. F major
3. G major
4. A major
5. D major
6. B♭ major
7. E major

Procedure:

1. Open a new file: File > New.
2. Create a software instrument track for each of the scales you will record and choose a regular piano sound.
3. Slow the click down to a speed where you can play the scale accurately, one note per click, without stopping.
4. Record one octave of C major scale on track 1, one note per click.
5. Quantize.
6. Play back and listen to the scale after you have recorded it.
7. Record one octave of F major scale on track 2.
8. Quantize.
9. Play back and listen to the scale after you have recorded it.
10. Continue recording and quantizing one scale per track.
11. Play back and listen to each scale after you have recorded each scale.

Analyzing a Remix 1

Remixing is a huge topic that can be the subject of an entire course of study. The next project briefly explores remixing using MIDI files for its music and technical educational value.

According to Eduardo Navas, "a music remix, in general, is a reinterpretation of a preexisting song, meaning that the 'aura' of the original will be dominant in the remixed version" (http://remixtheory.net/). Remixing comes in many different varieties, has evolved over many years, and is used in many different styles of music.

A cover song is a version of a song recorded by an artist other than the one who first recorded it. Remixing is the process of using portions of one piece of music and adding contemporary elements to create a new piece. In a sense, remixing creates a kind of cover song. The extent to which an artist maintains the integrity of the original or reinterprets sections of a prerecorded piece may determine whether or not the piece is "technically" a remix or a "cover." Each teacher will need to decide the extent to which he or she chooses to make these distinctions in the context of a classroom setting.

Early experiments with remixing can be traced back to technology experiments such as *Switched-On Bach,* an album created by Wendy Carlos and Benjamin Folkman. It was a re-creation of several pieces by Johann Sebastian Bach that were recorded using synthesizers. Although sounds were manipulated, it was basically Bach's work played on a contemporary instrument. Another venture into using technology with "classical" music was Walter Murphy's piece "A Fifth of Beethoven." It takes the original motive of the first movement of Beethoven's Symphony no. 5 and re-creates it using contemporary popular instruments, including a disco beat. The first lesson in this unit is an analysis of Beethoven's original and a comparison of it to Murphy's remix.

Today, remixing is a combination of using audio and MIDI and is an art form in and unto itself. Original audio recordings are cut up into sections and manipulated for tempo with a drum beat and other contemporary popular music instruments, and effects are added to change a piece from its original form to a contemporary one. Sometimes a contemporary song is remixed as a dance piece by adding drums and beats and changing the form. This style of remixing requires some advanced skills with audio and the technology and can be explored after a basic understanding of audio editing and manipulation is acquired through the lessons in part III.

Skills Required:

No technical skills required.

National Standards:

- Standard 6, Listening to, analyzing, and describing music.
- Standard 7, Evaluating music and music performances.
- Standard 8, Understanding relationships between music, the other arts, and disciplines outside the arts.
- Standard 9, Understanding music in relation to history and culture.

Objectives:

Students will demonstrate their knowledge of song form by analyzing and comparing two given pieces of music. Students will also discuss the musical elements that influence style and define the form and structure of a song.

Materials:

Audio recording of Ludwig von Beethoven's Symphony no. 5, first movement.
Audio recording of Walter Murphy's piece "A Fifth of Beethoven."
Song Analysis worksheet.

Procedure:

1. Play the audio of at least the exposition section of Beethoven's Symphony no. 5, first movement.
2. Ask students to describe the different elements of the music.
3. What is the main motive?
4. How does Beethoven use the motive?
5. Describe some of the elements that happen around the motive and main melodic ideas.
6. Play an audio recording of Walter Murphy's "A Fifth of Beethoven."
7. Ask students to map out the form of the piece using the Song Analysis worksheet.
8. Have students describe what happens in each section.
9. Some questions to be considered:
    a. How did Walter Murphy use Beethoven's motive?
    b. What makes the two pieces similar?
    c. What are the differences between the two pieces?
    d. What instruments were added or taken away?
    e. What are the different melodic lines?
    f. What is happening in the accompaniment?
    g. What, if anything, could be considered the "hook" or "chorus"?

Extensions:

1. Give students other pieces or have students find their own pieces that have been "remixed."
2. Let students work in groups or pairs to analyze the two pieces.

Modification:
Have the class work in teams to answer one question per team.

Analyzing a Remix 2

The original piece "Chocolate Rain," by Tay Zonday, was at one point the most watched You-Tube video. It is a simple two-part song. The professionally reconstructed remix takes the original elements and transforms the piece into classic hip-hop style. Some teachers may consider the video content of the remix inappropriate to use in their classrooms. An audio version can be used instead.

Skills Required:
No technical skills required.

National Standards:
- Standard 6, Listening to, analyzing, and describing music.
- Standard 7, Evaluating music and music performances.
- Standard 8, Understanding relationships between music, the other arts, and disciplines outside the arts.
- Standard 9, Understanding music in relation to history and culture.

Objectives:
Students will demonstrate their knowledge of song form by analyzing and comparing two given pieces of music. Students will also discuss the musical elements that influence style and define the form and structure of a song.

Materials:
Video or audio of "Chocolate Rain (www.youtube.com/watch?v=EwTZ2xpQwpA)."
Video or audio of "Cherry Chocolate Rain(www.youtube.com/watch?v=2x2W12A8Qow)."
Song Analysis worksheet.

Procedure:
1. Show the video clip of "Chocolate Rain."
2. Ask students to describe the different elements of the music, using these questions:
   a. What are the different melodic lines?
   b. What, if anything, could be considered the "hook" or "chorus"?
   c. What is happening in the accompaniment, that is, the piano, bass, drums?
   d. Does the accompaniment change at all? If so, when? How?
3. Show the video of "Cherry Chocolate Rain."
4. Have students describe what happens in each section of the piece as in number 2 above.
5. What musical elements make this hip-hop?

6. How did the person who remixed this piece use the original musical elements from "Chocolate Rain"?

Extensions:

1. Have students work in groups and have each group describe all the details of a specific section. One group works on the A section (verse), another on the B section (chorus), and so on.
2. Have students use the Song Analysis worksheet from unit 2 for both pieces and then write a few paragraphs comparing and contrasting the musical elements.

Modification:

Listen to and watch the video only for "Cherry Chocolate Rain" to discuss the elements that make up this version of hip-hop style.

MIDI Remix

This project is perfect for beginning students. Students can see and hear how others compose and arrange music by listening to MIDI files and have early success composing, recomposing, and arranging music while understanding the basics of MIDI technology. A student assignment sheet is given and should be customized by each teacher according to his or her students' needs.

Using MIDI files allows students to create pieces without having to start from scratch and to see how other composers treat elements of music including melody, harmony, accompaniments and form. MIDI files often also contain mixing data, such as volume and panning, so students can experience how others created a mix. When importing MIDI files, students will have no choice but to analyze the music to decide which parts they will use, edit, or delete. It is up to the teacher to decide whether to limit the amount of music material to be used from a MIDI file. For instance, limiting the use of up to eight measures of music at a time from the original MIDI file might be a good way to avoid having students simply importing the file and adding a drum beat.

Dance remixes usually take the audio track of a performance and add a dance beat to it. Dance remixes of popular music can include editing of the original audio file and a change to the form and structure of the original piece. Sometimes the audio is edited, but frequently it is simply cut into appropriate lengths. However, it should be noted that adding a beat as a significant element of the music that evolves and changes the form of the piece, extending the original music to several minutes in length, is a legitimate form of remixing and can be the foundation of exploring dance styles such as house and techno.

This project will take several class sessions to complete. Introduce each session by showing students the original version of a piece and a remix. Presenting a variety of original music and remix styles is a great opportunity for students to listen to music they might not otherwise be exposed to. Students will watch and be more engaged in the listening process with video. Show students videos of the first movement of Beethoven's Symphony no. 5 conducted by Arturo Toscanini, Leonard Bernstein, Herbert von Karajan, and Gustavo Dudamel. Students will listen to Beethoven three or four times watching the video!

An Internet search for remixes will provide plenty of examples. Here are some good originals and their remixes:

Beethoven's Symphony no. 5, first movement, and Walter Murphy's "A Fifth of Beethoven."
The Police, "Every Breath You Take" and Puff Daddy, "I'll Be Missing You."
Modest Mussorgsky's "Pictures at an Exhibition" and the Emerson, Lake and Palmer version.

A variety of free MIDI files is available at dozens of locations online. A specific piece can be found by typing in its name followed by "MIDI" in any search engine. A few more resources for MIDI files are:

Partners in Rhyme is a website that offers public domain music for free and available for purchase. It also has a collection of MIDI files divided into categories such as rock and pop, classical, hip-hop, dance/techno, jazz, Motown, Broadway, and many more. Instructions for downloading these MIDI files are on the website at www.partnersinrhyme.com/midi/index.shtml.

At www.midiworld.com, one may find not only a selection of MIDI files but also an active forum where users and creators of MIDI exchange ideas and have questions answered.

One of the largest collections of MIDI files is www.classicalarchives.com. This site requires users to sign up for a free or paid membership subscription.

Other large collections of classical MIDI files include www.classicalmidiconnection.com and www.midisite.co.uk.

Both Ken Simpson of Brookwood High School in Snellville, Georgia, and Scott Watson of Parkland School District in Allentown, Pennsylvania, have their students do holiday music covers and remixes every year. A portion of the proceeds from the sale of the CDs goes to charity. This is a great fundraiser for school and contributes something back to the community. Check with your school district about sales of CDs and permissions for students' music, and make sure that none of the music your students use has a copyright, or if it does, that you retain the proper permissions and pay all applicable fees and royalties. For details on copyright issues in the classroom, refer to *The Teacher's Guide to Music, Media and Copyright Law,* by James Frankel.

Some MIDI files are created with the intention for them to come as close to exactly reproducing a recorded performance as possible; others reinterpret the original. All the elements of recorded performance, including specific instruments, dynamics, panning, pedaling when appropriate, and a variety of other factors are included in the MIDI file. When importing MIDI into any software for music creation, all of these elements, called MIDI parameters, are also imported, whether or not they may be desirable for use in a student's new piece. Not all MIDI files are created equal. A good MIDI file for this project will contain information that was quantized and have few MIDI parameter changes through the piece. If there are a lot of velocity, volume, pedaling, and other MIDI parameter changes, it will take longer for the students to reset the file than you want it to. The focus for most beginning students should be on manipulation of the musical elements, not correcting or resetting MIDI parameters. College students may have different requirements in their classes. It might be a good idea to distribute a collection of prescreened MIDI files to your students. If students import their own MIDI files, encourage them to immediately delete the MIDI parameters, especially those of volume and panning, so they can make their own choices when it comes to mixing the piece. Common MIDI parameters to be aware of include program (instrument sound), velocity (volume), pan (signal directed to the right or left ear) and sustain pedal. MIDI parameters can be edited in a variety of ways, and these are specific to the software used. In general, software that has a MIDI Piano Roll/Matrix Editing window will have the MIDI parameter editing functions in that window. The software will also have MIDI parameter lists. Open the list and scan down, deleting any volume, panning, or other changes desired that are on the list. Check the software documentation for more details on how to edit MIDI parameters in the specific software you use.

More information on the history of MIDI and other topics on MIDI can be found at the MIDI Manufacturers Association website: www.midi.org/index.php.

On day 3 of this project, when students are ready to add their own music, it is up to each teacher to decide whether to allow students to add prerecorded loops from the Loops Library. This lesson and student assignment sheet assumes that students will not be using prerecorded loops and must create and record their own elements.

> **TIP**
>
> I have found that many beginning students benefit from my going through the details of a MIDI file with the whole class. As a class, the students define and divide sections and label them with markers, look at each track, define and label its role in the music (i.e. melody, bass, harmony 1, harmony 2, etc.), and notice any changes to these tracks in each section of the song. Some elements may move from one track to the next. Note what the change in orchestration/instrumentation makes to the sound between sections and the overall scope of the piece. This time spent on a MIDI file as a class helps students learn the elements of music.

101

Skills Required:
A basic understanding of how to edit MIDI in the software.

National Standards:
- Standard 6, Listening to, analyzing, and describing music.
- Standard 7, Evaluating music and music performances.
- Standard 8, Understanding relationships between music, the other arts, and disciplines outside the arts.
- Standard 9, Understanding music in relation to history and culture.

Objectives:
Students will demonstrate their understanding of how to manipulate MIDI to create an original piece based on an existing piece of music.

Materials:
MIDI files of various pieces.
MIDI Remix student assignment sheet.
MIDI Example.

Procedure:
Day 1:

1. Show an original piece and a remix at the beginning of each class during the scope of this project.
2. Explain how to find MIDI files.
3. Explain and demonstrate how to download and import MIDI files into the software.

4. Allow students time to search for and download MIDI files or choose from files distributed by the teacher.

Day 2:
1. Show an original piece and a remix at the beginning of each class during the scope of this project.
2. Review how to find, download, and import MIDI files into the software.
3. Demonstrate how to locate and delete MIDI parameters, such as volume and panning.
4. Identify different elements of the piece on each track, such as melody, harmony, bass lines, drums, and percussion.
5. Identify each section of the piece, such as introduction, verse, chorus, bridge, and coda.
6. Demonstrate how to split regions to delineate between each section of the piece. For instance, the melody track will probably be one long region. Split the region into multiple regions to have a separate region for the introduction, verse, chorus, bridge, and coda. You can split the regions of all the tracks at the same time to delineate sections.
7. Demonstrate how to rename each region.
8. Allow students time to delete MIDI parameters and identify and split regions according to elements in their files.

Day 3 and Beyond:
1. Show an original piece and a remix at the beginning of each class during the scope of this project.
2. Review editing and deleting MIDI parameters, identifying tracks according to musical elements and splitting and labeling regions.
3. Demonstrate how students can record their own music or add loops and other musical elements and sound effects to their pieces.
4. Circulate through the class and help students as needed.
5. Incorporate time for the class to listen to and comment on students' work.

Extension:

Students work in groups. Each group describes all the details of a specific section. One group works on the A section (verse), another on the B section (chorus), and so on.

Modification:

1. Distribute a file with MIDI already loaded in the software and free of MIDI parameters.
2. Allow students to use prerecorded loops with their MIDI file.

MIDI Remix

Remixing is the process of using portions of one piece of music and adding contemporary elements to create a new piece. Simply taking a piece of music, changing the sound of the instruments, and adding a contemporary drum beat is a very basic kind of remixing.

Assignment:

Remix a piece of music using a MIDI file.

Procedure:

1. Choose a MIDI file as the piece of music that will be used in your remix.
2. Listen to the file and label the sections: "A," "B," and so on, or "Chorus," "Verse," and so on.
3. Listen to each track in each section and label the regions according to its role in the music, that is, melody, bass line, harmony, drum beat, and so on.
4. Choose specific regions of the piece to use in your remix:
    a. You may use regions from a melody track, accompaniment tracks, or bass line track.
    b. You may use one or several sections with several tracks.
    c. You may change the music in these selections. Do not use the entire piece.
5. You may change MIDI parameters that may be in the original MIDI file. Some MIDI parameters include:
    Tempo (beats per minute).
    Instruments (program/patches).
    Volume (velocity).
    Panning (amount of sound in the left or right ear for each track).
6. You may add any music using any instrument, in any style that you like, by recording into new tracks.
7. Your piece should be a minimum of 64 measures long.

Eighth and Sixteenth Combinations

This lesson reviews reading of rhythms using Rhythm States (see unit 3) and introduces how to read and perform eighth- and sixteenth-note combinations.

Skills Required:
No prior skills required.

National Standards:
- Standard 1, Singing alone and with others, a varied repertoire of music.
- Standard 2, Performing on instruments, alone and with others, a varied repertoire of music.

Objectives:
Students will demonstrate an understanding of reading basic rhythms in standard music notation and in the Matrix Editor by singing, clapping, playing, or recording the rhythms on the Overheads 7, 8, 9 and/or 10 from the Appendix.

Materials:
Overheads 7, 8, 9 and/or 10 from the Appendix

Procedure:
1. Display the Reading Rhythms overhead via an overhead projector, whiteboard, iPad, computer projector, or Apple Remote Desktop. Any variation of display option can be used, as long as the teacher can freely point to the rhythms.
2. Explain basic rhythm notation of eighth and sixteenth notes and their relations to each other.
3. Have half the class say eighth notes ("U-tah") to a click track or prerecorded drum groove while the other half says sixteenth notes ("Mi-ssi-ssi-ppi") to a click track or prerecorded drum groove. Make sure they listen to each other to hear how the rhythms line up. Switch rhythms with groups.

4. Using Overhead 7, explain how two sixteenth notes equal one eighth note. The first two sixteenths ("Mi-ssi-") can be replaced with an eighth ("U-") forming a new pattern ("U-ssi-ppi"). Use Overhead 8 if you use a different counting method from Rhythm States.

FIGURE 12aLP1

5. Explain how the second two sixteenths ("ssi-ppi") can be replaced with an eighth ("-tah"), forming a new pattern ("Mi-ssi-tah").

FIGURE 12aLP2

6. Set a metronome to 80–90, depending on your students' experience and skill level.

7. Unsing Overhead 9, point to a rhythm and vary the rhythms at random, combining quarters, eighths, and sixteenths while students speak, play, or clap the rhythms in time to the metronome. Be sure to point to the rhythm before the click, on the second eighth of the beat, the upbeat, so students have time to read the rhythm and be able to perform it correctly on the beat.

8. Use Overhead 10 when student are comfortable with the rhythms.

Extensions:

1. Have one group of students clap steady quarters or eighths as the other group performs the random rhythms in steps 8 and 9. Switch groups.

2. Return to unit 4 and have students record the more advanced rhythms.

Modification:

Divide this lesson into two class sessions, one for each eighth/sixteenth combination.

Rhythmic Improvisation: Call and Response

The essence of composition can be said to begin with improvisation, either at an instrument or in one's head, after which developed musical thoughts are achieved by editing the original improvisations. Improvisation skills are often associated with jazz. However, experience and practice with improvisation enhances comfort with the language of music in every genre. Encouraging improvisation early makes it just another musical skill and nothing to be feared by the teacher or the student. Begin with rhythm; then add notes to create melodic improvisations.

Improvisation can be thought of as a language. The more vocabulary you have available to you, the easier it is to speak freely. Developing vocabulary in any language begins with imitation. One way to practice imitation is by using *instant dictations*. In this kind of exercise, the teacher plays a few beats or measures of either melodic or rhythmic material, and students immediately repeat it. No recording is required, although it is possible. This practice feeds students a vocabulary of material or reinforces previously learned material. *Instant rhythmic dictations* can be used to begin a class as a warm-up to the lesson or as an introduction to giving the assignments for rhythmic improvisation. Instant dictations can be accomplished with students in drum circle fashion, as a class, with students clapping, "playing" on their thighs like a drum, or using any number of percussion instruments, bought or made. If you have the capability for the entire class to hear everyone's audio at the same time (Korg GEC/Group Education Controller or Yamaha LC3 Music Lab Controller), students can play directly at their stations.

Group work can also be a great way for students to begin the process of improvisation. As part of the warm-up, try trading two- to four-bar phrases between the class/ensemble and a soloist. The class plays a constant and repeated groove that can have one or multiple overlapping rhythms (for advanced musicians, these can be authentic contemporary or various Latin grooves) and then, going around the room, each student can have a chance to improvise a solo, either over the grove or against a steady single drum beat—called the heartbeat in drum circles. This can be effective to stimulate short segments of improvisational material. Students will learn from listening to the improvisations of others and will try out material of their own. Live performance in real time with an audience is a much different experience from recording with headphones. Having students play improvised solos in front of the class is a double-edged sword. Be thoughtful of your students' needs and capabilities when asking for any form of solo in class. If students are experienced musicians or music majors, you have more leeway when having them solo in front of the class. It may be problematic to put non–music majors or beginning students on the spot, especially for younger students or those with developmental or emotional issues.

Discover and learn some of your students' favorite genres. Provide recorded accompaniments or prerecorded loops in those styles for students to improvise over. Contemporary popular genres such as hip-hop, techno, rock, and dub step all have their own distinct rhythmic patterns in their accompaniments. Do not forget to include some of the vast variety of

Latin music. Choose Latin styles from the countries represented in your own community. An Internet search will provide Western notation of these rhythmic patterns, either directly or from available books.

Given that this lesson should be tailored to students' individual needs and levels and should be repeated throughout the course with different rhythms and challenges, teachers will need to customize their own assignments. Make sure students record in one pass without stopping and without editing or quantizing. There are no wrong answers!

Below are five possible scenarios for students to record rhythmic improvisations:

1. Provide a file with three measures of rhythmic groove in any genre. MIDI, audio files, or prerecorded loops can be used for these three measures. Leave a fourth measure with just a pulse for students to record their own one-measure improvisation in. Repeat this pattern of three measures of groove and one measure for improvisation four times in the same track. Students will record three different improvisations in each of the one-measure spaces.

2. Produce a similar file, leaving two measures for students to improvise in. Repeat the grove several times in the track, so students can record several possible improvisations without stopping.

3. On a separate track, change the groove or genre.

4. Provide a file with a drum set groove in any genre. Leave one measure with just a pulse on the beats for students to record a one-measure drum fill. Repeat this pattern of three measures of groove and one measure empty for a drum fill several times on one track, so students can record improvisations in one pass.

5. Produce several files, so students can repeat this challenge with a three-beat, two-beat, and one-beat fill.

6. Create small ensembles, using the computers, laptops, or handheld devices such as iPads, in which students compose music and have opportunities to solo in their pieces.

Musicians spend a lifetime developing improvisation skills. There are entire methods for teaching improvisation, and a thorough exploration of it is outside the scope of this book. The following lessons are meant as a place to begin. Keep in mind that there are many ways to approach this topic and this is just one way. Explore the vast material available to teach improvisation and continue to add new teaching ideas to your lessons.

Skills Required:
Ability to record into the software.

National Standards:
• Standard 2, Performing on instruments, alone and with others, a varied repertoire of music.
• Standard 3, Improvising melodies, variations, and accompaniments.
• Standard 4, Composing and arranging music within specified guidelines.

Objectives:
Students will develop a comfort with and increase their vocabulary of rhythmic improvisation by recording rhythmic solos over a given accompaniment.

Materials:

Audio, MIDI, or preproduced software files of rhythmic patterns or grooves for students to improvise in.

Procedure:

1. Begin the class with a session of instant rhythm dictations to build vocabulary. Use simple rhythms and add more complex ones.
2. As an option, have the class create a beat or multiple overlapping rhythms (groove) in any genre and go around the room giving students an opportunity to improvise a two- or four-bar solo.
3. Distribute any MIDI or audio files that students are to improvise over.
4. Listen to the MIDI or audio files and demonstrate some improvisations using rhythms that students know or rhythms recently learned that need to be reinforced.

Extensions:

1. Have students record their own accompaniments and then improvise rhythmic solos on top of them.
2. Have students record the drum patterns in unit 3 or other drum patterns and create various one- to four-beat-length drum fills every fourth measure.

Modification:

Provide written rhythmic patterns for students to choose and read from as they record. Review the patterns in advance if needed.

Melodic Dictations

Dictations are something that should be done often and regularly during the school year. I do two kinds of dictation: formal and instant. In formal dictations, students listen to files of prerecorded examples of melodic material and record or notate the prerecorded material. For instant dictations, the teacher plays a few beats or bars of either melodic or rhythmic material and the students repeat it, instantly. When doing melodic instant dictations, use two to three notes and sing the notes using solfeggio syllables while playing them on the keyboard. Repeat as the students play along. Start each day with easy material and add more notes or more material (longer examples).

Several instant dictations are provided in this unit to give an idea of how they progress over time. Although they are written in C, they can be transposed to any key. If you are going to have students sing back the solfeggio syllables, you may need to transpose, depending on the age of your students. Formal dictation files that get gradually more difficult and challenging to help train the ear are also included. Use a routine that students can easily follow and adapt to, so dictations can be a regular part of the class routine. This lesson plan can be used to introduce formal dictations.

> **TIP**
>
> I have found that using a flute or violin sound for melodic dictations is preferable to using a piano sound. When using a flute or violin, students need to conscientiously hold the keys down to sustain sound for the proper rhythmic duration. They can't rely on the natural ring or sustain of a piano.

Keyboard Skills Required:
Basic understanding of the piano keyboard.
Basic understanding of how to record in the sequencer.
Basic notation skills (optional).

National Standards:
• Standard 2, Performing on instruments, alone and with others, a varied repertoire of music.
• Standard 5, Reading and notating music.

Objectives:

Students will demonstrate their understanding of melodic notation by accurately completing the Melodic Dictations exercises.

Materials:

Melodic Dictations student assignment sheet.
Melodic Dictations audio file.

Procedure:

1. Distribute the Melodic Dictations file.
2. Explain to the students that they will hear melodic material and they are to re-create that material by recording it in the sequencer. (Optional: Have students write down, i.e. notate, what they hear.)
3. Play an example from the Melodic Dictations audio track/file and demonstrate how to record in the sequencer or how to write the notation.

Extension:

Have students compose their own dictation for the class.

Modification:

Play the formal dictation or part of it for the students at the keyboard, so they can see what notes are being played. Record a video of yourself playing and distribute the video file for students to view.

Instant Dictation Examples: Do–Mi

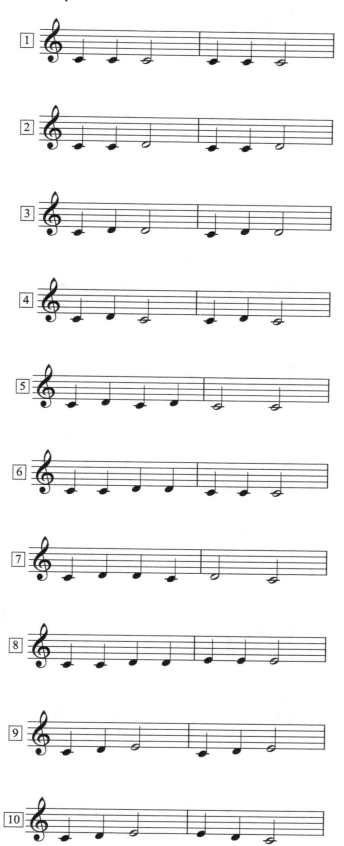

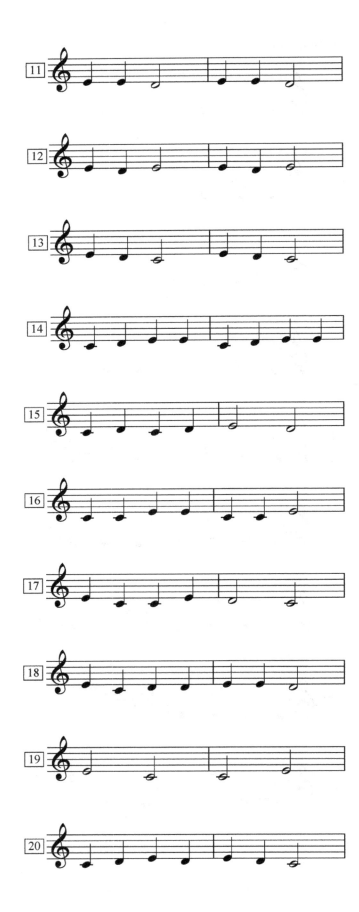

Melodic Dictations

"Dictation" means writing down what you hear. In this case, you will record what you hear.

Assignment:

Re-create what you hear in the Melodic Dictations file by recording it in the software.

Procedure:

1. Open a new file: File > New.
2. Save the file as: "Melodic Dictation _ _" (your two initials).
3. Create one software instrument track and choose either a flute or violin sound.
4. Set the metronome to 85.
5. Open the Melodic Dictations audio file in a playback software (iTunes, Real Player, etc.) or import the audio track into a track in the software.
6. Listen to the first example in the Melodic Dictations audio file.
7. Record the melodic material into the track you created.
8. You do not need to memorize the entire melody and record all at once. Record as much or as little as is comfortable for you. Rewind the audio file, listen to more material, and record more material.
9. Record as close to the click as possible.
10. Quantize your recording.
11. When you are finished with the first example, skip one measure and record the second example.
12. Proceed through all the examples in the Melodic Dictations audio file.

Creating Melodic Motives

Creating original melodies can be daunting for even the most advanced student. By combining the dictations in the previous lesson and short exercises that help guide creativity, students can develop melodic composition skills.

In Western art music ("classical"), the melody is at the core of the composition. This is not the case in many contemporary popular music styles. A solid drum beat and an engaging bass line are central to many contemporary genres. The exercises in this unit can also be used to create bass lines. Simply use a bass instrument and the bass range to complete the exercises. Students can compose and record a drum rhythm in a particular genre, use a prerecorded loop found in the software, or use one supplied by the teacher as a foundation for creating a bass line.

The exercises in this lesson can be given over several class sessions or a few per day as a warm-up activity. The lesson can also be a long-term, self-paced assignment. As an added bonus, collect all the motives created by students, distribute or project them to the class as notation, and have the students sing them as a class. You can also distribute them or project them to students as notation and have them play and record them. Distribute the students' motives as an audio file, and you have a plethora of one-measure dictations!

The exercises in this lesson develop melodic composition skills by limiting the students' choices of notes and then expanding and changing their choices. Limiting choices can actually allow for more creativity and be less frustrating, as students can create within a parameter and not have too many choices. The parameters given encourage tonic and dominant motive figures.

The teacher will notice that most students will explore and practice or "play around" with the different possibilities and combinations of the notes given. Some students will simply play and record whatever comes out, free-style. Either way, students are actually improvising. Improvising is the first step to composition, regardless of the genre, and should be encouraged and practiced whenever possible.

Students can also complete the assignment using standard notation on staff paper. If staff paper is used, the teacher should understand that the assignment becomes an exercise in notation knowledge and skill unless the students are proficient at sight-singing. This is perfectly acceptable but does not perform the same function as when students hear what notes they are choosing by recording their material into software. It is up to each teacher to determine the students' abilities and devise means for completing this, and other assignments like this, that are appropriate to the students' skill level and musical competency and the expectations of learning for the course.

It is suggested that students use a violin or flute sound. These sounds encourage sustaining long notes such as quarter and half notes. Students will need to keep the key suppressed for the duration of the rhythm to sustain a sound. This encourages long lines and conscientious performance of rhythms.

A note to music theorist purists: the short melodic material addressed here can be called a germ. The difference between a motive, a germ, and the usually longer material called a theme is how the material is treated in the overall melodic phrase. The first four notes of Beethoven's Symphony no. 5, first movement, are only two different pitches. The opening two bars could be called a germ, and the following two bars the germ in sequence. These four bars could be called the motive. The melodic material in the strings, beginning with measure 5, is a theme based on the motive in sequence, inverted. For beginning music students, this explanation can be overwhelming. For ease and simplicity, the short, one-measure melodic material referred to in this lesson is called a motive. College professors should use their discretion in the explanation of this material.

Skills Required:
Understanding of rhythms given.

National Standards:
- Standard 1, Singing, alone and with others, a varied repertoire of music.
- Standard 3, Improvising melodies, variations, and accompaniments.
- Standard 4, Composing and arranging music within specified guidelines.

Objectives:
Students will understand melodic motives by creating several of their own one-measure motives.

Materials:
Creating Melodic Motives student assignment sheet.

Procedure:
1. Define "motive" (French: *motif*): A short melodic idea.
2. Review the assignment on the Melodic Motives student assignment sheet, making sure students understand which portion is assigned for that day or series of days and the parameters of the assignment, including a clear understanding of the given rhythms.

Extensions:
1. Students can compose longer two-measure motives by combining any two measures on the student assignment sheet: measures a and b, c and d, a and c, for example, or any two others.
2. As different keys are explored in class, revisit this assignment for students to explore composing in these keys.

115

3. Collect all the motives and have the students sing them as a class.

4. Collect all the motives and distribute them to the class in notation and have students record them or re-create them in notation software as a notation reading assignment.

Modifications:

1. Instead of four rhythms (a–d), assign one or two rhythms at a time.

2. Limit the number of motives for each of the four rhythms such that instead of twelve motives, student will only create four, one for each rhythm.

3. Use one or two rhythms a day as a warm-up.

Creating Melodic Motives

A melody is an arrangement of pitches and rhythms that form a musical idea. Most melodies in Western music are several measures—often eight measures—long. There are many ways to construct a melody. One approach is to create a one-measure main motive that can be altered or repeated and then add other materials to make an eight-measure melody. The following exercises focus on the creation of the original motive.

Assignment 1: The First Three Notes of the Scale

For each of the four one-measure rhythms below, compose three motives (a total of 12 one-measure motives). Limit your selection of notes to the first three notes of the scale. In the key of C, only use C, D, and E.

Procedure:

1. Open a new file: File > New.
2. Save the file as: "Melodic Motives _ _ " (your two initials).
3. Add one software instrument track and choose a flute or violin sound.
4. The figure below has four different rhythms labeled a, b, c, and d. Compose three different one-measure motives using rhythm a, shown below.

5. Limit your note choices to the first three notes of the scale. In the key of C, only use C, D, and E (do, re, and mi).
6. Record your motive *one measure at a time.* Do not compose three measures at once.
7. Skip a measure between each composed motive.
8. Skip a few measures and compose three different one-measure motives using the rhythm b, shown above.
9. Record your motive *one measure at a time.* Do not compose three measures at once.
10. Skip a measure between each composed motive.
11. Repeat this procedure for rhythms c and d, shown above.
12. You will compose 12 one-measure motives.

Assignment 2: The First Five Notes of the Scale

Create three new motives for each of the same rhythms above (a total of 12 one-measure motives), but now increase your note choices to include the first five notes of the scale. The first note of each motive must be the first note of the scale or the third degree of the scale. In the key of C, the first five notes of the scale are C, D, E, F, and G. The first note for each motive could be a C or an E.

Procedure:

1. Open the file "Melodic Motives."
2. Add one software instrument track (track 2).
3. Choose a flute or violin sound.
4. Compose and record three different one-measure motives using the rhythm a above.
5. Limit your note choices to the first five notes of the scale. In the key of C, only use C, D, E, F, and G (do, re, mi, fa, and sol). Your first note must be the first or third note of the scale.
6. Record your motive *one measure at a time*. Do not compose three measures at once.
7. Skip a measure between each composed motive.
8. Skip a few measures and compose and record three different one-measure motives using rhythm b, shown above.
9. Record your motive *one measure at a time*. Do not compose three measures at once.
10. Skip a measure between each composed motive.
11. Repeat this procedure for rhythms c and d, shown above.
12. You will compose 12 one-measure motives.

Assignment 3: The Second Five Notes of the Scale

Create three new motives for each of the same rhythms above (a total of 12 one-measure motives). This time, your note choices are limited to the second five notes of the scale (in the key of C that's F, G, A, B, and C). The first note of each motive must be the fifth note of the scale and the last note of each motive must be the first or eighth note of the scale (in the key of C the fifth note of the scale is G and the first or eighth is C).

Procedure:

1. Open the file "Melodic Motives _ _" (your two initials).
2. Add one software instrument track (track 3).
3. Choose a flute or violin sound.
4. Compose three different one-measure motives using rhythm a, shown above.
5. Limit your note choices to the second five notes of the scale. In the key of C, only use F, G, A, B, and C (fa, sol, la, ti, and do). Your first note must be the fifth note of the scale and the last note must be the first or eighth note of the scale.
6. Record your motive *one measure at a time*. Do not compose three measures at once.
7. Skip a measure between each composed motive.
8. Skip a few measures and compose three different one-measure motives using rhythm b, shown above.
9. Record your motive *one measure at a time*. Do not compose three measures at once.
10. Skip a measure between each composed motive.
11. Repeat this procedure for rhythms c and d, shown above.
12. You will compose 12 one-measure motives.

Assignment 4: New Rhythms

Repeat assignments 1–3 above, using the four rhythms below.

Assignment 5: Original Rhythms

Create three original one-measure motives using any rhythm and combination of notes.

LESSON 14b

Motive Variations

Once students can create motives, the next step is to create variations of these motives. Some of the more common melodic variation techniques are given in this lesson. There are several, and exploring them in one class is daunting even for college music majors. It is recommended that the teacher explore one or two variations in each class lesson and have students complete the assignment for the variation discussed that day. For example, review Permutations and have students complete the assignment in which they alter their original motives using the permutations techniques to create variations. The next day, Transposition can be explored, and students can complete the assignment of altering their original motives using the transposition techniques to create variations. If students' abilities permit, or for advanced high school and college students, two or three melodic variation techniques can be explored in one day. As each variation technique is introduced, students can sing the original motive and then the variation on the student handout. To check for understanding, you can give your own motive and ask the class to create the variation and then sing both. As a modification on the entire topic of variations, the teacher may choose to explore fewer variations overall. If you wish, you can explore the Transposition variation only and then move immediately to the next lesson utilizing the motive sequences.

In class, students can complete variations for all of their original motives using each variation technique, or they can choose one or two motives for which they will complete all the variation techniques, so the teacher can check for understanding. The remaining motives can be assigned for homework.

As a warm-up or introduction to the lesson, do several instant dictations that use the rhythms and the notes given in each exercise.

The student assignment sheet instructs students to label their tracks. Students will need to know how to change the track names in the software. Refer to the software manual for specific instructions.

Skills Required:
Ability to read basic rhythmic notation of half, quarter, and eighth notes.
An understanding of basic generic intervals.
An understanding of the how to build and play the C Major scale on the piano keyboard.

National Standards:
- Standard 1, Singing, alone and with others, a varied repertoire of music.
- Standard 2, Performing on instruments, alone and with others, a varied repertoire of music.
- Standard 3, Improvising melodies, variations, and accompaniments.
- Standard 4, Composing and arranging music within specified guidelines.
- Standard 5, Reading and notating music.

Objectives:

Students will demonstrate their understanding of several types of melodic variation techniques by composing variations of their previously composed motives using the guidelines provided.

Materials:

Previously composed Melodic Motives from lesson 14a.
Motive Variations handout.
Motive Variations student assignment sheet.

Procedure:

1. Review the definition of melodic motives.
2. Define Motive Variations: a change to the original melody or motive.
3. Distribute the Motive Variations handout.
4. Review the Original Motive by playing it on an instrument, singing, or having the class sing it.
5. Choose which variation technique(s) are to be reviewed in this class session.
6. Explain and review the variation technique(s) by playing it on an instrument, singing it, having the class sing it, or any combination of these.
7. Distribute the Motive Variations student assignment sheet.
8. Choose the portion of this sheet that students are to complete for this class session.
9. Review this portion of the sheet.

Extensions:

1. Have students sing the examples on the student handout.
2. Have students record the examples on the student handout.

Modifications:

1. Choose two motives and have students complete one motive variation per class.
2. Students can work in pairs.

121

HANDOUT

Motive Variations

Here are brief descriptions of several techniques for creating melodic variations.

Original Motive

Examples of Variations:

1. Permutations: changing the order of the notes from 1, 2, 3, 4, 5 to 1, 3, 5, 2, 4; or 2, 4, 1, 3, 5; or 4, 5, 1, 3, 2; and so on.

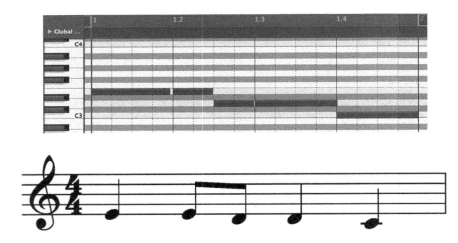

2. Transposition: shifting (moving) the motive to a higher or lower note while maintaining the intervals and staying in the key. Notice how all the Fs are natural, as in the key of C.

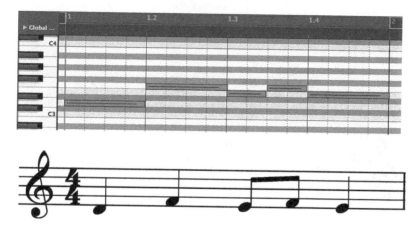

3. Inversion: upside down. Start with the first note (1), in this case an octave higher, so the notes fit on the staff. If in the original motive the second note went down a 2nd, then change it to go up a 2nd in the inversion. If the third note originally went up a 3rd from the second note, then change it to go down a 3rd, and so on.

4. Retrograde: play the motive backward, last note first: 5, 4, 3, 2, 1.

5. Retrograde inversion: start by creating an inversion; then play it backward.

6. Rhythmic augmentation: make the notes longer, in this case twice as long. One measure becomes two measures.

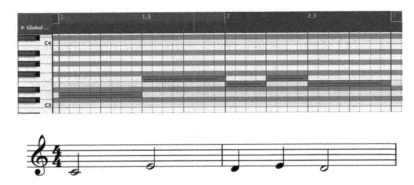

7. Rhythmic diminution: make the notes shorter, in this case twice as short. One measure becomes half a measure.

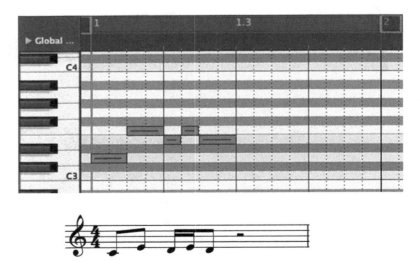

Motive Variations

An original motive can be altered using several techniques to create melodic variations. Some of the more common variation techniques are shown in the Motive Variations handout.

In the last lesson, you created several melodic motives. For this assignment, you will use your motives and create variations using the techniques on the Motive Variations handout.

Procedure:

1. Open the Melodic Motive file created in lesson 14a: "Melodic Motives."
2. Select any four motives and copy them to be added to a new file.
3. Open a new file: File > New.
4. Save the new file as "Variations _ _" (your two initials).
5. Add a software instrument track and select a flute or violin sound.
6. Paste the motives onto this new track, one motive per measure, leaving one measure between each motive.
7. Label the track "Motive."
8. Add another new software instrument track and choose a violin or flute sound.
9. Label the track "Permutation." Your file will look something like this:

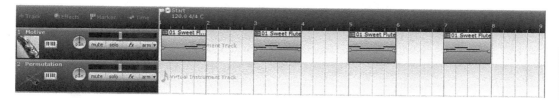

10. For each motive, create a permutation below the original motive on the second track and subsequent tracks. You can copy and paste the motive onto the new track, open it in the Piano Roll/Matrix Editing window, and manipulate the motive to create a transposition, inversion, retrograde, retrograde inversion, augmentation, or diminution.
11. Add a new track for each variation technique: transposition, inversion, retrograde, retrograde inversion, augmentation, and diminution and label the tracks according to the variation technique used.

12. Complete the variation technique for each motive on the respective track under the motive. Your file will look something like this:

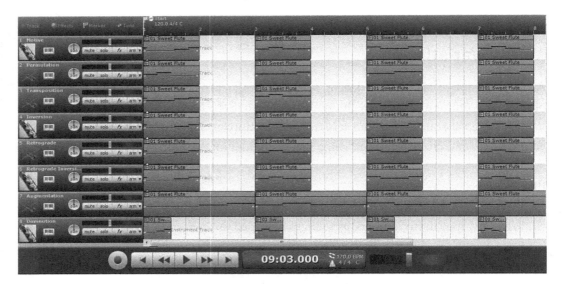

Motive Sequences

Combining a motive and its variations can form melodic phrases made up of multiple measures. A common occurrence is the motive and one or more transpositions in sequential order (one after the other). This treatment is called motive sequences or motive in sequence. Typically, no more than two transposed repetitions occur after the original motive. New melodic material follows the second repetition to maintain interest. This new material can move in the opposite direction of the sequence as a good way to create interesting melodic contour or shape to the phrase.

Some examples of melodies that have motives in sequence are:

"Angels We Have Heard on High"
"Do, Re, Mi" from *The Sound of Music*
Beethoven, Symphony no. 5, first movement

TIP

Transpositions can contain accidentals to maintain interval qualities between notes. In the end, it is what the composer wants to hear that counts.

Skills Required:
An understanding of the how to build and play the C major scale on the piano keyboard. An understanding of basic generic intervals.

National Standards:
- Standard 1, Singing, alone and with others, a varied repertoire of music
- Standard 2, Performing on instruments alone and with others, a varied repertoire of music.
- Standard 3, Improvising melodies, variations, and accompaniments.
- Standard 4, Composing and arranging music within specified guidelines.
- Standard 5, Reading and notating music.
- Standard 6, Listening to, analyzing, and describing music.
- Standard 7, Evaluating music and music performances.

Objectives:
Students will demonstrate their knowledge of creating sequences and how to transpose by generic intervals by completing the Motive Sequences assignment.

Materials:
Motive variations handout.
Motive Sequences student assignment sheet.

Procedure:

1. Review melodic motives.
2. Define "motive variations": a change to the original melody or motive.
3. Review the variation transpositions. The teacher can refer to the Motive Variations handout.
4. Explain how to a create transpositions at specific intervals of a 2nd or a 3rd.
5. Remind students that the new transposition needs to be in the same key. Demonstrate how to change "black notes" to "white notes" if in the key of C major.
6. Review the Motive Sequences student assignment sheet.
7. Demonstrate how to copy the motive and paste it into the adjoining measure and then transpose it by moving the material up or down, as required in the student assignment sheet, steps 5 and 6.
8. Check that the newly transposed material does not contain accidentals and is in the key.
9. Demonstrate how to do step 7 on the student assignment sheet. Highlight that the second transposition will be at the same interval as the first, a 2nd, or a 3rd up or down.
10. Demonstrate how to compose new material in the fourth measure of this phrase as required in the student assignment sheet, step 8.
11. Check for understanding by giving students a motive created by the teacher or another student and create the sequences as a class.

Extension:

Distribute or project students' work and have the class sing the final products, the original motive, and the sequences. Can they name at what interval the sequences were played?

Modification:

Give students some melodies that have motives and sequences and ask the students to circle the sequences. Can they name at what interval the sequences were played?

Motive Sequences

The example below is the traditional melody "Lightly Row." The first measure is the motive. The second measure is a transposition of the motive down a 2nd. This is called the "motive in sequence." The third measure is new melodic material, simply the first five notes of the scale ascending while the fourth measure repeats notes. The rhythm of the fourth measure is identical to that of the first and second measures. Notice how the motive in sequence (the motive and the transposition in measures 1 and 2) moves in a downward motion. Measures 3 and 4 move in the opposite direction, an upward motion. This melody has the original motive, a transposed sequence, and new material.

Can you describe what happens in measures 5–8?

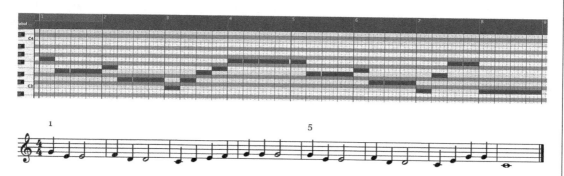

Assignment:

Create four melodic phrases, each four measures long, using melodic sequences with the motives created in lesson 14a. You will create two transpositions of the original motive and compose new melodic material to complete the four-measure phrase.

Procedure:

1. Open the Melodic Motive file created in lesson 14a: "Melodic Motives."
2. Select any four motives and copy to a new file: File > New.
3. Paste the motives into four tracks, one track for each motive and choose a flute or violin sound for each track.
4. Save the new file as "Sequences _ _" (your two initials).
5. For the first motive on the first track, create a variation by using the transposition technique. Copy and paste the original motive from measure 1 into measure 2 and again into measure 3.
6. In measure 2, move the motive up or down a 2nd or 3rd. Check that all the notes remain in the key. In other words, if you are in the key of C major, there should be no "black" notes (sharps or flats) after you move the motive up or down (transpose). If there are, change them to the "white" or natural note.

7. In measure 3, move the motive up or down the same generic interval you did in measure 2. If you moved measure 2 up a 3rd, move measure 3 a 3rd higher than measure 2. Check that all the notes remain in the key. In other words, if you are in the key of C major, there should be no "black" notes (sharps or flats) after you move the motive up or down (transpose). If there are, change them to the "white" or natural note.

8. Compose new material for measure 4 that is different from any of the material in measures 1–3.

9. Repeat steps 5–8 for tracks 2, 3, and 4.

Improvising Melodies

> When most people hear the word [improvisation] they think of two four-letter words, jazz and fear. What I am suggesting is that improvisation is essential to music learning and music making.
>
> —CHRISTOPHER AZZARA, PROFESSOR OF MUSIC EDUCATION AND
> AFFILIATE FACULTY OF JAZZ STUDIES AND CONTEMPORARY MEDIA,
> EASTMAN SCHOOL OF MUSIC

Improvisation is a powerful creative tool that can be practiced in any genre.[1] There are entire methods and complete courses of study on improvisation. This lesson is meant to be an entree into improvisation as a means of melodic discovery while reinforcing an understanding of keys and scales. This lesson should not be considered complete after one class session. These improvisation techniques can be used over the entire course of study as warm-ups and as supplements to learning new keys. As a variation, use these techniques to inspire further lessons or "discovery sessions" in which students are given a word cue: the word for a shade of color (dark, light), a texture (soft, smooth, rough, coarse), or an emotion (happy, playful, sad, sleepy, dizzy). On the word cue, students improvise over chord progressions given by the teacher or composed by the students.

At this point in the curriculum, students will have an understanding of several keys and their scales and arpeggios, as presented in the lessons and the piano supplement material. The basic idea for this lesson is to give students an opportunity to freely create melodic lines over a chord using the scale of that chord. For instance, if the underlying chord is F major, the student simply records melodic improvisations using the F major scale. For the first few times students try this, use one chord over several measures, four to eight. This gives students time to explore. Several MIDI files are provided on the companion website in C, F, and G major, and one file using C and G major. The files provided for this lesson are MIDI files, so students can choose instruments and practice at different tempos. Encourage students to simply hit the record button and begin. There are no wrong answers. If the software allows, use a record loop and let the chord progression repeat 16 or 32 bars. Again, there are no wrong answers. The idea that there are no wrong answers might be difficult enough for students to comprehend. The more they practice, the more comfortable they will become. Each new practice session can be over a different chord. After a few chords are explored, students can improvise over a simple progression. Eventually, students will be able to record their own chord progressions or use the progressions they record in units 18 and 19. If desired, add a drum track in different styles. Only one student assignment sheet is given as an example of the basic improvisation session.

---

1 The quotation in the epigraph is from Christopher Azzara, TEDxRochester talk, November 7, 2011, Rochester, New York, available at tedxtalks.ted.com/video/TEDxRochester-Christopher-Azzara.

> **TIP**
>
> The power of the exercises in this lesson should not be underestimated. It has been my experience that a majority of students have the most difficulty creating melodic material, especially melodic lines, that are more than two measures long. Giving students an opportunity to practice exploring and improvising melodic lines over chords makes it easier for them to create melodic material and to add melodic materials over chord progressions.

Students can be self-conscious about their creations. For these exercises, I only take a quick glance at the students' screens to make sure they are on task. I do not even listen to or grade these improvisations. I might listen to and make suggestions on students' improvisations much later in the course, as students become more comfortable and gain more confidence in their work.

Skills Required:
Understanding of scales and chords in a given key.

National Standards:
- Standard 2, Performing on instruments, alone and with others, a varied repertoire of music.
- Standard 3, Improvising melodies, variations, and accompaniments.
- Standard 4, Composing and arranging music within specified guidelines.

Objectives:
Students will practice melodic improvisation over chords by recording melodic material into the software.

Materials:

Improvising Melodies student assignment sheet.
Melodic Improvisation MIDI files:

     14d_1 C Major.mid
     14d_2 F Major.mid
     14d_3 G Major.mid
     14d_4 C_G.mid

Procedure:
1. Define "improvisation": spontaneous creation.
2. Demonstrate how to load the Melodic Improvisation MIDI into the software.
3. Describe the key the chord(s) in the MIDI.
4. Review the scale of the key(s) used in the MIDI.
5. Review the Improvising Melodies student assignment sheet.
6. Clarify that melodic improvisations create melody lines and do not just play up and down scales or arpeggios.
7. Demonstrate melodic improvisations over the MIDI.

Extensions:

1. Add a drum track or let students add a track of their own under the chords.
2. Have students record their own progressions.

Modifications:

1. Provide students with a file that has the MIDI or audio file already loaded.
2. Demonstrate a measure or two of improvised melodic material over the chords to the student and let the student imitate it. After the student is somewhat comfortable, ask the student to play a measure or two that you can imitate. Then ask the student to record several measures on his or her own.

STUDENT ASSIGNMENT SHEET

Improvising Melodies

Improvisation is simply spontaneously creating. There are no wrong answers. This is an opportunity for you to explore creating melodies using the scales in the key of the chords given.

Assignment:

Freely improvise melodic lines over the chords, using the notes of the scale in the key of the chord. For instance, if the chord is C major, use the note of the C scale to improvise a melody line. If the chord is F major, use the notes of the F scale to improvise a melody line. If more than one chord is used, use the appropriate scale for each chord when it is played. When a C chord is played, use a C scale; when a G chord is played, use a G scale.

Procedure:

1. Open a new file: File > New.
2. Name the file "Improvisation _ _" (your two initials).
3. Load the Melodic Improvisation MIDI or audio file.
4. Create a new software instrument track and choose a plain flute or violin sound.
5. Set the metronome to 85–95.
6. Record your improvisation. Do not go back and edit the material.
7. Record more takes as practice, improvising over the chords given.

Composing to Given Rhythms

Melody writing as an abstract exercise can be very difficult, especially for students who don't sing or play an instrument. This lesson gives specific guidelines for composing melodies and demonstrates important concepts in music.

This lesson will reinforce students' understanding of basic rhythms and gives them opportunities to compose short melodic figures. Rhythmic continuity allows them to have something to hold onto (the given rhythm) while they choose and combine notes with these rhythms.

As in lesson 14a, it is up to you to decide whether you would like your students to complete the assignment or to sketch possible responses to the assignment using standard notation. A worksheet is provided for notation.

Skills Required:

Ability to read standard notation of simple rhythms.
Understanding the five-finger position in a given key's scale or understanding of the entire scale.

National Standards:

• Standard 2, Performing on instruments, alone and with others, a varied repertoire of music.
• Standard 4, Composing and arranging music within specified guidelines.
• Standard 5, Reading and notating music.

Objectives:

Students will demonstrate their ability to read basic rhythms and to understand keys and scales by composing simple melodic figures to given rhythms.

Materials:

Compose to a Given Rhythm student assignment sheet.
Compose to a Given Rhythm worksheet (optional).

Procedure:

1. Review the five-finger or entire scale students are to use for this composition exercise.
2. Review the student assignment sheet, especially the rhythms, making sure the students understand them.

3. Explain to the students that they are to compose four melodies. Each melody is to use one of the rhythm examples given. For instance, in the first melody, they can use any combination of notes from the five-finger or entire scale given but must use the rhythms in example a. The second melody uses example b, and so on.
4. Remind students to keep it simple:
    a. Move in a stepwise motion.
    b. If you use leaps (skip a few notes), continue in stepwise motion.
5. Remind students that when you are choosing a note, the next note can either be the same note (repeated), something higher, or something lower.
6. Demonstrate an example.

Extensions:

1. Have students write the number of each beat over the example in the student assignment sheet.
2. Give students different starting and ending notes for each example.
3. Change keys.
4. Use the rhythms in the Extensions section on the student assignment sheet.

Modification:

1. Distribute a file with the rhythms recorded on one note, the tonic. Allow students to create their melodies by sliding the rhythms to different notes. Make sure students listen back to their melodies.
2. Let students compose only two measures at a time.
3. Have students complete only one or two of the given rhythms.

Compose to a Given Rhythm

Assignment 1:

Compose a melody in the key of C for each of the rhythms shown below. Start on the tonic, C (first degree of the scale), and end on the tonic, C (first degree of the scale).

Procedure:

1. Open a new file: File > New.
2. Save the file as "RhythmMelodies _ _" (your two initials).
3. Create one software instrument track and choose either a flute or violin sound.
4. Compose your first melody.
5. Edit and quantize as needed.
6. Skip one measure and compose your second melody.
7. Proceed this way until all four melodies are complete.

Assignment 2:

Compose a different melody to each of the four 4-measure rhythms above. This time, start on the tonic, C (first degree of the scale), and end on the dominant, G (fifth degree of the scale).

Procedure:

1. Open the file "RhythmMelodies _ _" (your two initials).
2. Create one software instrument track, track 2, and choose either a flute or violin sound.
3. Solo track 2 so this is the only track you hear when recording.
4. Compose your first melody.
5. Edit and quantize as needed.
6. Skip one measure and compose your second melody.
7. Proceed this way until all four melodies are complete.

Assignment 3:

Compose yet a different melody to the same four 4-measure rhythms above. This time, start on the dominant, G (fifth degree of the scale), and end on the tonic, C (first degree of the scale).

Procedure:

1. Open the file "RhythmMelodies _ _" (your two initials).
2. Create one software instrument track, track 3, and choose either a flute or violin sound.
3. Solo track 3 so this is the only track you hear when recording.
4. Compose your first melody.
5. Edit and quantize as needed.
6. Skip one measure and compose your second melody.
7. Proceed this way until all four melodies are complete.

Assignment 4:

Create four melodies, each eight measures long, by combining one 4-measure melody from assignments 1 or 2 and one from assignment 3 to create an eight-measure melody.

Procedure:

1. Open the file "RhythmMelodies _ _" (your two initials).
2. Create one software instrument track, track 4, and choose either a flute or violin sound.
3. Solo track 4 so this is the only track you hear when recording.
4. Select, copy, and paste one 4-measure melody from track 1 or track 2 and paste into track 4.
5. Select, copy, and paste one 4-measure melody from track 3 and paste into track 4 after the first four-measure melody, creating an eight-measure melody in track 4.
6. Listen to the melody.
7. Skip one measure and repeat step 4 above, creating a second eight-measure melody.
8. Proceed this way until all four melodies are complete.

Extensions

1. Use the same rhythms but different keys.
2. Repeat all the assignments (1–4) using the rhythms below:

Compose to a Given Rhythm WORKSHEET

Name_____   Date_____

1

2

3

4

5

Question-and-Answer Form

Melodies have form and structure. Understanding a few frequently used structures can help students write melodies.

In music theory and composition texts, question-and-answer form is called a parallel period, as two phrases are almost identical except for the cadences. The first period (the first four measures) ends in a half cadence. The second period (the second four measures) ends in a complete cadence. For instance, the melody by Stephen Foster "Camptown Races" is clearly in parallel period or question-and-answer form. However, the first four measures do not resolve in an upward movement, as is described and encouraged in this lesson.

140

FIGURE 16aLP

The explanation of implied cadences in melody is more than most beginning music students can understand or need to understand to compose music. These concepts and explanations can be covered in a more advanced music theory class. It will suffice to say that the first part of the melody ends on a note other than the tonic. The explanation and definitions below are differentiated for young or beginning students.

The question-and-answer form can be compared to a type of academic writing that students should be very familiar with. When doing homework or completing a test, students are encouraged to write their answers in full and complete sentences. For instance, if the question is "What is your favorite class in school?" the answer should not simply be "Music." A correct full-sentence answer, "My favorite class in school is music," includes part of the question. This analogy can be used to help explain question-and-answer form in music.

Below is the melody "Mary Had a Little Lamb." The first four measures represent a musical "question" and end with the melody going up, much as your voice does when you ask a question. The second four measures are a musical "answer" to the musical question in a full and complete musical "sentence," including material from the original question and ending emphatically on the tonic. The issue here is not one of lyrics but of musical tone, melodic shape, and use of musical content in both the first four measures and the second four measures of an eight-measure phrase.

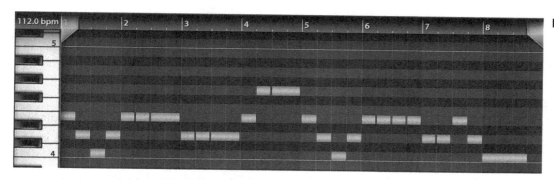

FIGURE 16aSA1

FIGURE 16aSA2

You can refer to "Camptown Races" as another example of question-and-answer form. Point out how the musical "question" (the first four measures) does not ascend but ends on a note that is not the tonic, thus giving a sense of incompletion.

Six examples are given in the Question-and-Answer MIDI file in different keys. You can transpose these to one key if preferred. You can distribute the Question-and-Answer MIDI file located on the companion website or load the MIDI file into your software, save the file as the Question file, and distribute this software file for students to use. If you prefer for your students to use music notation, they can use the notation provided and play or input their melodies into their computers, or write their notation directly on the student assignment sheet.

Skills Required:
Understanding of the piano keyboard.
Basic knowledge of how to record or step-input (draw music) into the software.

National Standards:
- Standard 1, Singing, alone and with others, a varied repertoire of music.
- Standard 4, Composing and arranging music within specified guidelines.
- Standard 6, Listening to, analyzing, and describing music.
- Standard 7, Evaluating music and music performances.
- Standard 8, Understanding relationships between music, the arts, and disciplines outside the arts.

Objectives:
Students will understand question-and-answer melodic form by composing the four-measure musical answers to the given four-measure musical questions of an eight-measure melody.

Materials:
Question-and-Answer Form student assignment sheet.
Question-and-Answer MIDI file.

141

Procedure:

1. Describe question-and-answer melodic form.
2. Show examples of question-and-answer melodic form such as "Mary Had a Little Lamb" and have students sing the melody where appropriate.
3. Review the materials in the Question-and-Answer MIDI file.
4. Review how in the first four measures, the musical question ends either by the melodic line moving upward like a question or on a note that sounds like the musical phrase is not complete.
5. Explain that in the musical answer, the melodic line usually resolves in such a way that makes the musical phrase sound complete or finished. Using the terms "tonic" or "home tones" might be helpful.
6. Explain to the students how they can either play the musical question over again or copy and paste it in measures 5–8.
7. Review how the musical answer, measures 5–8, will contain part of the musical question, but that the musical answer needs to be changed.
8. Explain to the students how they can change measures 5–8 by moving notes with the mouse or rerecording the measures.
9. Review compositional techniques that make the newly composed material in measures 5–8 relevant to the first four measures of the melody. Techniques to consider using that were discussed in lesson 14b:
   a. Repetition of musical elements, including rhythms and pitches.
   b. Melodic variations such as transposition or inversion of a melodic motive.
   c. Motive sequences.

Extensions:

1. Students can compose their own complete eight-measure melodies in question-and-answer format.
2. Have students compose their own four-measure questions, then have them pair up, trade with one another, and compose musical answers to complete each other's musical questions.
3. Distribute the musical questions as an audio file and have the students dictate them before completing the musical answers.

Modifications:

1. Have students work in pairs on the assignment.
2. Have students complete fewer than the six examples given.

Question-and-Answer Form

Many melodies have form and structure. One form is called "question and answer." An eight-measure melody can have two different four-measure sections. Simply having a four-measure melody and then repeating the same four measures is not an eight-measure melody but a four-measure melody repeated. In question-and-answer form, the first section is the musical question, and the second section is the musical answer. Just as in answering academic questions, a full and complete answer includes information from the question; however, material changes in the second four measures of the melody create a variation of the phrase.

Below is the melody "Mary Had a Little Lamb." The first four measures represent a musical "question" and end with the melody going up, much as your voice does when you ask a question. The second four measures are a musical "answer" to the musical question in a full and complete musical "sentence," including material from the original question and ending emphatically on the tonic.

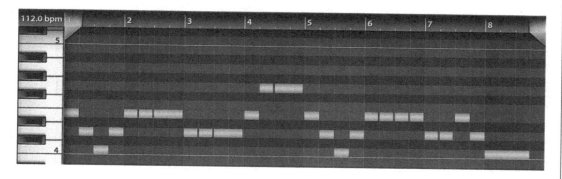

Assignment:

Turn each of the six 4-measure phrases given into an eight-measure melody using question-and-answer form.

Procedure:

1. Familiarize yourself with the four-measure phrase.
2. Either notate on the staves in the figure below or in the software, play, and record or copy and paste the four measures into the second four measures, measures 5–8.
3. Alter the second four measures, measures 5–8, concentrating on the last two measures, to have the new material resolve to the tonic/home tone, the first degree of the scale.
4. Repeat for each of the remaining examples, turning each of the six 4-measure phrases into eight-measure melodies.

144

AB Tonic/Dominant

There are common elements that make melodies pleasing to the listener in every culture. Although there are no formulas for writing timeless or "hit" melodies, there are some common practices. A widely used melody-writing technique is to utilize the relationship between the tonic and the dominant in a key. In an eight-measure melody, the first four measures hover around or pull strongly to the tonic, while the second four measures begin strongly in the dominant, or the fifth or second degree of the scale (implying the V of V), and resolves to the tonic.

The exercises in this lesson are similar to those in lesson 15b. Here, however, students will need to compose measures 5–8 in their entirety. As in lesson 15b, the six examples are given in different keys. You can transpose these to one key if preferred. You can distribute the AB Tonic-Dominant MIDI file located on the companion website or load the MIDI file into your software, save the file as "Tonic file," and distribute this software file for students to use. If you prefer for your students to use music notation, they can use the notation provided and play or input their melodies into their computers, or write their notation directly on the student assignment sheet.

This lesson is presented as practice in melodic writing, and students are expected to work with a single, monophonic line. However, if you choose, you can demonstrate how melodies work with I and V chords and provide students with a chord progression for them to listen to as they create their melodies. This may be a good idea for some less experienced or younger musicians. However, this approach could imply that only these chords can be used in melodic writing of this kind and that other chords may not be acceptable.

Skills Required:

Understanding of the piano keyboard.

Basic knowledge of how to record or step-input (draw music) into the software.

National Standards:

- Standard 1, Singing, alone and with others, a varied repertoire of music.
- Standard 4, Composing and arranging music within specified guidelines.
- Standard 6, Listening to, analyzing, and describing music.
- Standard 7, Evaluating music and music performances.

Objectives:

Students will understand the relationship between tonic and dominant, or 1-to-5 generic intervals, by composing the second four measures to follow the given first four measures of an eight-measure melody.

Materials:

AB Tonic/Dominant student assignment sheet.

AB Tonic-Dominant MIDI file.

Procedure:

1. Describe generic intervals and how to count the first note as 1 and count up to the fifth note.
2. Explain how the first note is known as the "tonic" or "home tone."
3. Explain how these change from key to key by playing some chords and short melodic lines and highlighting the tonic note or home tone.
4. Show examples of AB tonic-dominant melodic form such as "Twinkle, Twinkle," and have students sing the melody where appropriate.
5. Review the materials in the AB tonic-dominant file.
6. Play or sing the first four measures of each example and highlight how in the first four measures the listener's attention is drawn to the tonic or home tone.
7. Review how to find the tonic and dominant.
8. Review that students are to start on the second or fifth degree of the scale and end on the tonic.
9. As students work individually, go around the room and help students with each problem spot.

Extensions:

1. Create and distribute audio or MIDI files or use loops that contain four measures of a I chord and four measures of a V chord for students to compose their melodies over.
2. Students can compose their own complete eight-measure melody in AB tonic-dominant format.
3. Students can compose their own first four measures around the tonic, trade with another student, and compose the second four measures from dominant to tonic to complete the other students' first four measures.
4. Distribute the first AB Tonic-Dominant MIDI file as an audio file and have the students dictate them before completing the second four measures.
5. Remove the note given in measure 5 and have students locate the dominant themselves.
6. Allow students to change the rhythm of the given note in measure 5.

Modifications:

1. Have students work in pairs on each question and answer.
2. Give the students the dominant, second, or fifth degree of the scale in measure 5 and the tonic, first degree of the scale in measure 8.
3. Have students complete fewer than the six examples given.

AB Tonic/Dominant

Many melodies have form and structure. One melody form can be described as AB melody form and is very similar to the song form of the same name. An eight-measure melody can have two different four-measure sections. Simply having a four-measure melody and then repeating the same four-measure is not an eight-measure melody but a four measure-melody repeated. In AB melody form, the first four measures hover around or pull strongly to the first degree of the scale, known as the "tonic" or "home tone." The second four measures begin strongly in the dominant, or the fifth or second degree of the scale (the V of V), and resolve to the tonic.

Below is the melody "Twinkle, Twinkle." The first four measures begin and end on the first degree of the scale, also known as the tonic or home tone. This section can be labeled A. The next four measures begin on the fifth degree of the scale, also known as the dominant, and descend to the second degree of the scale. This section can be labeled B. Measures 8–12 are a repetition of the first four measures. The structure of this 12-measure melody can be said to be ABA.

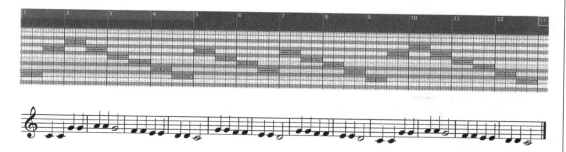

Assignment:

Complete each of the six 4-measure phrases given so as to create an eight-measure melody using AB melody form.

Procedure:

1. Familiarize yourself with the four-measure phrase.
2. Compose and notate on the staves in the figure below or record in the software new material beginning on measure 5. Measure 5 begins on the dominant, the fifth degree of the scale.
3. End your melodies on the tonic, the first degree of the scale.
4. Use compositional techniques that make your newly composed material in measures 5–8 relevant to the first four measures of the melody. Things to consider using:
    a. Repetition of musical elements, including rhythms and pitches.
    b. Melodic variations such as transposition or inversion of a melodic motive.
    c. Motive sequences.
5. Repeat for each of the remaining examples, turning each of the six 4-measure phrases into eight-measure melodies.

148

Rondo

Another melody composition technique that mimics a larger musical form is rondo form. This form uses a melodic motive that is repeated and alternates between new materials in an eight-measure melody. An excellent example of this form is the melody "Yankee Doodle." The motive is in measures 1, 3, and 5 and alternates with new and different material in measures 2, 4, 6, 7, and 8. The material in the final three measures can be described as a mini coda. The form of this piece can be described as ABACAD.

These exercises are similar to those in the previous two lessons. Students will compose new material for measures 2, 4, 6, 7, and 8. As in the previous lessons, the six examples are given in different keys. You can transpose these to one key if preferred. You can distribute the Rondo MIDI file located on the companion website or load the MIDI file into your software, save the file as the Rondo file and distribute this software file for students to use. If you prefer students to use music notation, they can use the notation provided and play or input their melodies into their computers, or write their notation directly on the student assignment sheet.

Skills Required:

Understanding of the piano keyboard.
Basic knowledge of how to record or step-input (draw music) into the software.

National Standards:

- Standard 1, Singing, alone and with others, a varied repertoire of music.
- Standard 4, Composing and arranging music within specified guidelines.
- Standard 6, Listening to, analyzing, and describing music.
- Standard 7, Evaluating music and music performances.

Objectives:

Students will understand the Rondo form by composing new music to the given previously composed material of an eight-measure melody.

Materials:

Rondo student assignment sheet.
The Rondo MIDI file.

Describe Rondo Melodic Form

1. Show examples of rondo melodic form such as "Yankee Doodle," and have students sing the melody where appropriate.
2. Review the materials in the Rondo file.

3. Review how the form can be described as ABACAD by labeling the measures appropriately. Review compositional techniques that make the newly composed material in measures 2, 5, 6, 7, and 8 relevant to the first four measures of the melody. Things to consider using are materials discussed in lesson 14b:
   a. Repetition of musical elements, including rhythms and pitches.
   b. Melodic variations, such as transposition or inversion of a melodic motive.
   c. Motive in sequence.
4. As students work individually, go around the room and help students with each problem spot.

Extensions:

1. Students can compose their own melodic motive (A).
2. Have students compose their own melodic motive, trade with another student, and compose the B, C, and D measures (2, 5, 6, 7, and 8).
3. Distribute the melodic motives as an audio file and have the students dictate them before completing the assignment.
4. These melodies can be complex and imply several possible chord changes. Have students add chords to the melody.

Modifications:

1. Have students work in pairs on the assignment.
2. Have students complete fewer than the six examples given.

Rondo

Many melodies have form and structure. One form can be described as rondo form and is very similar to the song form of the same name. This form uses a melodic motive that is repeated and alternates between new materials in an eight-measure melody. An excellent example of this form is the melody "Yankee Doodle." The motive is in measures 1, 3, and 5 and alternates with new and different material in measures 2, 4, 6, 7, and 8. The material in the final three measures can be described as a mini coda. The form of this piece can be described as ABACAD.

Below is the melody "Yankee Doodle." Measures 1, 3, and 5 contain the melodic motive and are identical. Notice how measures 2, 4, 6, 7, and 8 are different from the motive and from each other.

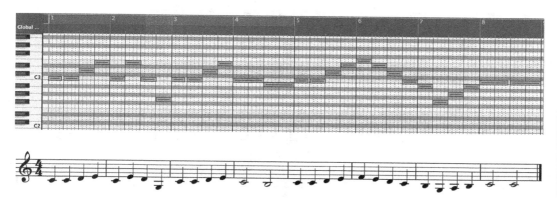

Assignment:

Complete each of the six 4-measure phrases given so as to create an eight-bar melody using rondo melody form.

Procedure:

1. Familiarize yourself with the melodic motive.
2. Compose and notate on that staves in the figure below or, in the software, record new material for measures 2, 4, 6, 7, and 8.
3. Use compositional techniques to make your newly composed material in measures 2, 4, 6, 7, and 8 are relevant to the motive in measures 1, 3, and 5. Things to consider using:
   a. Repetition of musical elements, including rhythms and pitches.
   b. Melodic variations such as transposition or inversion of a melodic motive.
   c. Motive sequences.
4. Repeat for each of the remaining examples, turning each of the six 4-measure phrases into eight-bar melodies.

The Ringtone Project

Nothing says "cool" like students hearing their self-composed ringtones on their cellphones. Since the musical material for ringtones needs to be relatively short, ringtones are great projects for students to understand the importance of melodies and the use of melodic motives.

A ringtone can be used for a few different things on a phone: the actual ring for a phone call, an alarm for a clock, notification for an email or SMS/Text message. What the ringtone will be used for can determine its length and content. An alert tone is usually short and repetitive. This is used for alarms that people might set in a calendar to alert themselves to a phone call or event or even as a morning wake-up. For phone calls, a 20- to 30-second ringtone is standard.

Old ringtones were monophonic melodies that used standard General MIDI instruments because of the playback limitations on the cellphones. There are still good examples of these on the Internet or on almost any cellphone. Monophonic ringtones are extremely effective, and on today's smartphones they can be recorded using the contemporary instruments in any sequencer and captured as an audio file. Most of today's smartphones can play back polyphonic ringtones and even sections of audio files of any piece of music available on the radio. Most students will want to compose a polyphonic, audio file ringtone.

Skills Required:

Basic understanding of how to record in the sequencer.
Understanding of how to compose simple melodies.

National Standards:

- Standard 4, Composing and arranging music within specified guidelines.
- Standard 7, Evaluating music and music performances.
- Standard 8, Understanding relationships between music, the arts, and disciplines outside the arts.
- Standard 9, Understanding music in relation to history and culture.

Objectives:

Students will gain understanding of the use of motives by composing a 30-second ringtone.

Materials:

The Ringtone Project student assignment sheet

Procedure:

1. Listen to some standard ringtones on various phones. Each phone manufacturer will preload several standard ringtones or ringtones can be heard off Internet sites that sell or distribute free ringtones.
2. Have students describe what works or doesn't work about each ringtone.
3. Ask students what are some of the elements that makes a melody good for a ringtone.
4. Review the Ringtone Project student assignment sheet.
5. Incorporate time for the class to listen to and comment on students' work.

Extension:

Compose a class or group "round robin" ringtone. Have one student start and then each student add something to the ringtone. One student will need to mix the final tracks.

Modification:

Have students compose a monophonic (single line) ringtone.

The Ringtone Project

Assignment:

Create a 30-second ringtone for use on a cellphone as a call notification ring.

Tips for Composing Ringtones:

1. You can either compose a piece that unfolds over the 30 seconds or a 15-second piece that loops.

2. Intros are not recommended, but if you have one, make sure it only lasts about two to three seconds.

3. Repeat elements and add elements that build tension as the ringtone progresses, informing the recipient that the call hasn't been answered.
   a. Double the melody in octaves on a different instrument.
   b. Create a parallel harmony by doubling the melody at an interval such as a 3rd or 6th.

4. As the ringtone progresses, some 7–10 seconds or more, add urgency.
   a. Speed up the tempo.
   b. Use rhythmic diminution.
   c. Layer elements.
   d. Offset motives (stretto).

5. Get to the point of your ringtone quickly. Most people pick up the call within a few seconds, so you'll want the highlight of your piece to be right up front.

6. It may be effective to start your motive on the fifth degree of the scale (in the key of C, the fifth degree of the scale would be G and would resolve to the tonic (C). This gives an effect of more tension or urgency, and as the piece plays, it resolves or releases to a more settled place.

7. Use instruments in a high register or that sound "bright" in pitch range and timbre (tone quality). There's a reason why a bell has been the telephone's ring sound for all these years: it cuts through a lot of background noise. Make sure your main melody cuts through. Compose in the c3–c5 range, depending on the instrument choice.

8. For polyphonic ringtones, spread your pitched instruments over three ranges, high, middle, and low, to allow each "sonic space" to be heard.

9. Bass is good, but forget those bass tones that rock the car. Remember, these rings are going to be heard through a tiny little speaker, and there just won't be enough to support a boomy or warble bass. As a matter of fact, a boomy bass could ruin those little speakers on your cellphone, so stay away unless you want to replace your phone!

155

Major and Minor Thirds

There are many ways to teach intervals. In general, thinking in terms of keys and the intervals that occur naturally in a scale can be an easier way to memorize intervals. For instance, in every major scale, the intervals created between the first note of the scale and subsequent degrees of the scale follow a pattern: major 2nd, major 3rd, perfect 4th, perfect 5th, major 6th, major 7th, perfect octave. In other words, 2nds, 3rds, 6ths, and 7ths are all major; 4th, 5th, and octave are perfect. Given that this is students' first exposure to an altered interval, flatting the 3rd to make a minor 3rd, understanding this small interval by counting half steps eliminates the need for understanding scale patterns at this point of learning and reinforces the understanding of the piano keyboard.

Skills Required:
Basic knowledge of the piano keyboard.

National Standards:
- Standard 5, Reading and notating music.
- Standard 6, Listening to, analyzing, and describing music.
- Standard 7, Evaluating music and music performances.

Objectives:
Students will demonstrate their understanding of the difference between major and minor 3rds by completing the Major and Minor Thirds worksheet.

Materials:
Major and Minor Thirds worksheet.

Procedure:
1. Review the layout of the piano keyboard.
2. Review the definition of half steps and whole steps:

    A half step is the closest any two notes can be on the piano keyboard: white to black key, black key to white key, and in two instances, white key to white key.

    A whole step is two half steps.
3. Define and demonstrate a generic 3rd: count the first note as 1 and count up to 3.

4. Define and demonstrate a major 3rd: four half steps (two whole steps).

5. Define and demonstrate a minor 3rd: three half steps (one whole step and one half step).

6. Check for understanding by asking questions of the class and eliciting verbal answers.

7. Review the Major and Minor 3rds worksheet.

Extensions:

1. Use computer-assisted instruction software or other worksheets for more examples.

2. During the lesson, have students sing up by half step to a major 3rd and to minor 3rds and then sing the interval of a major and minor 3rd, beginning on various notes in various ranges. Then do the same for each example of the worksheet after students complete it.

3. Have students record their triads both melodically and harmonically.

Modification:

Review major 3rds one day and minor 3rds another day. Check for understanding with verbal or written examples or using computer-assisted instruction software.

WORKSHEET **Major and Minor Thirds**

Name...

Date...

There are three basic groups of intervals: major/minor, augmented/diminished, and perfect. Major and minor 3rds are the foundation to understanding chord quality.

    To locate a generic 3rd up from any note, count the first note as 1 and count up to note 3. For instance, a 3rd up from D is F: D is one, E is two, and F is three. Thirds come in different varieties. A major 3rd can be described as four half steps above the first note. For instance, the distance from C to E is a major 3rd because E is four half steps above C. You can also think of a major 3rd as two whole steps:

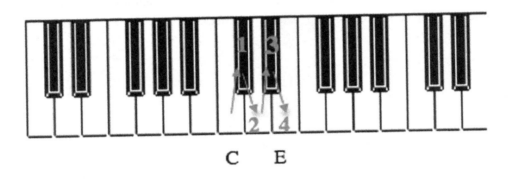

A minor 3rd is three half steps above the first note, or one and a half steps above the first note:

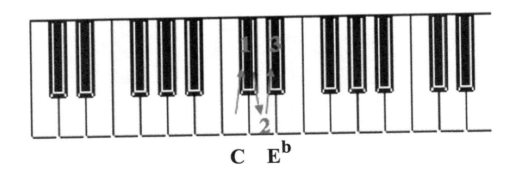

On the keyboard below, put an X on the notes given and indicate whether the interval is a major 3rd (M3) or a minor 3rd (m3).

Example:

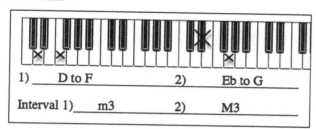

1) ____D to F_____ 2) ____Eb to G____

Interval 1)____m3____ 2) ____M3_____

1
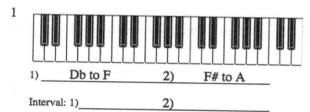

1) ____Db to F____ 2) ____F# to A____

Interval: 1)_____ 2)_____

2
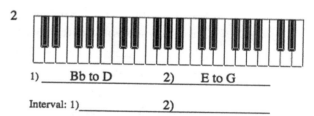

1) ____Bb to D____ 2) ____E to G____

Interval: 1)_____ 2)_____

3
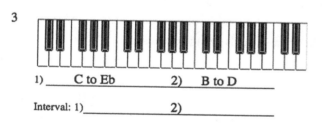

1) ____C to Eb____ 2) ____B to D____

Interval: 1)_____ 2)_____

4
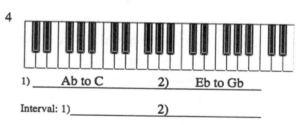

1) ____Ab to C____ 2) ____Eb to Gb____

Interval: 1)_____ 2)_____

5
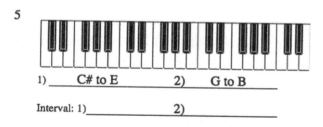

1) ____C# to E____ 2) ____G to B____

Interval: 1)_____ 2)_____

6
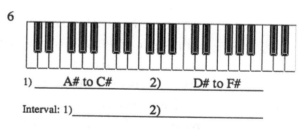

1) ____A# to C#____ 2) ____D# to F#____

Interval: 1)_____ 2)_____

7
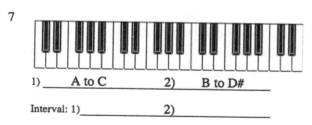

1) ____A to C____ 2) ____B to D#____

Interval: 1)_____ 2)_____

8
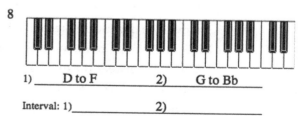

1) ____D to F____ 2) ____G to Bb____

Interval: 1)_____ 2)_____

9
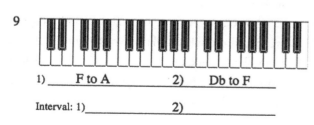

1) ____F to A____ 2) ____Db to F____

Interval: 1)_____ 2)_____

10
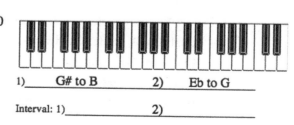

1) ____G# to B____ 2) ____Eb to G____

Interval: 1)_____ 2)_____

159

LESSON 18b

Understanding Triad Qualities

A thorough understanding of major keys and their scales is ultimately the best way to understand all keys, their variations, and the quality of the naturally occurring triads in scales. For instance, if you understand how a major scale is formed, you can alter certain scale degrees to form minor scales, that is, you can flat the third, sixth, and seventh, as appropriate to the specific minor scale desired. Taking this one step further, altering specific scale degrees produces new scales in different genres, for example blues. If you know how to alter a scale to form a basic blues scale (1, flat the third, 4, flat the fifth, 5, flat the seventh, 8) then you can form a blues scale in every key.

Altered scales produce triads of different qualities. The triad formed on the first degree of a major scale is always a major triad: I. The triad formed on the first degree of a minor scale produces a minor triad: i. Understanding quality of triads as they occur in keys reinforces an understanding of keys, their scales, and the relationship of one key to the next. This is, ultimately, the way to master advanced theory and the language of music.

Building triads on scale degrees produces naturally occurring major, minor, and diminished triads that remain constant for every major scale. For instance, in every major key, a triad formed on the first, fourth, and fifth degrees of the scale, without changing any notes in the scale, will produce major triads. Hence the use of capital Roman numerals to represent them: I, IV, and V. Triads formed on the second, third, and sixth degrees of the scale are minor triads and are represented by lowercase Roman numerals: ii, iii, and vi. The triad formed on the seventh degree of the scale is "diminished" and is represented with lowercase Roman numerals followed by the symbol for diminished chords: vii°. There are many ways to understand the differences between major, minor, diminished, and augmented triads.

For simplicity, this lesson concentrates on the most basic understanding of triads by stacking major and minor 3rds. The lesson also reinforces the previous lesson on major and minor 3rds. A triad is formed on a note called the root, with a note a 3rd above and then a note a 5th above. The qualities of the intervals between the root and the third and between the third and the fifth—major or minor 3rds—form triads of different qualities. A major triad consists of a major 3rd between the root and the third note and a minor 3rd between the third and the fifth note. A minor triad consists of a minor 3rd between the root and the third note and a major 3rd between the third and the fifth note. A diminished triad consists of a minor 3rd and then another minor 3rd. An augmented triad consists of two major 3rds.

You may prefer to teach this lesson in multiple days, spending one day on one or two triad qualities. A predesigned worksheet is provided, along with a blank worksheet for teachers to use for choosing their own chords. Use the blank worksheet to create a worksheet where students distinguish only between major and minor, or between major and diminished, or between major and augmented, or between any combination appropriate for students.

Skills Required:

Ability to distinguish major and minor triads.

National Standards:

- Standard 1, Singing, alone and with others, a varied repertoire of music.
- Standard 2, Performing on instruments, alone and with others, a varied repertoire of music.
- Standard 4, Composing and arranging music within specified guidelines.
- Standard 5, Reading and notating music.
- Standard 6, Listening to, analyzing, and describing music.

Objectives:

Students will demonstrate their knowledge of major, minor, diminished, and augmented triads, as defined by combinations of intervals of major and minor 3rds, by completing the Triad Qualities worksheet.

Materials:

Triad Qualities worksheet.

Procedure:

1. Review whole and half steps.
2. Define and review generic intervals: the distance between two notes defined by counting the distance between them.
3. Define and demonstrate a generic 3rd: count the first note as 1 and count up to note 3.
4. Define and demonstrate a major 3rd: four half steps (two whole steps).
5. Define and demonstrate a minor 3rd: three half steps (one whole step and one half step).
6. Define and demonstrate all four triads, starting on C: C major, c minor, c diminished, and C augmented.
7. Review the four qualities of triads using different roots.
8. Distribute and review the Triad Qualities worksheet.
9. Circulate in the room and check on student progress or answer any questions as they complete their worksheets and record their work.

Extensions:

1. Use the Triad Qualities blank worksheet to create more triads
2. When defining and demonstrating the different triads (item 6), have students sing them.
3. Have students record their answers from the worksheet into the software.

Modifications:

1. Use the Triad Qualities blank worksheet to create a page or half page of only major triads. Then create a page or half page of minor triads. Progress this way through diminished and augmented triads as appropriate to the students' needs.
2. Major and/or minor may be sufficient.

WORSHEET Triad Qualities

Name...

Date...

On the keyboards below, mark an X on each key to form the triad, write the note names on the line provided under the keyboard, and draw in the notes on the staff.

Example: C Major triad

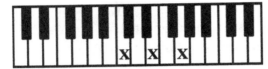

Note names: ___C___E___G___

Example: c minor triad

Note names: ___C___E___G___

1) f minor triad

Note names: _____

2) D flat Major triad (D)

Note names: _____

3) Eb Major triad (E♭)

Note names: _____

4) B flat minor triad (b⁰)

Note names: _____

162

5) B diminished triad (b⁰)

Note names:_____

7) C Augmented triad (C⁺)

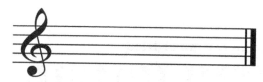

Note names:_____

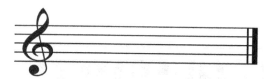

9) F Augmented triad (F⁺)

Note names:_____

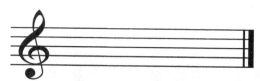

6) D Major triad (D)

Note names:_____

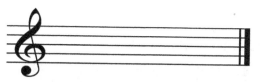

8) A minor triad (a)

Note names:_____

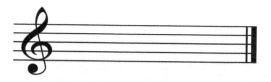

163

10) A diminished triad (a)

Note names:_____

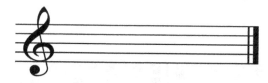

Name..

Date...

On the keyboards below, mark an X on each key to form the triad, write the note names on the line provided under the keyboard, and draw in the notes on the staff.

Example: C Major triad

Note names: C E G

Example: c minor triad

Note names: C E♭ G

1) _____

Note names: _____

2) _____

Note names: _____

3) _____

Note names: _____

4) _____

Note names: _____

Note names:_____

Note names:_____

Note names:_____

8)_____

Note names:_____

9)_____

10_____

Note names:_____

Note names:_____

LESSON 18c

Building Triads on Scale Degrees

Using the piano supplement material in the appendix and on the companion website will reinforce standard and common chord progressions. It is important for students to understand that there's more to harmony than just three chords. Triads are easy to construct and use.

This lesson provides a generic worksheet that the teacher can choose keys for and use at different points throughout the course. The worksheet can be a template from which students play and record their chords. It can also serve as a template for use with unit 19 on chord progressions.

An added bonus for advanced and college students is to have them solfège each triad in the key. For instance, sing: do mi sol mi do, re fa la fa re, mi sol ti (si) sol mi, and so on.

Skills Required:
Understanding the piano keyboard.
Understanding basic intervals.

National Standards:
- Standard 1, Singing, alone and with others, a varied repertoire of music.
- Standard 2, Performing on instruments, alone and with others, a varied repertoire of music.
- Standard 3, Improvising melodies, variations, and accompaniments.
- Standard 4, Composing and arranging music within specified guidelines.
- Standard 5, Reading and notating music.

Objectives:
Students will demonstrate their understanding of how to build triads on each scale degree by completing the Building Triads on Scale Degrees worksheet.

Materials:
Building Triads on Scale Degrees worksheet.

Procedure:
1. Explain how triads are constructed; root, third, fifth.
2. Demonstrate how a triad can be built on any scale degree.
3. Distribute the Building Triads on Scale Degrees worksheet and explain how to complete it.
4. Give students sufficient time to complete the worksheet.
5. Have students play and record each chord in succession.

Extensions:

1. Use the Building Triads on Scale Degrees worksheet for different keys as they are explored in class.
2. Sing the triads in the keys given.

Modification:

Give students a limited number of scale degrees each day.

WORSHEET Building Triads on Scale Degrees

Name..

Date..

On the keyboards and staves below:

1. **Mark a X on each key to form the triad on each degree of the scale in the key given.**

2. **Write the note names on the line provided.**

3. **Draw the notes on the staff.**

Key:_____

First Degree: _____

Example Key: C Major
First Degree: C Major

Note names:_____C___E___G_____

Second Degree: _____

Note names:_____

Third Degree: _____

Note names:_____

Fourth Degree: _____

Note names:_____

Note names:_____

Fifth Degree: _____

Note names: _____

Sixth Degree: _____

Note names: _____

Seventh Degree: _____

Note names: _____

Eighth Degree: _____

Note names: _____

Basic Chord Progressions

This lesson begins a series that focuses on chords and progressions. Adding melodic material is not discussed here. However, it is suggested that you consider having students add melodies to every chord progression produced. This encourages an understanding of harmonies, melody writing, and voice leading, and adding melodies to harmonies is a common problem encountered in high school Advanced Placement and college music theory courses. Adding melodies to harmonies also addresses a legitimate approach to composition that many songwriters, pianists, and guitarists encounter when they compose chord patterns before melodic material. A great deal of time can be spent on this subject, especially when addressed in conjunction with the use of the nonharmonic tones in unit 22.

The assignment for this and subsequent lessons on chord progressions does not specifically address the use of inversions. If the teacher is using the piano supplement material in the appendix and the companion website, chords and their inversions will be addressed. It is up to the teacher to decide when it is appropriate for students to utilize inversions in the assignments in units 19–21.

This and most of the assignments are in major keys. Adding at least the parallel minor key would be a good reinforcement of keys and key relations. Add minor keys at your discretion.

Skills Required:

Ability to record in the software.

Ability to edit in the software.

Understanding of how to build and play triads in root position.

National Standards:

- Standard 2, Performing on instruments, alone and with others, a varied repertoire of music.
- Standard 4, Composing and arranging music within specified guidelines.
- Standard 6, Listening to, analyzing, and describing music.
- Standard 7, Evaluating music and music performances.

Objectives:

Students will understand basic chord progressions using the I, IV, and V chords in C major in various combinations.

Materials:

Basic Chord Progressions student assignment sheet.

The Building Triads on Scale Degrees worksheet (unit 18c) can be used as a reference.

Procedure:

1. Review how to create a triad using the root, third, and fifth.
2. Review the I, IV, and V triads in the key of C major.
3. Review and demonstrate various combinations of I, IV, V progressions, using four chords in each progression (i.e., I, IV, V, I; or I, V, IV, V; or V, I, IV, V; etc.).
4. Demonstrate how to record a chord progression in the software. Students can record all four chords in one pass without stopping the recording. They can also use a technique called "punching in": recording into a recording. In this case, students will record each chord individually, stop the recording after each chord, find the next chord, hit the Record button, and record one chord at a time, each in its proper location.
5. Review the Basic Chord Progressions student assignment sheet.

Extensions:

1. Notate the chord progressions.
2. Give other keys for students to use to form the progressions.
3. Have students add melodies to their progressions.

Modifications:

1. Provide progressions for students to record.
2. For a visual reference to record with, provide a keyboard worksheet on which students can mark X on the keys to form the triads.
3. Students can step-input or draw the notes into the Piano Roll/Matrix Editing window.

Basic Chord Progressions

Chords can be formed on any note of a scale. Triads are three-note chords. The most basic triads are formed from the first degree of the scale (the I chord), the fourth degree of the scale (the IV chord), and the fifth degree of the scale (the V chord).

Create and record four four-chord progressions using I, IV, and V chords in any combination. For example: I, IV, V, I; or I, V, IV, V; or V, I, IV, V; or others.

Procedure:

1. Open a new file: File > New.
2. Save the file as "Basic Chords _ _" (your two initials).
3. Add four software instrument tracks and use a basic piano sound for each track.
4. On one of the tracks, play the I triad, the IV triad, and the V triad in the key of C major, to make sure you understand how the chords are formed and played.
5. On the first track, record a four-chord progression using these three chords. You will need to repeat one of the three chords in the four-chord progression. Record one chord per measure, each chord as a whole note that lasts for four beats. You will have four measures in the track. You do not need to record all the chords in one pass. You can stop the recording after the first chord, find the second chord on the keyboard, and record each chord separately.
6. Solo the second track and record the same three chords in a different order, creating a new progressions of the I, IV, and V chords. Record one chord per measure. You will have four measures in the track.
7. Repeat this process for tracks 3 and 4, using different combinations of the same three chords.
8. You will have four tracks each with four measures of chords. Each track will have a different combination of I, IV, and V chords.

Twelve-Bar Blues

The I–IV–V progression is the foundation for several styles of music. The blues is the foundation of much contemporary song and an important genre for students to understand. This lesson explores the basic 12-bar blues chord progression.

Skills Required:

Ability to record in the software.

Ability to edit in the software.

Understanding of how to build and play triads in root position.

National Standards:

• Standard 2, Performing on instruments, alone and with others, a varied repertoire of music.

• Standard 4, Composing and arranging music within specified guidelines.

• Standard 6, Listening to, analyzing, and describing music.

• Standard 7, Evaluating music and music performances.

Objectives:

Students will gain understanding of the basic 12-bar blues chord progression by recording it into the software using the MIDI keyboard.

Materials:

Twelve-Bar Blues student assignment sheet.

The Building Triads on Scale Degrees worksheet (unit 18c) can be used as a reference.

Procedure:

1. Review how to create a triad using the root, third, and fifth.

2. Review the I, IV, and V triads in the key of C major.

3. Play a variety of songs or pieces that use the 12-bar blues.

4. Review and demonstrate the 12-bar blues chord progression. Notice that each bar/measure has one chord and the chords are grouped in four-bar (four-measure) phrases: I–I–I–I , IV–IV–I–I, V–V–I–I.

5. Demonstrate how to record a chord progression in the software. Students can record the entire 12-bar blues in one pass without stopping the recording, or they can record in smaller four-bar phrases. They can also "punch in" : recording into a recording. In this case, students will record each chord individually, stop the recording after each chord, find the next chord, hit the Record button, and record one chord at a time, each in its proper location.

6. Review the Twelve-Bar Blues student assignment sheet.

Extensions:

1. Students can use standard music notation to write out the chord progressions.

2. Give other keys for students to use to form the progressions.

3. Have students add or improvise melodies to their progressions. Incorporate time for the class to listen to and comment on students' work.

Modifications

1. Provide a keyboard worksheet for students to mark "x" on the keys to form the triads in any key given for a visual reference to record with.

2. Students can step-input or draw the notes into the Piano Roll/Matrix Editing window.

Twelve-Bar Blues

Chords can be formed on any note of a scale. Triads are three-note chords. The most basic triads are formed on the first degree of the scale (the I chord), the fourth degree of the scale (the IV chord), and the fifth degree of the scale (the V chord).

An important chord progression is the 12-bar blues. This progression is based on the three chords I, IV, and V in a specific order and is played over 12 bars or measures of music.

Assignment:

Record a 12-bar blues progression.

Procedure:

1. Open a new file: File > New and save the file as "12 Bar Blues __ __" (your two initials).
2. Add one software instrument track and use a basic piano sound.
3. Play the I triad, the IV triad, and the V triad in the key of C major, to make sure you understand how the chords are formed and played.
4. Record the 12-bar blues progressions: I–I–I–I , IV–IV–I–I, V–V–I–I.
5. On the first track, record a four-chord progression using these three chords. You will need to repeat one of the three chords in the four-chord progression. Record one chord per measure. You will have four measures in the track. You do not need to record all the chords in one pass. You can stop the recording after the first chord, find the second chord on the keyboard, and record each chord separately. This process is called punching in.

You will have one track with 12 measures of chords.

175

LESSON 19c

Given Chord Progressions from the Simple Chord Map

The Simple Chord Map by Steve Mugglin (available at Chordmaps.com) is an excellent tool for students to use to create chord progressions. The chord formed on the seventh degree of the scale is omitted because, according to Mugglin, this is a "simple" map. A more advanced map and detailed maps for various keys are available (http://mugglinw.ipower.com/chordmaps/chartmaps.htm).

How to Use the Simple Chord Map:

These are Mugglin's instructions: to use the map, remember two things. First, you may jump anywhere from I. Second, if a chord appears at more than one place, there is an "imaginary tunnel" connecting both spots, so you can move from one to the other. Start anywhere and then follow the arrows.

Skills Required:

Ability to record in the software.
Ability to edit in the software.
Understanding of how to build and play triads in root position.

National Standards:

- Standard 2, Performing on instruments, alone and with others, a varied repertoire of music.
- Standard 4, Composing and arranging music within specified guidelines.
- Standard 6, Listening to, analyzing, and describing music.
- Standard 7, Evaluating music and music performances.

Objectives:

Students will understand basic chord progressions using the Simple Chord Map by recording a variety of progressions given.

Materials:

Simple Chord Map.
The Building Triads on Scale Degrees worksheet (unit 18c) can be used as a reference.
Given Chord Progressions from the Simple Chord Map student assignment sheet.

Procedure:

1. Review how to create a triad using the root, third, and fifth.
2. Review the triads in the key of C major and how each chord is built on a scale degree. The Roman numerals refer to each scale degree.
3. Review the Simple Chord Map and how to "read" it.

4. Review the following chord progressions in C major or in the key the students are to use and refer to the Simple Chord Map:

I IV V IV

I V vi IV

I iii vi IV

I vi IV V

I ii V vi

5. Demonstrate how to record a chord progression in root position in the software. Students can record all four chords in one pass without stopping the recording. They can also use "punching in": recording into a recording. In this case, students will record each chord individually, stop the recording after each chord, find the next chord, hit the Record button, and record one chord at a time, each in its proper location. Some software allows the user to cycle a section, repeat over and over, and record multiple takes over one another. The multiple takes can then be merged together.

6. Review the Given Chord Progressions from the Simple Chord Map student assignment sheet.

Extensions:

1. Students can notate the chord progressions.
2. Give keys other than C major for students to use to form the progressions.
3. Have students add melodies to their progressions.

Modifications

1. For a visual reference to record with, provide a keyboard worksheet on which students can mark X on the keys to form the triads in any key given.
2. Distribute a worksheet with multiple copies of the Simple Chord Map and have students circle and draw arrows between chords.
3. Students can step-input or draw the notes into the Piano Roll/Matrix Editing window.

The Simple Chord Map

To use the map, remember two things. First, you may jump anywhere from I. Second, if a chord appears at more than one place, there is an "imaginary tunnel" connecting both spots, so you can move from one to the other. Start anywhere and then follow the arrows.

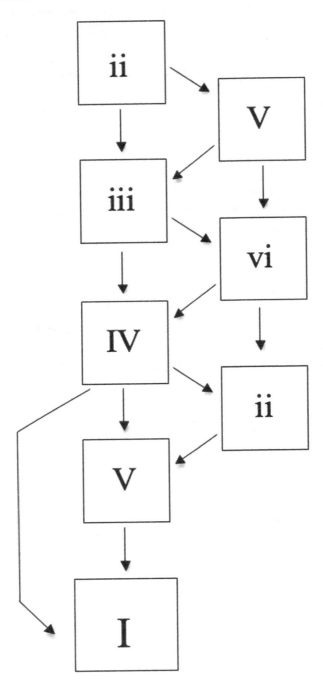

Given Chord Progressions from the Simple Chord Map

Chords can be formed on any note of a scale. Triads are three-note chords. Triads can be formed on each degree of the scale. These chords are referred to using the Roman numerals that correspond to their scale degree. For instance, the triad formed on the first degree of the scale in C major is called the I chord. A triad formed on the second degree is called the ii chord. Capital and lowercase Roman numerals are used to distinguish major from minor chords.

Assignment:

Record the following four-chord progressions based on the Simple Chord Map:

I IV V IV

I V vi IV

I iii vi IV

I vi IV V

I ii V vi

Procedure:

1. Open a new file: File > New and save the file as "Given Chords __" (your two initials).
2. Add five software instrument tracks and use a basic piano sound for each track.
3. On the first track, record these progressions in the key given: I–IV–V–IV.
4. Record one chord per measure. You will have four measures in the track. You do not need to record all the chords in one pass. You can stop the recording after the first chord, find the second chord on the keyboard, and record each chord separately. This process is called punching in.
5. Solo the second track and record these progressions: I–V–vi–IV.
6. Record one chord per measure. You will have four measures in the track.
7. Repeat this process for track 3, using these progressions: I–iii–vi–IV.
8. Repeat this process for track 4, using these progressions: I–vi–IV–V.
9. Repeat this process for track 5, using these progressions: I–ii–V–vi.
10. You will have five tracks each with four measures of chords.

LESSON 19d

Common Chord Progressions Not on the Simple Chord Map

There are many different combinations of chord progressions that do not follow the rules of the Simple Chord Map. Below are some of these; they are found in many styles of music.

Skills Required:
Ability to record in the software.
Ability to edit in the software.
Understanding of how to build and play triads in root position.

National Standards:
- Standard 2, Performing on instruments, alone and with others, a varied repertoire of music.
- Standard 4, Composing and arranging music within specified guidelines.
- Standard 6, Listening to, analyzing, and describing music.
- Standard 7, Evaluating music and music performances.

Objectives:
Students will understand basic chord progressions by recording a variety of progressions given.

Materials:
The Building Triads on Scale Degrees worksheet (unit 18c) can be used as a reference.
Given Chord Progressions 2 student assignment sheet.

Procedure:
1. Review how to create a triad using the root, third, and fifth.
2. Review the triads in the key of C major and how each chord is built on a scale degree. The Roman numerals refer to each scale degree.
3. Review the following chord progressions in C major or in the key the students are to use. Notice that these do not follow the rules of the Simple Chord Map:

   I V ii IV
   I vi V IV
   I VII IV
   I ii V I

4. Demonstrate how to record a chord progression in root position in the software. Students can record all four chords in one pass without stopping the recording. They can also use "punching in": recording into a recording. In this case, students will record each chord individually, stop the recording after each chord, find the next chord, hit the Record button, and record one chord at a time, each in its proper location.
5. Review the Given Chord Progressions 2 student assignment sheet.

Extensions:

1. Students can notate the chord progressions.
2. Give keys other than C major for students to form the progressions.
3. Have students add melodies to their progressions.

Modifications:

1. Provide a keyboard worksheet for students to mark X on the keys to form the triads in any key given for a visual reference to record with.
2. Distribute a worksheet with multiple copies of the Simple Chord Map and have students circle and draw an arrow between chords.
3. Students can step-input or draw the notes into the Piano Roll/Matrix Editing window.

STUDENT ASSIGNMENT SHEET

Given Chord Progressions 2

Chords can be formed on any note of a scale. Triads are three-note chords. Triads can be formed on each degree of the scale. These chords are referred to using Roman numerals equivalent to their corresponding scale degree. For instance, the triad formed on the first degree of the scale in C major is called the I chord. A triad formed on the second degree is called the ii chord. Capital and lowercase Roman numerals are used to distinguish major from minor chords.

Assignment:

Record the following four-chord progressions. Notice that these progressions do not follow the rules of the Simple Chord Map:

I V ii IV
I vi V IV
I ii V I
Extra credit: I VII IV

Procedure:

1. Open a new file: File > New and save the file as "Given Chords 2 _ _" (your two initials).
2. Add three software instrument tracks and use a basic piano sound for each track.
3. On the first track, record these progressions in the key given: I–V–ii–IV.
4. Record one chord per measure. You will have four measures in the track. You do not need to record all the chords in one pass. You can stop the recording after the first chord, find the second chord on the keyboard and record each chord separately. This process is called punching in.
5. Solo the second track and record these progressions: I–vi–V–IV.
6. Record one chord per measure. You will have four measures in the track.
7. Repeat this process for track three using these progressions: I–ii–V–I.
8. For extra credit:
    a. Can you form a vii° triad in the key given?
    b. What note would it start on?
    c. What would the 3rd be? How do you make the chord major?
    d. Record these progressions for extra credit in track 4: I–vi–IV–V.
    e. You will have three or four tracks each with four measures of chords.

Accompaniment Patterns

The patterns given in this lesson are some of those more commonly found in accompaniments. There are more kinds of accompaniment patterns, and students should be encouraged to explore and create their own.

Accompaniment patterns should not be confused with *harmonic rhythms*: the rhythmic rate of changing harmonies or chords. Accompaniment patterns add texture to music by *creating movement within* the harmonic rhythm. For instance, on the Accompaniment Pattern handout, broken chord type 3, Alberti bass, has a harmonic rhythm of a whole note because the chords change every bar (whole note) even though the notes of the chord are played as eighth notes. It is the specific pattern of the order in which they are played—root, fifth, third, fifth—that defines the accompaniment pattern as an Alberti bass. The term "harmonic rhythm" refers to when the chord changes, not to the rhythm in which the notes of the chord are played, whether in eighths, quarters, or any other rhythm.

Although all four accompaniment patterns presented in this chapter may be introduced in one class session, the exercises may be best approached over several. It is recommended that single class sessions or homework assignments be devoted to each variation. College teachers may choose to give all the materials for homework in a single week.

The assignment for this lesson has students record a basic I–IV–V progression using the various accompaniment patterns. It is desirable for students to play the accompaniment patterns as they record; however, some may not have these piano skills. Students may record the basic progression and then edit the notes to create the accompaniment pattern. To add exercises to each assignment, students can access their previously recorded chords from their assignments in lessons 19a (Basic Chord Progressions), 19b (Twelve-Bar Blues), 19c (Given Chord Progressions from the Simple Chord Map), and 19d (Common Chord Progressions Not on the Simple Chord Map). Of course, students can create new chords for this lesson.

This lesson and assignment can be used each time a new key is explored in class.

> **TIP**
>
> I think it is best for students to record the accompaniment patterns by performing on a MIDI or piano keyboard. I do not insist that my students perform with the correct fingering, as long as they record in real time. They may record as slowly as they like and edit as necessary.

Skills Required:

Ability to record MIDI into the software.

Basic MIDI editing skills.

National Standards:

- Standard 4, Composing and arranging music within specified guidelines.
- Standard 6, Listening to, analyzing, and describing music.
- Standard 7, Evaluating music and music performances.

Objectives:

Students will demonstrate their knowledge of various accompaniment patterns by recording these patterns according to the rhythms given in the student assignment sheet.

Materials:

Accompaniment Patterns handout.

Accompaniment Patterns student assignment sheet.

MIDI files on the companion website.

Procedure:

1. Define "accompaniment": music that supports the melody.
2. Introduce each accompaniment pattern and use the Accompaniment Patterns handout and the MIDI examples or other examples to demonstrate each pattern. Below is a list of recommended pieces. Those in the public domain are on the companion website.
   a. Block chord patterns: Mozart, *Eine Kleine Nacht Music*; Jerry Lee Lewis, "Whole Lotta Shakin' Going On."
   b. Oompah : Jaromír Vejvoda, "Modřanská polka" (Beer Barrel Polka)"; Prokofiev, "Dance of the Knights" from *Romeo and Juliet*
   c. Arpeggiation: Beethoven, "Moonlight Sonata"; "Aqua Harp." from the video *Animusic 1*, available at www.animusic.com
   d. Alberti bass: Mozart, Piano Sonata no. 16 K. 545, Allegro.
3. Review the accompaniment pattern to be focused on in each class session.
4. Review the student assignment sheet.
5. As students work individually, go around the room and help students with each problem spot.

Extensions:

1. Students can create their own chord progressions to use for the accompaniment patterns.
2. Students can create their own rhythmic patterns to be used for the accompaniment patterns.
3. Students can use prerecorded chord progressions from unit 19.

Modifications:

1. The teacher provides a file with prerecorded chord progressions.
2. Students can copy and paste the chord progressions and manually manipulate the rhythms to create the desired patterns.
3. Limit students to one rhythmic example per accompaniment pattern.

Accompaniment Patterns

Block Chords

When all the notes of a chord are played simultaneously, this is called a block chord. Block chords can be repeated using different rhythmic patterns. Strumming a chord on a guitar creates *block chord patterns*. Any rhythmic pattern can be used, and they can vary from measure to measure, for example by playing on the downbeat holding the chord for one measure or two beats, or mixing up rhythms as in the examples shown.

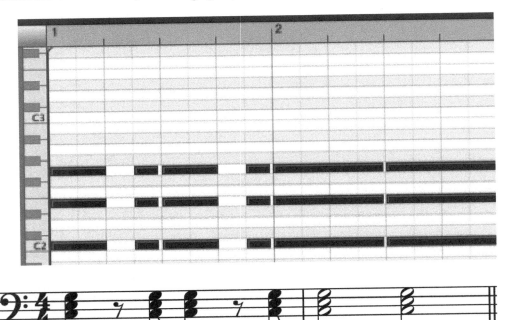

Broken Chord Type 1: "Oompah"

A very simple way to break up a chord for accompaniment is to play the root of the chord first and then the remaining two notes, the third and fifth ones, together. This broken chord pattern is also called an "oompah" accompaniment. You can use quarter notes, as in measures 1 and 3, or eighth notes, as in measures 2 and 4. Measures 1 and 2 show the pattern in "closed" position. Notice how the order of root, third, fifth is maintained. Measures 3 and 4 are in "open" position; the third has been transposed up an octave, so it is above the fifth.

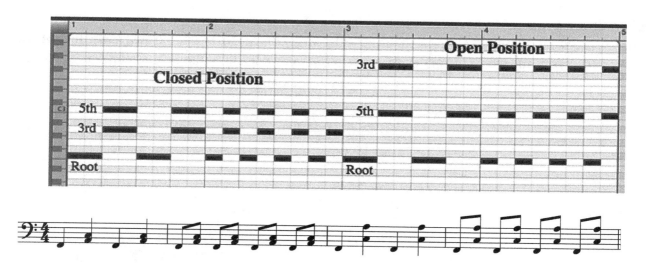

A more sophisticated version of the oompah pattern has the bass note (the lowest note) alternating between the root and the fifth.

Broken Chord Type 2: Arpeggiation

An arpeggiation makes for a simple but interesting accompaniment pattern. The chord is played melodically (one note at a time in succession) rather than harmonically, as in the block chord pattern. Measure 1 shows a single-direction pattern using eighth and half notes. Notice in measure 2 how the first three notes go up, then the fourth note goes down, and finally the fifth note goes up again, making this measure a mixed-direction pattern. Measure 3 uses eighth notes where the notes go up and then down, forming a wave-shaped pattern.

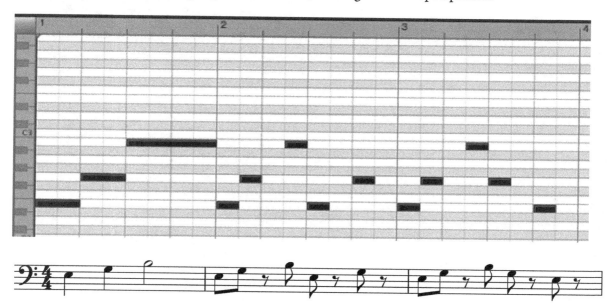

Broken Chord Type 3: Alberti Bass

Created by composer Domenico Alberti in the eighteenth century, the Alberti bass is still used today. This pattern is similar to the arpeggiation but follows a specific format; root, fifth, third, fifth. This example shows two different chords using the Alberti bass pattern: D minor in measure 1, and G major in measure 2.

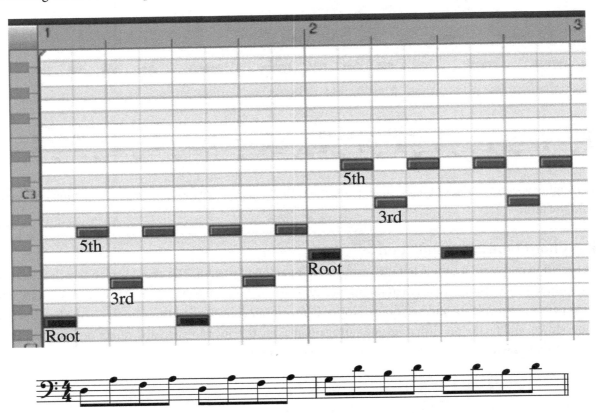

Accompaniment Patterns

The rhythmic rate at which chords change, a whole note, half, quarter, or other rhythm, is called the harmonic rhythm. Accompaniment patterns are ways to play chords to add rhythm and texture to the harmonic rhythms of a piece.

Procedure:

1. Create a new file: File > New; name and save as "AccompPatterns _ _" (your two initials).
2. Record the following accompaniment patterns, using I–IV–V chord progression in the key of C major.

Block Chords

1. Add a software instrument track and choose a basic piano sound.
2. Record each chord using a block chord pattern and using the following rhythms, skipping one measure between each pattern, A, B, and C.

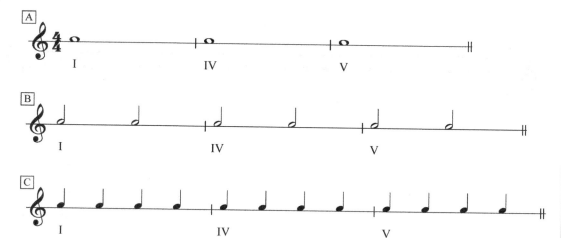

Broken Chord Type 1: Oompah

1. Add a software instrument track and choose a basic piano sound.
2. Record each chord using an oompah pattern and using the following rhythms, skipping one measure between each pattern, A and B.

Broken Chord Type 2: Arpeggiation

1. Add a software instrument track and choose a basic piano sound.

2. Record each chord using an arpeggiation pattern, either mix direction or wave, and using the following rhythms, skipping one measure between each pattern, A and B.

Broken Chord Type 3: Alberti Bass

1. Add a software instrument track and choose a basic piano sound.

2. Record each chord using an Alberti bass pattern and using the following rhythms, skipping one measure between each pattern, A and B.

Composing Four-Measure Melodies

This unit puts it all together, melody, harmony, and bass lines. This top-down approach is based on music that focuses on melody and harmony rather than on rhythm and bass. However, the teacher may choose a different approach and have students compose chord progressions first (unit 19) and then add melody and the subsequent lessons in unit 20. A combination of both approaches for college music majors is advised to keep them on their toes!

Students who want to focus purely on contemporary popular styles that rely heavily on rhythm (drums) and bass may struggle with or resist this approach. Even if students insist that they only want to be the producers of the "groove," drums and bass, we must remind them that there isn't a single piece of music on the top of most contemporary music charts that does not have a melody in it. Even if the "hook" is the bass and drums or some melodic ostinato, a melody looms within, either as a portion of a section or as an ostinato, and is essential to the success of the tune. In the end, we have a responsibility as teachers to expose students to the totality of music.

Many styles of contemporary pop music do not contain extended melodic material. This is why students whose musical experience is limited to these styles find it more difficult to write long melodic lines. The melody writing drills elsewhere in this book help develop skills for creating longer melodic lines based on certain guidelines or restrictions. This lesson allows students to create without restrictions and with few guidelines.

For this first lesson in the unit, it is recommended that students use a flute or violin sound, as these instruments have clear, simple sounds that require the student to keep the key pressed to sustain sound, encouraging conscientious rhythmic choices. However, at this point in the curriculum it might be advantageous to allow students to chose their own instruments. Instrument selection (timbre) can inspire composition. Instrument ranges and which octave to place the melody in are not a concern until accompaniments (harmony, countermelodies, bass lines, etc.) are composed.

The assignments for this lesson are similar to those students had for creating melodic motives, although rhythms are not given. The teacher can choose to use all or any one of the exercises for the student assignments. As stated in unit 14, the exercises develop melodic composition skills by limiting the students' choices of notes and then increasing and changing their choices. Limiting choices can actually allow for more creativity and be less frustrating, as students can create within a parameter and not have to face too many choices. The parameters given encourage tonic and dominant melodic figures. If using standard music notation, teachers can project or distribute all student melodies to be sung and reviewed by the class.

The assignments in this lesson require only four-measure melodies. After these melodies have been composed, teachers can revisit unit 15 and use students' material to turn the newly composed four-measure melodies into eight-measure melodies using the melodic form techniques discussed in that unit. Alternately, for more advanced students, the initial assignment can be for students to create eight-measure melodies. In addition, repeat all the assignments in this lesson requiring the melodies to be written in the relative minor: A minor.

This unit can also be a foundation for college teachers who have ensemble writing as part of their curricula. Key choices and harmonization across instruments or voice types will depend on the ensemble. This unit can be an entire semester of study when students are assigned both major and minor keys and add accompaniment patterns from unit 20. It can also be the core of a one-semester college music composition course or songwriting course for students with some music background.

Each teacher will decide when it is appropriate to have students share their creations with the class and have a class listening and peer evaluation session.

Skills Required:
Understanding the piano keyboard.
Ability to record in your software of choice.

National Standards:
• Standard 2, Performing on instruments, alone and with others, a varied repertoire of music.
• Standard 4, Composing and arranging music within specified guidelines.

Objectives:
Students will demonstrate their ability to create simple melodic figures in the key of C by composing several four-measure melodic phrases.

Materials:
Composing Four-Measure Melodies student assignment sheet.

Procedure:
1. Start the class with two-measure instant dictations in C as a warm-up. This will reinforce the concept of melodic figures.
2. Explain that there are several assignments that will occur over several class sessions. Students will compose short melodic figures and will learn how to harmonize these melodies and how to create accompaniments, bass lines, and drum patterns.
3. Handout or open the Composing Four-Measure Melodies student assignment sheet.
4. Review the student assignment sheet.
5. Review possible solutions for four-measure melody compositions, including motive and motive variations.
6. As students work individually, go around the room and help students with each problem spot.

Extensions:

1. Have students record eight-measure melodies.
2. Give a starting note and/or an ending note for each of the melodic figures.
3. Require two of these melodic figures be the key of in C minor or A minor.
4. Use all of the assignments in this unit in a different key to explore keys other than C.

Modifications:

1. Give C as the starting note. Some students require more guidance with where to begin.
2. Give students a one-measure motive.
3. Have students record one measure at a time. Can they string two together to create a two-measure phrase?
4. Require all four melodies to be only two measures long.

Composing Four-Measure Melodies

Each exercise requires you to record four melodies, each four measures long, using the parameters given.

Assignment 1: The First Five Notes: C, D, E, F, G

Record four melodies, each four measures long, using only the first five notes of the scale in the key of C major (C, D, E, F, G). For each melody, your first note must be a C or an E.

Procedure:

1. Create a new file: File > New.
2. Save the file as "C Exercises __" (your two initials).
3. Create a new software instrument track and choose any flute or violin sound.
4. Record the first four-measure melody using only the first five notes of the scale in the key of C major (C, D, E, F, G). You do not have to use all five notes. For each four-measure melody, your first note must be a C or an E. You may use any rhythm combinations that you like, but you are encouraged to keep it simple.
5. Quantize.
6. Skip one measure.
7. On the same track, record the second melody, starting on measure 6.
8. Quantize.
9. Skip one measure.
10. Record the third melody, beginning on measure 11.
11. Quantize.
12. Skip one measure.
13. Record the fourth and last melody, beginning on measure 16.
14. Quantize.

Assignment 2: G to C

Create four melodies, each four measures long. This time, your note choices are limited to the second five notes of the scale (in the key of C, that's F, G, A, B, C). Your first note must be the fifth degree of the scale (in C, this is G). your last notes must be the tonic or first degree of the scale (in C, this is C).

Procedure:

1. Either skip a measure and begin this series of exercises on measure 21 or create a new file: "C Exercises 2 __" (your two initials) and begin this exercise on measure 1 of the new file.
2. Record the first four-measure melody using only the second five notes of the scale (in the key of C, that's F, G, A, B, C). You do not have to use all five notes. You may use any rhythm combinations that you like but you are encouraged to keep it simple.

3. Quantize.

4. Skip one measure.

5. On the same track, record the second melody starting on measure 26.

6. Quantize.

7. Skip one measure.

8. Record the third melody beginning on measure 31.

9. Quantize.

10. Skip one measure.

11. Record the fourth and last melody beginning on measure 36.

12. Quantize.

Assignment 3: Any Note You Choose in the Key

Repeat this exercise of creating four melodies, each four measures long, using any note in the scale of choice or as assigned by the teacher.

Procedure:

1. Either skip a measure and begin this series of exercises on measure 41 or create a new file: "C Exercises 3 __ __" (your two initials) and begin this exercise on measure 1 of the new file.

2. Record the first four-measure melody using any notes of the scale in the key given by the teacher or of your choice. You do not have to use all the notes of the scale. You may use any rhythm combinations that you like, but you are encouraged to keep it simple.

3. Quantize.

4. Skip one measure.

5. On the same track, record the second melody starting on measure 46.

6. Quantize.

7. Skip one measure.

8. Record the third melody beginning on measure 51.

9. Quantize.

10. Skip one measure.

11. Record the fourth and last melody beginning on measure 36.

12. Quantize.

LESSON 21b

Drone

There are many ways to teach parallel harmony, including interval relations, transposition by key, or clef replacement. This and the rest of lessons in this unit use a method that reinforces the understanding of intervals and major scales and keys. Numbers are used here, but teachers can use solfeggio syllables if desired.

If you are using standard music notation, you can project or distribute all student melodies and drones reviewed by the class. Have students sing or play the melody in unison; then the drone in unison; then in parts.

In this and the rest of lessons in this unit, teachers may choose to make connections to the historic development of polyphony and harmony. Early polyphony began with drones and then organum, doubling the melody at the 5th below or the octave. Later developments in polyphony added parallel melodies at the 3rd and 6th.

Skills Required:
Ability to record and edit in the software.
Knowledge of how to construct a major scale.
Knowledge of the key used.

National Standards:
- Standard 1, Singing, alone and with others, a varied repertoire of music.
- Standard 2, Performing on instruments, alone and with others, a varied repertoire of music.
- Standard 4, Composing and arranging music within specified guidelines.

Objectives:
Students will demonstrate their understanding of intervals in a specified key by creating a drone to a previously composed melodic figure.

Materials:
Drone student assignment sheet.

Procedure:
1. Review lessons 10a: Whole and Half Steps; 10b: Understanding Basic Generic Intervals; and 10c: Understanding Major Scales, if necessary. Explain that an interval is the distance between two notes. The first note is always counted as 1; then you count up. A 3rd above the note C is the note E (C is 1, D is 2, and E is 3). A 6th above C is A.
2. Define "drone": a sustained or repeated note.
3. Demonstrate a drone. Play a melody with a drone or use any recording of a bagpipe or hurdy-gurdy player.

4. Explain how drones can be any notes. For this assignment, students will use the fifth and first degree of the scale of the key.

5. Review how to find the first, fifth, and eighth degrees of the scale in the key used.

6. Demonstrate how each of these may sound when used with a melody.

7. Review the Drone student assignment sheet.

Extensions:

1. Have students combine their use of the first, fifth, and eighth degrees of the scale in the same melody.

2. Have students create different rhythmic patterns for their drones.

3. Have students sing or play their melodies and drones with other students or with the whole class.

Modification:

Limit students to either the fifth or first degree of the scale to record with their melodies.

Drone

A drone is a sustained or repeated note played with a melody. Several instruments play drones with the melody, including the bagpipe and the hurdy-gurdy.

A drone can be played on any interval, but most often is played on the first or the fifth degree of the scale.

Unlike the bagpipe and hurdy-gurdy, which play the same note as the drone all the time, in the example below the drone is played on the fifth degree of the scale in the first measure and then on the first degree of the scale in the second measure. In addition, the notes are one long sustained sound. Half notes are used. Any rhythm can be used.

Assignment:

Create a drone in your "C Exercises" file to be played with your melodies.

Procedure:

1. Open your "C Exercises" file.

2. Add a new software instrument track and select a violin or flute sound, one that is different from the first track.

3. Record a drone using half notes on the fifth or first degree of the scale.

4. Quantize.

5. Listen to the melody and drone together:

    a. Do you like the drone above or below the melody?

    b. Can you combine the use of the fifth or first degree of the scale?

Generic Parallel Intervals

When a musical line moves in the same rhythmic pattern and follows the same generic interval contour of the melody but has different notes, it is said to move in *parallel motion*. Parallel melodies create instant harmony. Adding a drone creates more complex harmonies and texture with little effort.

If you are using standard music notation, you can project or distribute all student melodies and the corresponding harmonies to be reviewed by the class. Have students sing or play the melody in unison, then the harmony in unison, and then in two or multiple parts, adding other parallel harmonies or drones as appropriate.

Harmonies can certainly be above the melody, but for the purposes of maintaining clarity of the melody line for beginning students, the assignments require students to create parallel harmonies below the melody. Descants are addressed in the next lesson.

Skills Required:

Ability to record and edit in the software.
Knowledge of how to construct a major scale.
Knowledge of the key used.
Knowledge of intervals.

National Standards:

- Standard 1, Singing, alone and with others, a varied repertoire of music.
- Standard 2, Performing on instruments, alone and with others, a varied repertoire of music.
- Standard 4, Composing and arranging music within specified guidelines.

Objectives:

Students will demonstrate their understanding of intervals in a specified key by creating a parallel melody to a previously composed melodic figure.

Materials:

"C Exercises" file.
Parallel Intervals student assignment sheet.

Procedure:

1. Review lessons 10a: Whole and Half Steps; 10b: Understanding Basic Generic Intervals; and 10c: Understanding Major Scales, if necessary.
2. Explain that an interval is the distance between two notes. The first note is always counted as 1; then you count up. A 3rd above the note C is the note E (C is 1, D is 2, and E is 3). A 6th above C is A.

3. Explain how melodies follow a certain contour or pattern on the keyboard. Does a melody move one step after the other? Are there leaps? The pattern of a melody can be thought of as a series of successive intervals.

4. Demonstrate the pattern as a series of numbers, for example 1, 3, 4, 5, 2. These numbers can represent note degrees of the scale. If you re-create the same series but start on the number 3, the pattern will be 3, 5, 6, 7, 4. For teachers who use them, solfeggio syllables can be used.

5. Explain how to maintain the relative interval relation between notes when starting on a new pitch. For instance, in the series of notes 1, 3, 4, 5, 2, the distance between the first and second notes is a 3rd. If we start the same melody on the note E, the distance between the first and second pitches will still be a 3rd, so the second pitch will be G. Starting on an E, the pattern will be 3, 5, 6, 7, 4, and the pitches will be E, G, A, B, F.

6. If maintaining the same key is desired, explain that only the notes in the key are to be used and no accidentals.

7. Review the Generic Parallel Intervals student assignment sheet.

8. As students work individually, go around the room and help students with each problem spot.

Extensions:

1. Record the interval of a 6th and a 3rd above the melodic line. In this case, moveable *do* is very helpful, as long as students sing and play in the new minor key.

2. Record at intervals of a 4th and/or a 5th. These are nontraditional harmonies that were very popular among twentieth-century composers, including Aaron Copeland. Many students will be familiar with these harmonies, and most will find them very appealing aesthetically.

3. Have students sing or play their melodies, harmonies, and drones with other students or with the whole class.

Modification:

Allow students to copy and paste the melodies onto a new track and drag or mechanically edit the intervals using the computer software. If maintaining the key is desired, make sure students check that no accidentals have been added due to the copy/paste, or mechanical edit.

Generic Parallel Intervals

When a musical line moves in the same rhythmic pattern and follows the same generic interval contour of the melody but has different notes, it is said to move in *parallel motion*.

An interval is the distance between two notes. The first note is always counted as 1; then you count up. A 3rd above the note C is the note E (C is 1, D is 2, and E is 3). A 6th above C is A.

Melodies follow a certain contour or pattern on the keyboard. Does a melody move one step after the other? Are there leaps? The pattern of a melody can be thought of as a series of notes on scale degrees. Numbers can represent note degrees of the scale, for example 1, 3, 4, 5, 2. If you re-create the same series but start on the number 3, the pattern will be 3, 5, 6, 7, 4.

Melodic lines can be duplicated and move parallel to the melody at intervals of a 3rd, a 6th, or any number of possibilities. In the example below, notice how the melody begins on C and the harmony begins on E, a 6th below. If the melody is re-created using the exact same intervals, the harmony, the parallel 6th below, will contain accidentals: F# and G#. Below, the generic intervals remain constant, although the notes F# and G# have been altered to F and G to maintain the key.

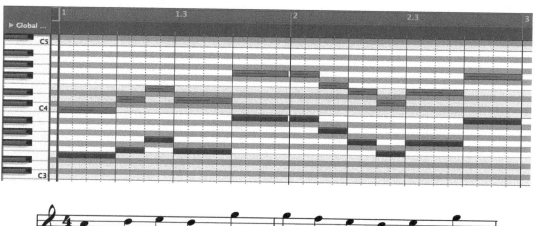

Assignment:

Create parallel harmonies in your "C Exercises" file. One track will have the harmony a 6th below the melody. Another track will have the harmony a 3rd below the melody.

Procedure:

1. Open your "C Exercises" file.
2. Add a new software instrument track (track 3) and select a violin or flute sound, one that is different from the first track.
3. Play the same melodic pattern a 6th lower. If you start on C, your new pattern will start on E.
4. Record the new pattern into your new track, making sure you are playing in the key. In the key of C, there will be no sharps or flats.
5. Quantize.
6. Listen to the two tracks together. Do you like the sound? Are there notes that don't sound good together to you?
7. Add a new track (track 4) and select a violin or flute sound, one that is different from the first track.
8. Play your original melodic pattern a 3rd lower. If you start on C, your new pattern will start on A.
9. Quantize.
10. Listen to the two tracks together. Do you like the sound? Are there notes that don't sound good together to you?

Countermelody

A countermelody is a melody that can stand on its own as a separate melody, as well as harmonizing the main melody. Countermelodies produce polyphonic textures in what might otherwise be homophonic music, chords, and melodies. This should not be confused with counterpoint as a technique of composing two or more completely independent yet simultaneous melodies, though counterpoint also creates a polyphonic texture. The study of counterpoint is beyond the needs of beginning composition students. However, countermelodies have become prevalent in some contemporary music styles, including hip-hop. Short two- to four-measure melodic material that is repeated over and over again creates a melodic ostinato and is sometimes used independently as a variation in what is otherwise repetitive music.

This lesson can be a good time to distinguish between homophonic and polyphonic textures in music. The most basic example of polyphonic texture in music is the round. Although each melodic line is the same, the entrance of each voice creates an independent musical line that stacks on top of the others. Singing rounds in class helps students understand polyphonic texture. Another form of countermelody can be found in Dixieland music. Each instrument plays its own distinct melody, creating an intricate weave of texture in and around the main melodic line. The most sophisticated form of polyphony can be found in any fugue by Bach. For the inexperienced listener, these can be difficult to listen to and understand. A little easier on the ear and probably well known by most students is Pachelbel's Canon.

A simple form of countermelody can be demonstrated by listening to the descant in hymns and gospel music. Usually in the last stanza of the hymn and in the soprano line, a descant adds color and excitement, moving the music to the end of the piece. In contemporary popular music, for example hip-hop, countermelodies are treated as melodic ostinati that are placed in the accompaniment. Sometimes multiple ostinati are used, often resembling sections of counterpoint and, at times in the piece, with one or the other dropping out and then being layered again on top of one another for a thicker sound.

For most classes, the rules of classic Fux counterpoint and nineteenth-century music theory need not apply unless the teacher wishes. There is no single way to compose anything, including countermelodies. For the most part, students will do well to keep in mind a few ideas about how to approach composing a countermelody:

1. Examine your original melody and notice the rhythmic movement. Does it move in long, sustained lines (quarter, half, and whole notes) or is it rhythmically active (quarter, eighth, and sixteenth notes)? The countermelody will do well to have an opposite rhythmic movement from the original melody. If the melody is active, the countermelody might have longer rhythms. If the melody has long lines, the countermelody can have shorter and possibly syncopated rhythms. The idea is to create rhythmic space and independence for each melody.

2. If the melody is low, begin the countermelody higher. The fifth degree of the scale or the octave are good places to begin.

3. Contrary motion is encouraged, and parallel motion should be kept to a minimum.

4. Try muting the melody track and improvising to compose a new melody or melodic fragment.

5. Try muting all the tracks except the melody and improvising to compose a new melody or melodic fragment.

6. Consider using some of the techniques in unit 14.

Skills Required:

Basic melodic compositional skills.

National Standards:

- Standard 3, Improvising melodies, variations, and accompaniments.
- Standard 4, Composing and arranging music within specified guidelines.
- Standard 6, Listening to, analyzing, and describing music.
- Standard 7, Evaluating music and music performances.

Objectives:

Students will understand countermelodies by composing countermelodies to an existing melody.

Materials:

"C Exercises" files.
Countermelody student assignment sheet.

Procedure:

1. Define "homophony": when two or more parts move together in the same rhythms, creating harmony, as in a church hymn or chord accompaniments with a melody line.

2. Define "polyphony": when two or more parts move together in different rhythms and different pitches, creating two or more distinct and independent melodies.

3. Define "countermelody": a melody that harmonizes the main melody and can also stand on its own as a separate melody.

4. Explain and demonstrate contrary motion.

5. Play some examples of polyphony. Sing rounds as an example, if appropriate.

6. Play some examples of countermelody.

7. Review the Countermelody student assignment sheet.

8. As students work individually, go around the room and help students with each problem spot.

Extension:

Provide students with MIDI or audio files (or have them record it themselves) of a Bach chorale and have students create a countermelody.

Modifications:

1. Give students melodies you create for this assignment.
2. The "C Exercises" file may contain several melodies. Limit the number of melodies to have countermelodies added.

STUDENT ASSIGNMENT SHEET

Countermelody

A countermelody is a melody that is played or sung with the main melody and harmonizes the main melody.

Assignment:
Create a countermelody for your previously recorded melodies in your "C Exercises" file.

Procedure:
1. Open the "C Exercises" file.
2. Create a new software instrument track under or above the melody, track 1. You will now have four tracks in your "C Exercises" file.
3. Compose and record a countermelody for each of your four 4-measure melodies.
4. Keep the following in mind when composing countermelodies:
   a. Examine your original melody and notice the rhythmic movement. Does it move in long sustained lines (quarter, half, and whole notes) or is it rhythmically active (quarter, eighth, and sixteenth notes)? The countermelody will do well to have an opposite rhythmic movement from the original melody. If the melody is active, the countermelody has longer rhythms. If the melody has long lines, the countermelody can have shorter and possibly syncopated rhythms. The idea is to create rhythmic space and independence for each melody.
   b. If the melody is low, begin the countermelody higher. The fifth degree of the scale or the octave are good places.
   c. Try muting the melody track and improvising to compose a new melody or melodic fragment.
   d. Try muting all the tracks except the melody and improvising to compose a new melody or melodic fragment.
   e. Employ some melodic variation techniques such as inversions, retrograde, rhythmic diminution or augmentation, and so on.

Adding Chords

The previous lessons have focused on melody and chords independent of one another. Adding the two together can be approached either from the melody side, analyzing a melody and then adding chords to that melody, or from the harmony side, creating a chord progression and then adding a melody. Experience has shown that students readily create bass lines or melodic ostinati. Most young composers do not realize that when they write a bass line or melodic ostinato they are composing implied harmonies. This lesson focuses on how to analyze melodic content for chord tone content to determine chord progressions. The first step is to identify harmonic tones in the melody and chords, simply identify notes in the melody where a chord is to be played, and choose chords that contain that melody note. Alternately, students can choose chords and create chord progressions by improvising chords to the melody. They can choose to use chords that do not contain the notes in the melody, and then the melodic material contains nonharmonic tones. There is no right way. It is up to you to determine whether you want to restrict students to locating shared chord tones or to allow students to choose their own harmonies and progressions. Restricting students to using only primary chords (I, IV, V) at first can help students develop this skill of harmonizing melodies and help them focus on harmonic rhythms. Later allowing the use of secondary chords (ii, iii, vi, and vii°) expands the composer's options. College teachers may want students to further analyze melodies for cadential features and use chords that support specific cadences. It is up to the teacher to determine whether students should record all the chords as root position triads or use inversions and/or open voicing. This will depend on the skill levels of the students and how much the teacher wants to adhere to eighteenth-century harmony practices.

Most beginning students will want to compose what sounds "good" to them. Sometimes, this contains dissonance between the melody and harmony or uncommon chord progressions. These creations come from a twenty-first-century ear having been exposed to many different tonalities. It can be a big surprise for students to find out that certain common twentieth-century tonalities such as parallel fifths and octaves are forbidden in college music theory classes on the basis of eighteenth-century rules of harmony. It is important for the teacher to decide whether to require students to adhere to eighteenth-century tonal theory practices, as is expected in the high school Advanced Placement music theory course and many college beginning music theory classes. If the teacher chooses, this lesson can be done two ways: restricting students to eighteenth-century theory practices, and again with no restrictions.

This lesson further exposes students to basic harmonic rhythms, which are the rhythmic rate at which harmonies or chords change. The harmonic rhythms most often occur on the strong beats. The Adding Chords student assignment sheet requires students to create harmonic rhythms on the downbeat of each measure and on beats 1 and 3 of each measure, emphasizing the main and secondary strong beats of a measure in common time.

207

When one is freely composing harmonies/chords to a previously composed melody, the harmonic rhythm can also be influenced by the melodic rhythm. In addition, many genres of music, especially dance forms, have specific harmonic rhythms and progressions that are idiomatic to the specific genre. Bass lines for the genre often highlight or outline the harmonic rhythms. Teachers are encouraged to explore specific genres and cultural styles that may be of interest to their communities.

> **TIP**
>
> The assignment requires students to change harmonies at a very fast rate. This rate is not necessarily recommend or encouraged for their personal compositions. It is simply required here to be expeditious for the assignment. Please encourage students to consider using long, sustained harmonic rhythms of even several measures in their personal work.

At this point the students will need to be conscientious about what octave the melody and harmony are in. If they are using instruments with similar or blending timbres, having the melody and harmony/chords in the same octave can make it difficult to hear the melody. Changing octaves, having two contrasting instruments, or having a simple alteration of the track volume can help clarify the melodic line when chords are played with it. Exploring panning, compression, and EQ can also help if the teacher is comfortable with these topics now. However, the assignments in this unit are composition exercises, and the technology need not be a barrier to developing solid composition skills.

Skills Required:
Understanding the piano keyboard.
Ability to record in the software.

National Standards:
- Standard 2, Performing on instruments, alone and with others, a varied repertoire of music.
- Standard 3, Improvising melodies, variations, and accompaniments.
- Standard 4, Composing and arranging music within specified guidelines.
- Standard 6, Listening to, analyzing, and describing music.
- Standard 7, Evaluating music and music performances.

Objectives:
Students will demonstrate their ability to harmonize melodic figures by adding triads to their previously composed melodic figures in the "C Exercises" file, using the harmonic rhythms specified.

Materials:
Adding Chords student assignment sheet.
Previously completed Building Triads on Scale Degrees worksheet (lesson 18c).
"C Exercises" file.

Procedure:

1. Explain that there are different ways to choose which chords to use with a melody. Ultimately, what the student-composer thinks sounds good is what counts.

2. Demonstrate how to analyze the melody, determine what notes are in the melody, and choose chords that share the note when the chord is to be played (the beginning of the harmonic rhythm). For instance, if the first note of the melody is a C, determine what triads contain a C, and use one of those chords. If the first note of the second measure is an E, determine what triads contain an E, and use one of those chords. Explain that you can play a chord to determine whether you want to use it; play a chord with the melody to determine whether it is to be used or changed; try different chords that contain the note in the melody. Listen to the melody and play several chords at random (improvise) to hear what sounds pleasing.

3. Demonstrate how to analyze the melody and choose possible chords, or demonstrate improving chords with a melody.

4. Define "harmonic rhythm": the rhythmic rate at which harmonies or chords change. Emphasize that harmonic rhythms are not the rhythms played by the accompaniment, the instrument playing the harmonies, but the rate of change of a chord.

5. Review the Adding Chords student assignment sheet.

6. Point out that each assignment will use a different harmonic rhythm, whole notes for the original four melodies, and half notes for the duplicate melodies.

7. Review whole and half notes, if necessary.

8. As students work individually, go around the room and help students with each problem spot.

9. Integrate time for students to share and comment on each others' work.

Extensions:

1. Have students record or edit their chords into an accompaniment pattern, as discussed in unit 20.

2. Have students analyze the chords and notice whether their progressions follow or do not follow the Simple Chord Map (lesson 19c).

3. Have students re-voice their root position triads and use inversions or open chords for good voice leading.

Modifications:

1. Give students melodies you have created to use for this assignment.

2. Give students a limited selection of chords to choose from, for example I, IV, and V.

3. Assign students only the I and/or V chord to use at any time in the melody or during a specific measure as determined by the teacher.

Adding Chords

Assignment:

Add chords to your previously recorded melodies.

When adding chords to melodies, follow these steps:

1. Analyze what note is being played in the melody at the time the chord is to be played.
2. Determine which chords contain that note.
3. Choose one of the chords that contain that note.
4. Notice the other notes in the melody that will be heard while the chord is being played.
5. Ask yourself:
    a. Are they part of the chord you chose?
    b. When you play the chord, does the chord sound good to you while all the notes of the melody are being played?
    c. Does this chord sound good when played with the other chords and melody from the beginning?
    d. Would using another chord be more appealing to use for this portion of the melody?

Procedure:

1. Open the file "C Exercises."
2. Add a new software instrument track and choose a regular piano sound. You will now have five tracks in your "C Exercises" file.
3. Analyze your first melody to determine what the notes are.
4. Choose at least three different chords for each melody. Each chord will be recorded on the downbeat of each measure and will last for one measure, giving it a harmonic rhythm of one whole note.
5. Record one chord on the first measure of each bar, for a total of four chords. See example 1.
6. Quantize.

Example 1: Harmonic Rhythm of one whole note or every four beats using three different chords.

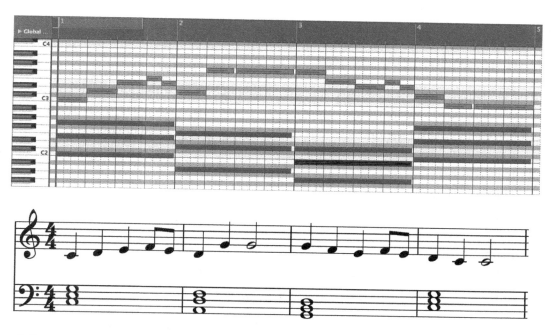

7. Repeat steps 3–6 for all four melodies.

8. Copy and paste all four of your melodies further down the file at about measure 21, making a duplicate of all four of your four-measure melodies.

9. Under these duplicate melodies, record new chords.

10. Record one chord every two beats, using a harmonic rhythm of a half note and using at least five different chords in each melody. See example 2 below.

Example 2: Harmonic rhythm of one half note or every two beats with five different chords

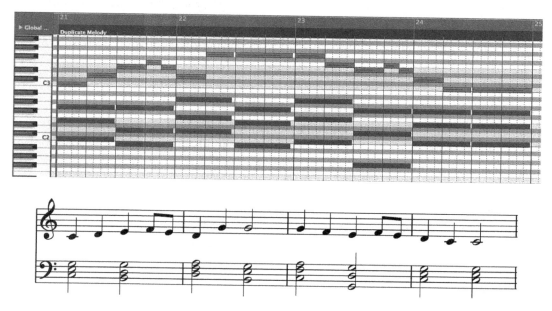

Understanding Bass Notes

The foundation of knowing how to create simple bass lines to go with a previously composed chord progression is the ability to recognize the roots of triads. Lessons 21f–h take the student through a series of explorations of bass lines based on triads and chord progressions.

Skills Required:
Basic keyboard knowledge.
Basic knowledge of triads.

National Standards:
• Standard 4, Composing and arranging music within specified guidelines.
• Standard 6, Listening to, analyzing, and describing music.

Objectives:
Students will demonstrate a basic knowledge of recognizing triads and locating roots of a triad one octave lower than the given triad by completing the Understanding Bass Notes worksheet.

Materials:
Understanding Bass Notes worksheet.

Procedure:
1. Define and review triads: chords made of three notes: the root, the third, and the fifth.
2. Review the first page of the Understanding Bass Notes worksheet.
3. Check for understanding by observing students playing the chords on exercise 1 of the worksheet.
4. Review exercise 2 of the worksheet.
5. Give students time to complete the worksheet.
6. Have students play their completed worksheets to hear the bass notes they have created.
7. As students work individually, go around the room and help students with each problem spot.

Extensions:
1. Students can create bass notes from the chords they created in unit 19.
2. Students can use standard notation to write the chords and the bass notes.

Modifications:
1. Give students the bass notes and have them play and record them.
2. Have the students work in pairs, one playing the chord and the other playing the bass note. Switch.

Using the roots of chord progression and adding a rhythmic figure can create a bass line. In the keyboard below, the notes with the darker dots form a C major triad. The note with the lighter dot is a C, the root of a C major triad, an octave lower than the chord.

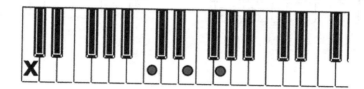

The keyboards below form an F triad and a G triad, with the bass note below each triad in red:

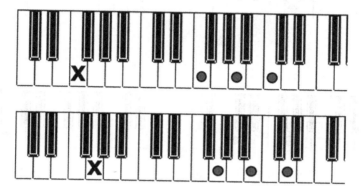

The following is a view of the chord progression I–IV–V in C major (C, F, G) in the Piano Roll/Matrix Editing window:

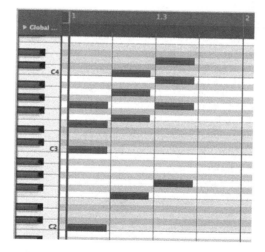

When recording, it's best to know how to play the triads in the right hand and the bass note in the left hand, but you can always copy the roots of the chords from the chord, paste them into the piece, and drag them down an octave, if necessary. Most software also has a pencil tool that you can use to draw in the notes. You can also record the bass line onto a separate track.

Exercise 1. On the keyboards below, put an X on the key that would form the bass note (the root of the chord an octave lower). Then play the chords with the bass note on your keyboard.

1

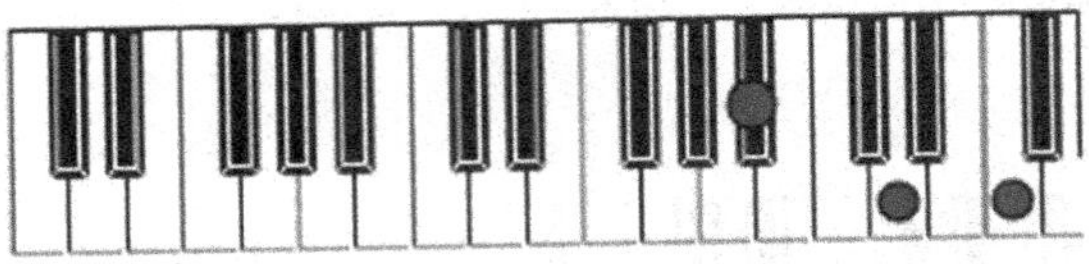

2

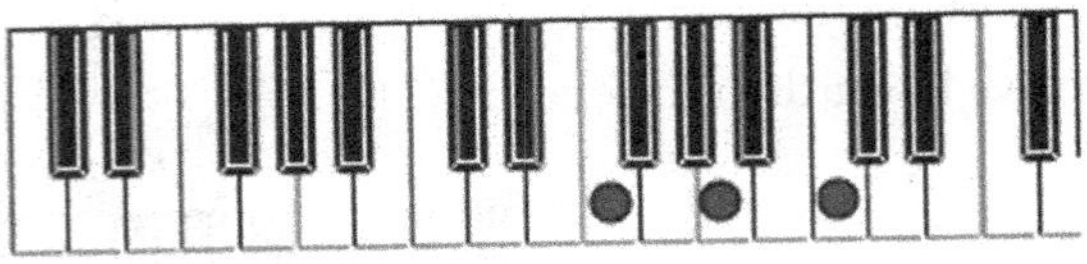

3

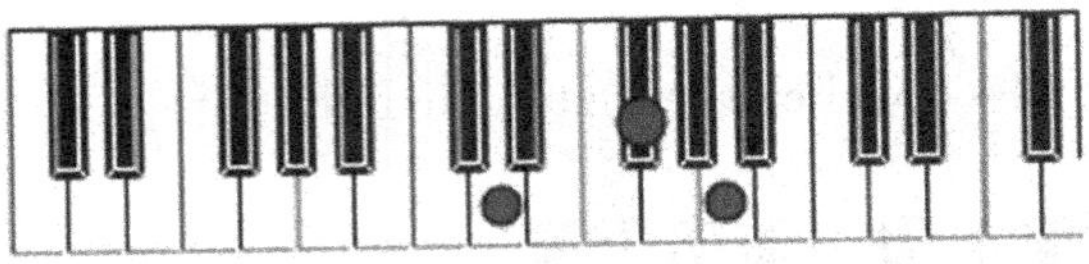

4

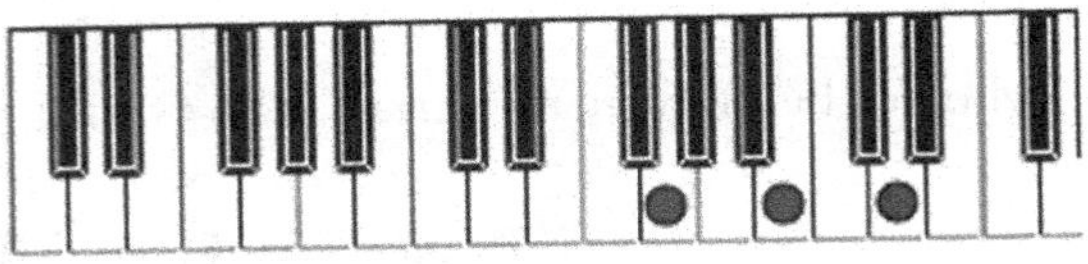

5

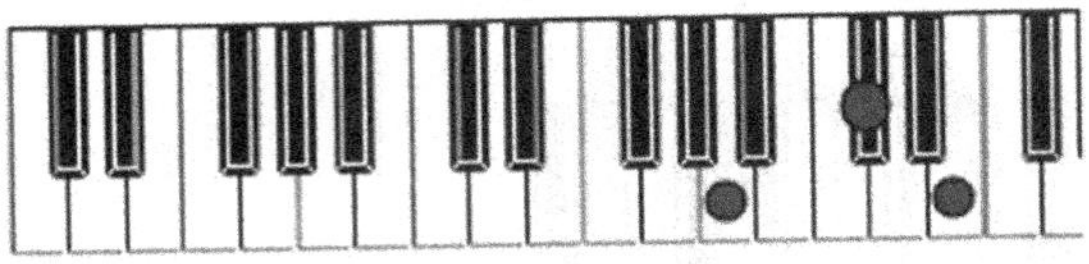

6

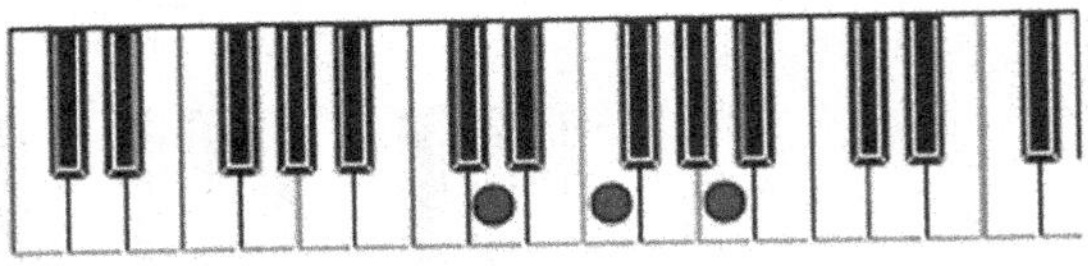

Exercise 2. In the Piano Roll/Matrix Editing window, draw in the bass note, the root of the chord an octave lower (that would be where the red note above would go):

1

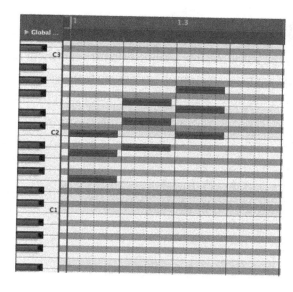

2

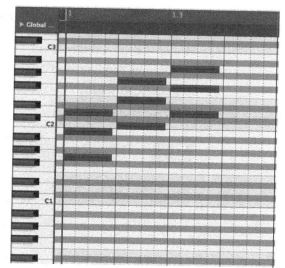

3

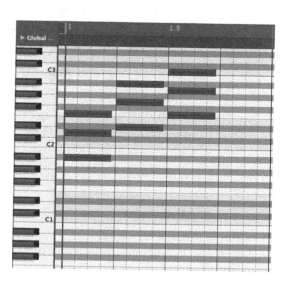

4

LESSON 21g

Creating Bass Lines from Roots

Students will record roots of triads into the software. It is assumed that students will record in real time. Modifications include having students step-input by drawing in notes or copying from the chords already recorded, pasting the notes onto a new track, and then moving the notes down an octave.

> **TIP**
>
> Use the Understanding Bass Notes worksheet (lesson 21f) to reinforce students' understanding of how to find the root of the chord and how to locate it in the bass range.

Skills Required:
Ability to record into the software.
Understanding of triads and how to locate the root.

National Standards:
- Standard 4, Composing and arranging music within specified guidelines.
- Standard 6, Listening to, analyzing, and describing music.
- Standard 7, Evaluating music and music performances.

Objectives:
Students will demonstrate their ability to recognize roots of triads and create bass notes by adding root notes to their previously composed melodic figures and harmonies in the "C Exercises" file.

Materials:
"C Exercises" file.
Creating Bass Lines from Roots student assignment sheet

Procedure:
1. Review triads and how to locate the root on the piano keyboard, in the Piano Roll/Matrix Editing window and/or in standard music notation.
2. Demonstrate how to add a software instrument track and select a bass instrument.
3. Demonstrate how to locate the root of the triad in a previously recorded triad.
4. Demonstrate how to record the root of the chords on the new track in the bass range.
5. Review the student assignment sheet.
6. As students work individually, go around the room and help students with each problem spot.

Extensions:

1. Have students improvise rhythmic patterns on the root of the triad, allowing octave leaps if desired.
2. Have students add a drum beat and imitate the rhythmic pattern of the bass drum in the bass line.

Modifications:

1. Instead of recording the bass notes, students can select the root note out of the triad, copy and paste into the new bass track, and then drag the note down one octave, if appropriate.
2. Have students "step-input" or draw the notes into the Piano Roll/Matrix Editing window.
3. Give the students a rhythmic pattern to follow.
4. Assign or allow for only one or two melodies to be completed.

Creating Bass Lines from Roots and Fifths

Create a bass line by using the roots of chords.

Assignment:
Create bass lines by placing the root of a triad in an instrument in the bass range.

Procedure:
1. Open your "C Exercises" file.
2. Add a software instrument track and choose any bass sound. You will now have six tracks in your "C Exercises" file.
3. Note that for this assignment, the bass line is going to be the root of the triads you used in the chords track.
4. Look at the chords you recorded for your first melody.
5. Record the root of the chords on the new track in the bass range.
6. Quantize.
7. Look at the chords for the second melody.
8. Record the roots of the chords on the new track in the bass range.
9. Repeat steps 4–6 for the remaining melodies.

Creating Bass Lines from Roots and Fifths

Locating the root and adding the fifth is a simple way to begin to create bass lines.

Skills Required:

Understanding triads and how to locate the root and fifth.

National Standards:

- Standard 4, Composing and arranging music within specified guidelines.
- Standard 5, Reading and notating music.
- Standard 6, Listening to, analyzing, and describing music.
- Standard 7, Evaluating music and music performances.

Objectives:

Students will understand the use of the root and the fifth of a chord when creating bass lines by composing bass lines to a given rhythm.

Materials:

"C Exercises" file.
Creating Bass Lines from Roots and Fifths student assignment sheet.

Procedure:

1. Review triads and how to locate the root and the fifth on the piano keyboard, in the Piano Roll/Matrix Editing window and/or in standard music notation.
2. Review and demonstrate how to add a software instrument track and select a bass instrument.
3. Review and demonstrate how to locate the root and fifth of the triad in a previously recorded triad.
4. Review the Creating Bass Lines from Roots and Fifths student assignment sheet.
5. As students work individually, go around the room and help students with each problem spot.

Extensions:

1. Have students improvise rhythmic patterns on the root and fifth of the triad allowing octave leaps if desired.
2. Have students add a drum beat and imitate the rhythmic pattern of the bass drum in the bass line.

Modifications:

1. Instead of recording the bass notes, students can select the root and the fifth out of the triads, copy and paste into the new bass track, and then drag the note down one octave and edit if appropriate.

2. Students can step-input or draw the notes into the Piano Roll/Matrix Editing window.

3. Assign or allow for only one or two melodies to be completed.

Creating Bass Lines from Roots and Fifths

Locating the root and adding the 5th is a simple beginning to creating bass lines.

Assignment:

Create a bass line for each of the three rhythms for each of the chord progressions.

Procedure:

Assignment 1

1. Open your "C Exercises" file.

2. Add a new software instrument track (track 7) and choose any bass sound.

3. Mute the previously recorded bass track (track 6) that contains the bass line with just the roots of the triads.

4. For this assignment, the bass notes are going to be the root and the 5th of the triads you created in the chords track 5 that used whole notes for the harmonic rhythm.

5. Look at the chords you recorded for your first melody.

6. On track 7, record in the bass range the following rhythm, using the root of the chords for the first half note and the 5th of the chord placed below or above the root for the second half note:

7. Quantize.

8. Listen to your new bass line with the melody, chords, and any other tracks or combination of tracks.

9. Create a bass line as in steps 4–7 for the remaining three melodies. Don't forget to listen to your bass lines with the melody, chords, and any other tracks or combination of tracks.

Assignment 2

1. Add another software instrument track (track 8) and choose a bass instrument.

2. Mute the bass track 7 that you created for assignment 1.

3. For this assignment, the bass notes are going to be the root and the 5th of the triads you create in the chords track 5 using quarter notes and quarter note rests.

4. Look at the chords you recorded for your first melody.

5. On this new track 8, record in the bass range the following rhythm, using the root of the chords for the first quarter note and the 5th of the chord placed either below or above the root for the second quarter note:

6. Quantize.
7. Listen to your new bass line with the melody, chords, and any other tracks or combination of tracks.
8. Create a bass line as in steps 3–6 for the remaining three melodies. Don't forget to listen to your bass lines with the melody, chords, and any other tracks or combination of tracks.

Assignment 3
1. Add a new software instrument track (track 9) and choose a bass instrument.
2. Mute bass track 8 that you created for assignment 2.
3. For this part of the assignment, the bass line is going to be the root and the 5th of the triads you create in the chords track 5 using quarter notes.
4. Look at the chords you recorded for your first melody.
5. Record in the bass range any combination of root and 5th of the chord using the following rhythm:

6. Quantize.
7. Listen to your new bass line with the melody, chords and any other tracks or combination of tracks.
8. Create a bass line as in steps 3–6 for the remaining three melodies. Don't forget to listen to your bass lines with the melody, chords, and any other tracks or combination of tracks.

Adding Drums and Syncing the Bass

Rhythmic patterns of bass lines often mimic the bass drum pattern in a drum set part. This is why the bass player and the drummer are often next to each other in ensembles of all genres, to make sure they are playing together and syncing up. If the bass drum pattern is complex, the bass line might only frame the pattern, or vice versa. This is left up to the composer. In the end, the only justification for any part of a composition is that the composer liked it.

Skills Required:

Ability to record into the software.

Understanding of basic rhythmic patterns using quarters and eighths.

National Standards:

- Standard 4, Composing and arranging music within specified guidelines.
- Standard 6, Listening to, analyzing, and describing music.
- Standard 7, Evaluating music and music performances.

Objectives:

Students will demonstrate their ability to recognize basic rhythmic patterns using quarters and eighths by editing bass lines to match these in their previously harmonized melodic figures in the "C Exercises" file.

Materials:

"C Exercises" file.

Adding Drums and Syncing the Bass student assignment sheet.

Procedure:

1. Demonstrate how to add a drum pattern to the "C Exercises" file by recording it, or copy and paste from another piece, using drums or the drum patterns created in lesson 3d. It is best to make certain that the bass drum part is on a separate track from the other drum parts such as the snare drum and any cymbal parts.
2. Demonstrate how to show both the bass drum region and the bass region in the Piano Roll/ Matrix Editing window. (This is not possible in all software programs.)
3. Demonstrate how to use the bass rhythmic pattern in the bass line.
4. Explore several options of using the exact rhythm, outlining the large beats or implied subdivisions and/or accents.
5. Explore how changing notes (5th and octave) of the bass line might be desirable.
6. Explore several possibilities for adding or subtracting notes and changing rhythms.
7. Review the Adding Drums and Syncing the Bass student assignment sheet.

Extension:

Add other notes to the bass line that are not the 5th or octave, for example the 3rd of the triad, ornaments, passing tones, or parts of the melodic line at the octave or other interval creating parallel harmony.

Modifications:

1. Have students step-input the bass notes.
2. Give the students a rhythmic pattern to follow.
3. Assign or allow for only one or two melodies to be completed.

Adding Drums and Syncing the Bass

Rhythmic patterns of bass lines often mimic the bass drum pattern in a drum part. This is why the bass player and the drummer are often next to each other in ensembles of all genres, to make sure they are playing together and syncing up.

Assignment:

Add drums to your harmonized melodies and sync the bass to the drums.

Procedure:

1. Open your "C Exercises" file.
2. Add as many tracks as you need, starting at track 5, to add a drum pattern of your choice, or copy and paste a drum pattern from a previously recorded file.
3. Edit the drum part to four measures.
4. Make sure the bass drum part in your drum pattern is on a separate track from the snare drum, cymbals, and any other drums or percussion.
5. Open the bass drum and the bass parts in the Piano Roll/Matrix Editing window, if possible.
6. Change the rhythm of the bass line to match the bass drum rhythm.
7. Quantize.
8. Listen to the bass and drum parts separately and then with all the other parts (mute track 3, the bass notes).
9. Change the rhythm and notes of the bass lines, if desirable.
10. Repeat steps 3–9 for the remaining three melodies; use a different drum part with a different bass drum pattern for the other melodies in the "C Exercises" file.

PART III Developing More Advanced
Composition Skills

Melodic Nonchord Tones

Melodies can be made of any combination of notes. When a note in the melody is also a note in the chord composed with the melody, those notes are called chord tones. When a note is not part of a chord, then the notes are called nonchord or nonharmonic tones. Understanding all the different nonchord tones in this lesson may be overwhelming for many beginning students. However, at this point of the curriculum, students may not be beginners any more. It depends how much the teacher has covered up to this point and the abilities of the students.

The examples on the Melodic Nonchord Tones worksheet use chords in root position. The voice leadings do not adhere to nineteenth-century harmonic rules and contain parallel harmonies. Root position triads are the most basic form of chords that most students should be able to recognize at this point in the curriculum.

This lesson has a worksheet and a MIDI file with the same music information as on the worksheet. The teacher can distribute the MIDI file and have students import it into the software, or the teacher can create a file in the software and distribute it to the students. This gives the teacher an opportunity to select some or all of the types of nonchord tones to be used in the lesson and gives students an opportunity to complete the worksheet in the software and hear the examples.

Skills Required:
Understanding of notes of the scale and chords in the key given.

National Standards:
- Standard 4, Composing and arranging music within specified guidelines.
- Standard 7, Evaluating music and music performances.

Objectives:
Students will demonstrate their knowledge and understanding of notes of the scale and chords in the given key and how to use specific nonchord tones in melodies by completing the Melodic Nonchord Tones worksheet and/or the file provided by the teacher.

Materials:
Melodic Nonchord Tones worksheet.
Melodic Nonchord Tones MIDI file.

Procedure:

1. Review the scales and chords in the key of C.
2. Define nonchord/nonharmonic tones.
3. Define and demonstrate a passing tone.
4. Define and demonstrate an upper neighbor and lower neighbor tone.
5. Define and demonstrate an escape tone.
6. Define and demonstrate an anticipation tone.
7. Review the Melodic Nonchord Tones worksheet and/or MIDI file.

Extension:

Distribute sheet music, MIDI file, or software file of the chords and melody of a song and have students identify the nonchord tones in the melody.

Modification:

Break down the different nonchord/nonharmonic tones into several different lessons, or only demonstrate passing tones and neighbor tones.

Melodic Nonchord Tones　WORKSHEET

Melodies can be made of any combination of notes. When a note in the melody is also a note in the chord composed with the melody, those notes are called chord tones. When a note is not part of a chord, the notes are called nonchord or nonharmonic tones. To determine whether a note is a nonchord tone, first figure out what the chord tones are for each chord. Notes that are not part of the chord are nonchord tones. For instance, if you have a melody with the notes C, D, and E, and there is a C major chord (C, E, G) with those melody notes, then D is the nonchord tone (D is not part of the C major chord). Nonchord tones come in a few varieties. Although nonchord tones can be any note between chord tones, including chromatics (C# and D# for the example above), for these exercise only use notes in the key, in this case, C major.

Passing Tones

A passing tone is a note that is between two chord tones. You "pass through" the nonchord tone to the chord tone. In the example below, the "highlighted" notes in the melody are passing tones. Notice how they are not part of the chord given below the melody line:

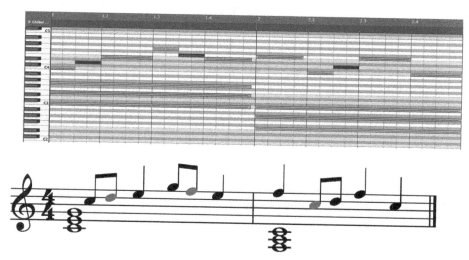

Exercise 1:

Draw in passing tones in boxes a, b, c, and d below.

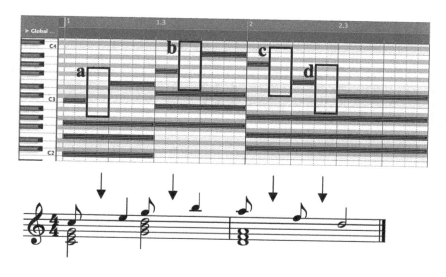

231

Neighboring Tones

A neighboring tone is a nonchord tone a step above (upper neighbor) or below (lower neighbor) a chord tone:

Exercise 2:

Draw in neighboring tones in the boxes below. Use two upper neighbors and two lower neighbors.

Escape Tone

An escape tone is a nonchord tone that is between two chords. It most commonly occurs as step upward (escaping away from the chord tone) and resolves down by a skip (a third) to the second chord.

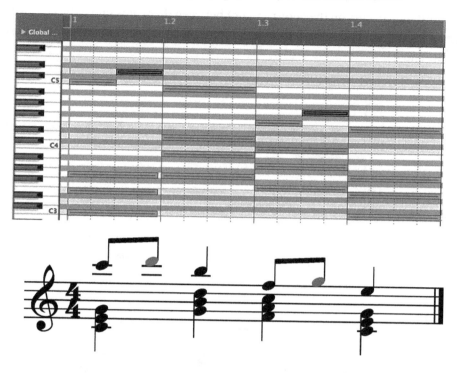

Exercise 3:

In the example below, the first chord tone is given over the first chord. Draw in the escape tone and the resolution tone for the second chord.

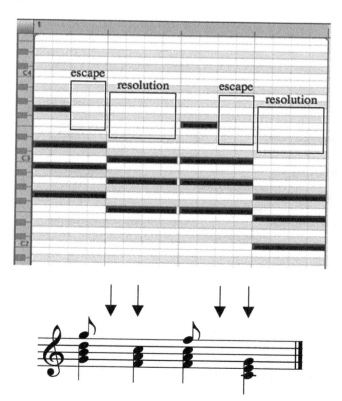

Appoggiatura

An appoggiatura is the opposite of the escape tone. It is a nonchord tone made by a skip and resolved by a step in the opposite direction to a chord tone. An appoggiatura is also different in that it occurs on the chord not between them. When a nonchord tone occurs on the chord and not between them, it is said to be *accented*. Notice how the nonchord tone, the appoggiatura, is accented. It occurs on the chord, while the resolution occurs after the chord has been played (unaccented).

Exercise 4:

In the example below, the first chord tone is given over the first chord. Draw in the appoggiatura and the resolution tone for the second chord.

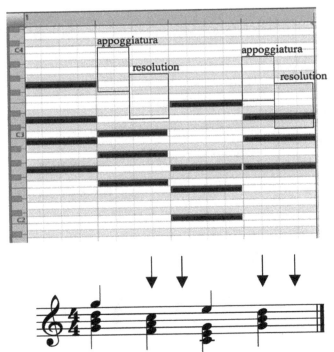

Anticipation

An anticipation is a nonchord tone that is a step above or below the chord tone and remains the same in the next chord. It is basically a note of the second chord played early and not on the beat.

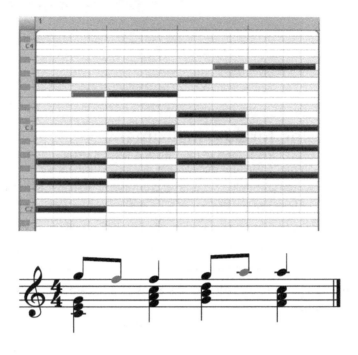

Exercise 5:

In the example below, the first chord tone is given over the first chord. Draw in the anticipation and the resolution tone for the second chord.

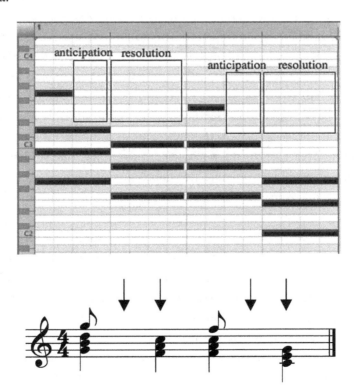

Composing for Solo Instrument

Composing a piece for one instrument is a difficult task for even the most experienced composer. The added difficulty for young composers is that this project forces students to eliminate their tendency to use drums as a crutch.

This project will take several class sessions. Each class session can be introduced with the listening and analysis of a different piece of music to explore form, melodic variations, and techniques for composing for certain instruments. This is also a good opportunity to review techniques discussed in unit 14. The same techniques used in motive variations can be used for longer phrases of music.

Other variation techniques can be explored by reviewing and analyzing Mozart's "Ah vous dirai-je, Maman," K. 265/300e, or what are known as the Twinkle Variations. Although this is written for piano, it is a good example of melodic variations. The *Twelve Fantasies for Solo Flute* by Georg Philipp Telemann are excellent examples of solo flute music. A MIDI file is provided on the companion website. Load it into the software to demonstrate how this kind of music appears in the Piano Roll/Matrix Editing window.

This would be a good time to introduce and explore the use of melodic ornamentation. Traditional Western ornaments include the trill, turn, mordent, glissando, and various grace notes such as the appoggiatura and acciaccatura. Ornamentation also exists in Irish and Indian music, and these may offer good examples for students to hear and explore.

The teacher can choose any instrument. Some students may be instrumentalists, and it would be appropriate to allow these students to compose for their own instruments. It is suggested, however, that for the purposes of this project that students compose for traditional band or orchestral instruments. This constrains students to monophonic texture. It is more challenging to create material without the use of chords available in instruments such as guitar and piano.

Students will also have to prepare manuscript for live performance. For most high school students, properly preparing music manuscript for performance is difficult. Although most software for creation has good notation capabilities, it is recommended that software that was created to produce printed music manuscript, such as Sibelius, Finale, Noteflight (noteflight.com), or MuseScore (musescore.org), is a wiser choice than GarageBand, Logic, or ProTools. However, use what is available as best you can.

I suggest that a soloist be invited to demonstrate the instrument as part of the early lessons for this project. The students can ask any questions of the performer. The performer can return to play the pieces and make comments on the compositions.

TIP

Even if students are adept at reading and performing from standard music notation, properly preparing a manuscript for another person to perform from is challenging at best. I have always found this to be a "teacher time" consuming task. It is well worth the effort, but know going into this project that it will take a while for you to go through the files before anything gets printed. You may also consider having all students compose in the software and select just a few student pieces to be performed live off the printed page. This will save you time preparing manuscript.

Skills Required:

Advanced composition skill.
Notation skills.

National Standards:

- Standard 3, Improvising melodies, variations, and accompaniments.
- Standard 4, Composing and arranging music within specified guidelines.
- Standard 5, Reading and notating music.
- Standard 6, Listening to, analyzing, and describing music.
- Standard 7, Evaluating music and music performances.

Objectives:

Students will demonstrate advanced composition skills and technical abilities of using notation software (optional) by composing and preparing a piece for a solo instrumentalist to perform.

Materials:

Piece for Solo Instrument student assignment sheet.
Solo Flute or Violin Piece MIDI file.

Procedure:

1. Demonstrate a piece or two for solo instrument every day students work on this project.
2. Review melodic composition and variation techniques.
3. Demonstrate how these techniques are accomplished in the pieces shown in class.
4. Demonstrate how articulations are accomplished in the Piano Roll/Matrix Editing window.
5. Review the Solo Flute or Violin Piece student assignment sheet.
6. Incorporate time for the class to listen to and comment on students' work.

Extensions:

1. Students can work completely in music notation software.
2. Students can be paired with other students in or out of the class to be coached on the techniques, possibilities, and limitations of the instrument.

3. Students can compose for trios and quartets. The teacher will have to decide if and how students will work with transposing instruments.

Modifications:

1. Limit the length of the piece in terms of measures.
2. Have less experienced students collaborate with more experienced students in the music notation software to produce manuscript for live performance.

Piece for Solo Instrument

Assignment:

Create a piece for a solo instrument such as flute or violin. The piece must be a minimum of two minutes long.

Procedure:

1. Open a new file: File > New and name it "Solo Piece _ _ " (your initials).
2. Check the instrument ranges for your instruments.
3. Do not use the extreme ranges of the instrument unless you play the instrument and can comfortably play these notes with good tone and technique.
4. Use monophonic texture, only one note at a time.
5. Consider using different melody variation techniques to develop your music ideas, including the use of ornaments.
6. Consider changing key centers in different sections.
7. Remember that wind and brass players need to breathe!

The Art Project: Rondo Form

This project reinforces students' understanding of a specific form of music. The same project can be used without the restriction of rondo form to allow students more freedom when composing. The artwork can evoke a story in the student's imagination. Students can write a paragraph to explain the story and represent this story musically. This project can even be modified for very young or inexperienced students to use prerecorded loops that are available in the software or prerecorded songs/pieces of music. Change this to a multimedia project by having students use a program like iMovie or iPhoto to add images and scan over the specific sections of the artwork represented in the music while their piece is being played. Students' abilities, experience with music composition, and basic music knowledge should be considered when determining the specifics of this project.

College students can compose to art from a specific era using music techniques typical of that era. For instance, a baroque painting can be represented by an ensemble using polyphony. An artwork from the eighteenth century can be represented by a student-composed piece of music emulating the classical styles prevalent in that era, such as piece for string quartet utilizing the theory and idiomatic music practices of that time. A more challenging task is to use poetry from the same era for lyrics to a song.

There are many examples of composers using art as inspiration for their music, including Modest Mussorgsky's *Pictures at an Exhibition,* inspired by a collection of works by Victor A. Hartman, Franz Liszt's *Totentanz,* inspired by Andrea Orcagna's *Il trionfo della morte,* and Igor Stravinsky's *Rake's Progress,* inspired by William Hogarth's *Rake's Progress.*

> **TIP**
>
> As the "lessons" become projects, fewer instructions are given. This lesson doesn't even need to be in rondo form. It's just a convenient way to introduce a new musical form to students! At this point in the curriculum, students will have a good handle on basic music theory and music composition skills. I truly believe that at some point you need to leave kids alone. They need to be free to create. If you really feel compelled to attach a rubric and give a grade, there is ample opportunity in every lesson, assignment, and project. But do you really need to do that? Maybe just listening and giving the students suggestions and a good pat on the back is what they really need. Or the contrary is finding students off task and guiding them back with a firm hand. For me, the goal is to have students stay on task and compose as best they can, as close to the assignment as possible and within their ability. That's an A in my book every time.

Skills Required:

Basic understanding of how to record and edit in the software.

Understanding of how to compose simple melodies.

National Standards:

- Standard 4, Composing and arranging music within specified guidelines.
- Standard 8, Understanding relationships between music, the arts, and disciplines outside the arts.
- Standard 9, Understanding music in relation to history and culture.

Objectives:

Students will demonstrate an understanding of rondo form by composing a piece of music based on their interpretation of an artwork.

Materials:

An image of a two-dimensional artwork such as a drawing or a painting; www.art.com/ is a good source for images.

The Art Project: Rondo Form student assignment sheet.

Procedure:

1. Explain simple rondo form: ABACAD, and so on.
   a. "Yankee Doodle" can be used as an example of rondo form in a melody.
   b. Mozart's "Romance" from *Eine Kleine Nacht Music* is another example of rondo form.
2. Discuss techniques used by the artist to create the artwork, such as short and pointed or long brush stokes, the use of dark or bright colors, the size of the work, the specific images in the work, and how music can capture these aspects (major/minor, staccato/legato, specific instrumentation and number of instruments, etc.).
3. Review The Art Project: Rondo Form student assignment sheet.
4. Give students plenty of time to work on their own before you check work.
5. As students work individually, go around the room and offer to listen and give comments.
6. Incorporate time for the class to listen to and comment on student work.

241

Extensions:

1. Do not restrict students to rondo form.
2. Allow students to create sections that may use elements from other sections.

Modifications:

1. Students use artwork provided by the teacher.
2. Students use melodies they have previously composed in unit 16 and/or material they composed in unit 21.
3. Students use prerecorded music.

STUDENT ASSIGNMENT SHEET

The Art Project: Rondo Form

In rondo form, a musical section is repeated with different music between the repetitions. This order of letters is an example: ABACA.

Assignment:

Compose a piece of music that has been inspired by a painting, sketch, or drawing of your choice using rondo form. Artwork can be viewed at www.art.com and must be approved by your teacher.

Procedure:

1. Choose an image to be approved by the teacher.
2. Open a new file: File > New.
3. Name the file the name of the artwork followed by your two initials.
4. Choose three "subjects" in the artwork. A "subject" can be a person, an item, a shape in the image, or an emotion evoked by the image or portion of the image.
5. When composing, consider the art:
   a. How was the artwork produced? What is the medium and technique? Is it a watercolor painting, a pencil sketch, a pastel drawing? Does this suggest texture that can be recreated in the music?
   b. What brush techniques does the artist employ? Are there long, smooth strokes, pointillist dots, combinations of techniques? Can you emulate this in the music?
   c. Do the colors or lack of colors suggest instruments (dark or bright) or registers (high or low)?
   d. Are there primary or secondary subjects in the art? Can you use themes, melodies, or recurring melodic or rhythmic patterns to suggest subjects in the artwork or their interactions with one another?
   e. Consider how music can capture these subjects (major/minor, staccato/legato, specific instrumentation and numbers of instruments, etc.)
6. Compose a melody for each of the subjects, keeping in mind that they will be used in rondo form.
7. Compose accompaniments for each of the melodies as you like.
8. Arrange and edit your piece in rondo form.

The Speech Project

This lesson is a great way to introduce audio, audio editing, and plug-ins and is really a project over several classes rather than a specific lesson. The ability to change and alter audio allows for a plethora of compositional possibilities.

Below is the basic outline for the project. The teacher will need to spend some time explaining how to import and edit audio. If the software allows, the speech can be altered to use specific pitches or contours of sound. Each of the demonstrations listed below can take place over a few class sessions to allow students some time in each class session to research their audio and to compose some music. A few lessons on plug-ins such as EQ and Compression should be included in this unit. A lesson on EQ follows this project's lesson plan. It can be used as a template to teach other plug-ins like compression.

The guidelines for the Speech Project are simple. The purpose in limiting the length of audio used is to make sure students aren't taking long sections of speech and just putting some groove under it. However, allow some leeway with the parameters of the assignment if a student uses a longer audio clip effectively.

TIP

This may be the first project your students do using words. Below is one of my classroom rules. Please feel free to use it in its entirety or edited to your needs:

"When using songs, song lyrics, poetry, or literary excerpts, no swearing (cursing), offensive slang, remarks that are derogatory, condescending, or explicitly or implicitly sexual, or any other comment, sound, or imagery that might be offensive or degrading to a group or individual. Please use your common sense. This is a school and a place of business and not a nightclub or the street."

Skills Required:

Intermediate composition skills (for beginning students, use prerecorded loops).

National Standards:

- Standard 4, Composing and arranging music within specified guidelines.
- Standard 5, Reading and notating music (if you use notation software).

- Standard 8, Understanding relationships between music, the other arts, and disciplines outside the arts.
- Standard 9, Understanding music in relation to history and culture.

Objectives:

Students will demonstrate a basic knowledge of editing and processing audio by creating a piece of music incorporating segments of prerecorded audio.

Materials:

Audio files of speeches (available at www.americanrhetoric.com).
The Speech Project student assignment sheet.

Procedure:

1. Review the use of speech in music. Some examples:
   a. An excerpt of Aaron Copland's *Lincoln Portrait.*
   b. Sergei Prokofiev's *Peter and the Wolf.*
2. Have students listen to several speeches, poems, or literary excerpts and choose a few for use in their pieces. One to three speeches are recommended.
3. Demonstrate how to load audio into the software.
4. Demonstrate how to edit audio in the software.
5. Demonstrate some possible rhythmic uses of audio. For instance, an audio region edited to one eighth note in length and repeated to create an eighth-note pattern.
6. Demonstrate how to load audio into the software's sampler instrument (i.e., in Logic, the EXS24).
7. Demonstrate how to alter the pitches or add effects to the audio.
8. Review the appropriate school use of language and imagery created by language, sounds, and music.
9. Review The Speech Project student assignment sheet.
10. As students work individually, go around the room and encourage students to stay on task and within the guidelines and rules of the assignment.
11. Incorporate time for the class to listen to and comment on students' work.

Extensions:

1. Have students record their own speeches, poems, or literary excerpts.
2. Have students load clips of audio into a sampler instrument to trigger the audio off the MIDI input device (MIDI keyboard).

Modifications:

1. Allow students to use the software's prerecorded loops.
2. Let students work in pairs.

The Speech Project

The spoken word can sometimes evoke emotions or ideas that can be represented musically. When combining speeches, poetry, or literary excerpts, the original intention of the author can be reinforced, or it can be opposed or changed. Music can support this "rewriting" of the speech. Speech can also be edited and used musically or rhythmically.

Create a piece using prerecorded audio of speeches, poetry, or literary excerpts. The piece should be a minimum of two minutes in length. The music should reflect the speech or the point the composer is trying to make when combining speeches.

Procedure:

1. Open a new file: File > New.
2. Save the file as "Speech Project __ __" (your two initials).
3. Choose and use prerecorded audio of speeches according to the following guidelines:
    a. You can use any number of speeches or recorded poetry to be incorporated into a piece of music.
    b. You are limited to using five-second audio clips (regions) of speech at any given time.
    c. The audio clip can be short segments to be used for its dramatic content and imagery, or it can be used rhythmically.
4. Load the audio into the software.
5. Edit the audio to be part of the music, and limit each audio clip (region) to a maximum of five seconds.
6. Add the audio into the Arrange window.
7. Compose appropriate music. The music needs to match the mood of the speech or the dramatic intention of the composer.
8. Add plug-ins to the audio to clarify the vocal line, that is, EQ, Compression, Reverb, and so on.
9. Add plug-ins to the music as appropriate.

EQ

Mixing is the combination and interplay between many different elements. The very basics of these include volume, panning, frequency equalization, also called EQ, and reverb. Compression is a common tool in contemporary recording techniques, especially in popular music styles, and is used to manipulate volume. It also has an effect on the EQ. When you manipulate any one of these elements in a track, it will have an effect on the levels desired for the other elements. When mixing, you'll need to adjust these elements constantly until you reach the desired sound for the track individually and for the track in the context of the overall mix (with all the other tracks). Mixing can take five times longer or more than actually composing!

The basics about EQ and some standard techniques for adjusting EQ for specific instruments and voices are essential. There are a few good resources in the bibliography, and a quick Internet search will provide many printed and video resources. Understanding EQ is really about understanding the physics of sound. It is up to you to decide the extent to which you discuss the history and physics of EQ in your class. Here are a few tips to get you started.

First and foremost, trust your ears. EQ is basically the ability to slightly adjust the timbre of an instrument. It is very similar to an instrumentalist being able to make a note sound brighter or darker. When listening to individual instruments, make a decision about the overall quality of that instrument. If it is too bright or too dark or the pitches of the notes are not coming through clearly, change the EQ. Keep in mind that the playback speakers, volume, and environment will have a great deal of impact on what something sounds like. A recording will sound different on a pair of earbuds and a $200 pair of headphones. A recording played back on computer speakers, a car sound system, or an auditorium or club sound system will sound different in each case. All of these will sound different at different volumes. What to mix for is the art part. Experience and practice will help with these decisions.

A three-decibel (3 db) change to anything is a lot. If students start cranking the EQ of a bass drum in the low frequencies, maybe they should consider choosing a different instrument or changing the overall sound design of that instrument.

Don't use EQ for overall volume changes. If an instrument isn't coming through the mix clearly and a volume change is the answer, do it in the track, or double the instrument in a new track. Better yet, turn down the other instruments.

For almost all aspects of mixing, keep in mind that less is more. Subtractive EQ is when you attenuate (cut) certain frequencies. This is often done to clarify tone color and to allow space for it to come through in other instruments. A note is made up of several sounds, the fundamental tone and the related harmonics. EQ can also be thought of as the ability to manipulate harmonics. Removing or cutting back on the prevalence of certain harmonics can allow those harmonics to come through in other instruments. In contemporary dance music, certain instruments should not have certain harmonics (EQ). As an example, some producers believe that a bass drum sound should not contain any of the high frequencies. When a DJ decides to cut all the high frequencies, there won't be any artifacts in the bass drum.

As a preliminary class, give students an opportunity to play with EQ outside the context of a musical piece. Provide students with audio or MIDI files of different instruments. A bass drum, a cymbal, an acoustic guitar, a piano, a flute, and several different voice ranges of singing or speech are good places to start. Choose instruments and voices that your students use or will use in the popular genres of your community. Load the file into the software, and add an EQ unit. Students can use an analyzer that can be found in most EQ units to determine which frequencies are more or less prevalent in each instrument or voice. Another technique for finding frequency ranges is to have the students sing the notes being played or sung by the instrument or voices and locate these pitches on the EQ chart. This will give the general frequency area of these notes. Remember, notes contain harmonics, so an octave higher is double the frequency, and an octave lower is half the frequency. For instance, the A above middle C is 400 Hz. An octave above is 880 Hz, and an octave below is 220 Hz.

Each EQ unit will have presets that will change one or several parts along the EQ spectrum. These are good for seeing how these changes affect the instrument or voice. Another good experiment is to increase the EQ a few decibels at any frequency (band pass filter) and sweep across the frequencies to hear the effect it has on each audio file. This method is often used to find the exact place in the frequency range to change. (A great two-minute introductory video on EQ can be found at www.winksound.com/video/2051288/winksound-live-at-tainted. More information on EQ can be obtained in the books and articles referenced in the bibliography.)

It might make good sense to discuss EQ much earlier in a course. For many electronic musicians, mixing and altering sounds using EQ and other plug-ins is as much a part of the composition process as anything else. It is placed here as a more advanced subject to allow the teacher time to discuss other musical elements. It is up to you to decide on the importance of this topic with regard to the overall scope of the course you are teaching.

Skills Required:
Ability to load a plug-in into the software instrument track.

National Standards:
- Standard 1, Singing, alone and with others, a varied repertoire of music.
- Standard 6, Listening to, analyzing, and describing music.
- Standard 7, Evaluating music and music performances.

Objectives:
Students will demonstrate their understanding of EQ manipulation by making EQ adjustments to at least three tracks in their Speech Piece.

Materials:

The Speech Project file.

EQ student assignment sheet.

Instrument Range/EQ Chart in the appendix.

Procedure:

1. Explain EQ.
2. Demonstrate EQ boosts and cuts using several different audio or MIDI files containing a variety of instruments and voice types.
3. Allow students time to experiment with changes to EQ on these files, if desired.
4. Review the EQ student assignment sheet.

Extensions:

1. Have students use an EQ on all tracks.
2. Have students use an EQ on the master track after the mix is complete.

Modifications:

1. Provide students with specific presets in the software plug-in to choose from.
2. Provide students with specific parameter changes to make in the EQ unit in the software. For instance, on the speech track with a male speaker, boost the EQ between 350 and 500 Hz.

EQ

In music, frequency equalization (EQ) is the process of adding or subtracting along the spectrum of sound. Musical travels in waves. The frequency of these waves per second is measured in hertz. For instance, the note A above middle C is called A-440 because the waves of the note travel at 440 cycles per second, or 440 Hz. One thousand hertz are a kilohertz or kHz. The more cycles per second or the higher the frequency, the higher the pitch. An A that is one octave above an A-440 is A-880. An A that is one octave below A-440 is A-220.

The height of each wave is amplitude. The higher the wave, the louder the sound. Boosting or cutting EQ is measured in decibels (db). Plus or minus 3 decibels makes a big change.

Below is an example of a graphic equalizer that is used to raise or lower specific frequencies.

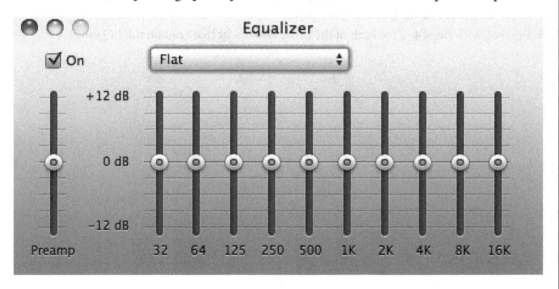

In general, the following can be used as a guide to find frequency ranges:

Bass: 20 Hz–140 Hz. Few instruments play lower than 60 Hz. Changes to the bass frequencies are most noticeable between 60 Hz and 90 Hz.

Mid-Bass: 140–400 Hz. Many instruments include this range, including the male voice.

Low Mids: 400 Hz–2.6 kHz. Except for the few lowest instruments, all instruments and voices include these frequencies.

Upper Mids: 2.6–5.2 kHz Few instruments play actual notes as high as this, but most music and sounds are affected by changes to this range.

Highs: 5.2–20 kHz. This is the range of frequencies that adds what is called "shimmer" to a sound. It is also the range that can make something sound harsh or squeaky. Most people over the age of 50 can't actually hear above 15 kHz, but the addition or subtraction in this range can still have a great impact on the quality of sound.

Assignment:

Add an EQ unit to three tracks in your "Speech Project" file and boots, or attenuate (cut) EQ to clarify the sound of that track. One of the tracks must contain some of the prerecorded speech used for this project.

Procedure:

1. Open your "Speech Project" file.
2. Locate three tracks to add an EQ unit to clarify sound. One track must contain speech audio.
3. Add an EQ plug-in from your software for each of the three tracks.
4. Solo one track of the tracks with the added EQ unit.
5. Experiment with adding or subtracting EQ along the spectrum.
6. Deselect the solo setting for the track you have been working on and listen to the track with the EQ setting.
7. Return to the EQ unit and adjust along the spectrum to hear how the EQ affects the track in the context of all the tracks in your piece.
8. Proceed with steps 4–7 for each of the other two tracks that contain the EQ unit.

The Radio Commercial Project

In addition to learning the basics of audio recording, this lesson requires a variety of musical and technical skills to complete. Students will record music and audio and mix the two together to create a radio commercial. Many of the needed skills may have been developed in previous lessons, and some can be learned while producing the final product. This project also requires students to work with other students. As the "producer," the student must learn necessary skills to make the "talent" comfortable and work with them to evoke the best performance possible.

When choosing pairs, you can select students you know might work well together or pair students at random by having them choose numbers from a hat.

When teaching how to use the recording equipment, the teacher can demonstrate to the entire class; however, it is a good idea to review with each pair of students.

Information about audio recording in the classroom for this and the following lessons can be found in the introduction starting on page xxxi.

> **TIP**
>
> It doesn't matter how many times I demonstrate to the class how to set up a microphone, adjust volume levels, or route signal, every pair of students is going to need help and guidance in the recording booth. Then, after they are recording for a few minutes, inevitably, several pairs find themselves off task. I can appreciate that they are having a good time, and there is nothing wrong with that. There is much to be gained by most of what I find my students doing; however, unless you have multiple spaces for students to record, it's important to keep pairs on task so other students have equal time in the booth.

This lesson is another chance to review the class rules about appropriate language and content!

Skills Required:

Ability to create music for the background of the commercial.
Ability to edit audio.

National Standards:
- Standard 4, Composing and arranging music within specified guidelines.
- Standard 8, Understanding relationships between music, the arts, and disciplines outside the arts.
- Standard 9, Understanding music in relation to history and culture.

Objectives:
Students will learn to record audio by creating their own radio commercials.

Materials:
The Radio Commercial Project student assignment sheet.

Procedure:
1. Review The Radio Commercial Project student assignment sheet.
2. Review the use of the recording equipment.
3. Review how to edit audio in the software.
4. Review how to change the tempo of the piece in the software to make the final product exactly 30 seconds long.
5. Review the use of EQ, compression, and reverb for the recorded audio track (spoken word).
6. Incorporate time for the class to listen to and comment on students' work.

Extensions:
1. Create a video to be added to the audio and music.
2. Work with the school's business department on a product they might be using in class.
3. Use the school, music department, or your class as the product.
4. Create a public service announcement or school announcements.

Modifications:
1. Have students work in small groups to create the product and copy. Break down the assignment by tasks and assign each student a job to do that is part of the finished product.
2. Allow students to use the software's prerecorded loops to create the music.

The Radio Commercial Project

Assignment:

Create one 30-second audio commercial.

You will write the words for the voice-over (copy), compose music appropriate to the product and intended audience, be the recording engineer and producer for the voice-over recording session, and mix and finalize your radio commercial.

You will work in pairs. For your commercial, you will be the producer and will work with another student who will be the "talent." The producer's job is to work the recording equipment and make sure the talent is speaking the words of the commercial the way you want them to. Consider the volume, the inflection of the speaker's voice, the speed and pace of the words and energy. Remember, as the producer, you have to get the talent to produce what you need from them. Be careful how you speak to the talent.

Once one of you has completed recording the audio for your commercial, you will switch roles as producer and talent.

Procedure:

1. Create your product. You must create a fictional product, so we can post these on the Internet or put them in a podcast. You cannot choose an existing product, store, or service.
2. Your product must be "Disney Rated G" and approved by the teacher.
3. Write the copy (what is going to be said on the commercial). It must be "Disney Rated G" and approved by the teacher.
4. Write music appropriate to the product and age group you are trying to sell it to.
5. Add any sound effects as desired. They must be "Disney Rated G" and approved by the teacher.
6. The final product, the radio commercial, must be *exactly* 30 seconds long. Not a nanosecond longer or shorter!

Remember, you are trying to sell a product or service. The music and supporting audio should help you sell the product, so they should have something to do with the product or target audience.

Answer the following questions as a guide to help you in writing your copy (the spoken part of the commercial). Use the spaces provided.

1. What age groups are trying to sell your product to?

2. Say the product name or store name, address, and phone number.
   Use the school address (your school's address here):

Use the following phone number: 1 (800) 555-1234.

3. Describe your product.

4. What is special about your product or service?

5. Say the product name or store name, address, and phone number.
   Use the school address (your school's address here):

Use the following phone number: 1 (800) 555-1234

6. Are you offering any special deals now?

7. Say the product name or store name, address, and phone number.
   Use the school address (your school's address here):

Use the following phone number: 1 (800) 555-1234.

8. What is the last thing you want to leave in people's minds about your product?

Be sure to say the product name and how people can buy it or the location and address at least *three* times in the commercial!

The Podcast

A podcast is a short, prerecorded radio-style show available over the Internet. Enhanced podcasts use still pictures and video podcasts, also called vidcasts or vodcasts, are available. It is a relatively new format that goes back to 2004, when people could access these shows and download them onto their iPods to listen to whenever they wanted. The podcast gives students a chance to record their own voices, edit audio, and produce an entire show. Encourage students to name their show and compose their own theme music. Podcast shows are easily created and loaded on to a website. Followers can subscribe to them and have them sent to their music aggregator, such as iTunes, whenever new episodes become available. Free podcast hosting sites include PodOmatic.com, MyPodcast.com, and PodBean.com.

This project has students present their own previously composed music. However, a podcast can use anything that is recorded. Older students can work with younger students to record their creative writing stories or other essays. Care should be taken when using copyrighted materials if the show is to be posted on the Internet. Teachers should always review student scripts and listen to the final recorded product before posting to the Internet.

Students will be challenged by contrast in volume levels between recorded music and the spoken word. Volume adjustments and automation between tracks may be necessary. The automated process of lowering the volume of one track when another track begins is called ducking. Some programs include a simple tool or box that can be checked off to accomplish this task. It is a valuable lesson to look at how the automated tool accomplished raising and lowering volumes between tracks. However, more advanced students are encouraged to make their own choices. Even if a ducking tool or automation is used, advanced students should check the automation points and manually adjust volume when necessary.

The Podcast worksheet is included to help students prepare before they begin editing music and recording voice-overs. A sample podcast release form is included as an example of what might be used. Please consult your school's legal department before using any forms of this nature.

TIP

If students will be permitted to use copyrighted material, this can be a good time to discuss copyright issues in music. There are many Internet resources with good information for students about copyright, including the Library of Congress, (at www.loc.gov/teachers/copyright mystery/), an informative comic book from Duke University Law School (www.law.duke.edu/cspd/comics/zoomcomic.html), and an interactive site with cartoon characters by the Copyright Society of the U.S.A. (www.copyrightkids.org). More information for teachers on what can and cannot be used in the classroom can be found in James Frankel's *Teachers Guide to Music, Media, and Copyright Law.*

In my experience, most students have no idea how money generated from the sale of a song or CD is distributed. They have no idea that most artists do not make any money at all on a song or CD sales. They have no idea of the impact that "bootlegging," or taking music without paying for it, has on an artist's future with a record company. Not buying a song or CD sends a powerful message to the record company that you do not want to hear any more of an artist's work. If enough people don't purchase the music, why would a record company invest in a second CD? Often they don't, and careers are lost. Taking an item that is for sale from any source and using it for your own needs is stealing. As Jim Frankel often says in his clinics on copyright: "Most students would never think of shoplifting but that's exactly what they do every time they click on the mouse and download a file without paying for it."

This lesson is another good opportunity to review the class rules about appropriate content. You just can't do this too many times!

Skills Required:
Ability to record voice in the software.
Ability to add and edit audio in the software.

National Standards:
• Standard 4, Composing and arranging music within specified guidelines.
• Standard 6, Listening to, analyzing, and describing music.

Objectives:
Students will demonstrate their knowledge of audio recording and editing by producing a podcast of their original music.

Materials:
Prerecorded original pieces of music.
The Podcast student assignment sheet.

Procedure:
1. Explain and demonstrate a podcast. Podcasts can be retrieved from the websites listed on the previous page or through iTunes.
2. Review how to import audio into the software.
3. Review how to record audio in the software.
4. Divide students into pairs.
5. Allow time for students to work together to choose music and script their podcast.
6. Review the appropriate school use of language and imagery created by language, sounds, and music.
7. Review the Podcast student assignment sheet.
8. Schedule recording time for students if microphones or recording booth space are limited.
9. As students work on their projects, check to make sure they are on task and observing the guidelines and rules.
10. Incorporate time for the class to listen to and comment on students' work.

Extensions:

1. Students can work individually
2. Create a series of podcasts on a specific topic.

Modifications:

1. Provide students with music to use.
2. Provide students with a script.
3. Have more advanced students edit the audio.

The Podcast

A podcast is a short, prerecorded, radio-style show available over the Internet.

Assignment:

Create a podcast that is no more than 12 minutes total in length. Use the following guidelines and the worksheet below to help produce your podcast.

Procedure:

1. Use three to five pieces of music.
2. You cannot use material that has a copyright. If you bought it, it is copyrighted. If you got it off the Internet, it is copyrighted. If someone else created it, it is copyrighted.
3. If you use music created by other students in this or other classes, you must obtain written permission.
4. Using the Podcast worksheet, script every section of your podcast.
5. Record your podcast voice-over material.
6. Add your prerecorded music.
7. Edit the podcast paying careful attention to volume levels between the voice-over and the music.
8. Export your podcast as a single audio file.

Podcast WORSHEET

Producers: ....

Title/name of your podcast: ....

Brief description: ....
....
....
....

Approximate Outline/Timeline:

1. Intro music: 10–15 seconds. What piece or portion of a piece are you using? ....
....

2. Intro speaking: no more than 15 seconds.

   Who is speaking? ....

   What general ideas do you want to convey in your Intro? ....
   ....
   ....

Try to limit each piece of music to 3.5 minutes.

Music pieces:

1. Title: ....

   Composer: ....

   Performers (if any): ....

   Do you have a release signed? Yes or No.

   Attach the release to these pages.

   Ideas you want to say about this piece or the composers: ....
   ....
   ....

2. Title: ....

   Composer: ....

   Performers (if any): ....

   Do you have a release signed? Yes or No.

   Attach the release to these pages.

   Ideas you want to say about this piece or the composers: ....
   ....
   ....

3. Title: ....

    Composer: ....

    Performers (if any): ....

    Do you have a release signed? Yes or No.

    Attach the release to these pages.

    Ideas you want to say about this piece or the composers: ....

    ....

    ....

4. Title: ....

    Composer: ....

    Performers (if any): ....

    Do you have a release signed? Yes or No.

    Attach the release to these pages.

    Ideas you want to say about this piece or the composers: ....

    ....

    ....

5. Title: ....

    Composer: ....

    Performers (if any): ....

    Do you have a release signed? Yes or No.

    Attach the release to these pages.

    Ideas you want to say about this piece or the composers: ....

    ....

    ....

Ending:

Do you want to end with speaking or music? (circle one)

What do you want to say to conclude your podcast? ....

....

Who do you want to thank? ....

....

Do you want to remind your audience about anything? ....

....

....

I hereby consent to the photographing of myself and the recording of my voice and the use of these photographs and/or recordings singularly or in conjunction with other photographs and/or recordings for advertising, publicity, commercial, or other business purposes. I understand that the term "photograph" as used herein encompasses both still photographs and motion picture footage.

I further consent to the reproduction and/or authorization by .... to reproduce and use said photographs and recordings of my voice, for use in all domestic and foreign markets. Further, I understand that others, with or without the consent of.., may use and/or reproduce such photographs and recordings.

I consent to the photographing of myself, recording of my voice, and use of my music and the use of a pictures for these and/or recordings for advertising, publicity, commercial, or other business purposes and/or recordings singularly or in conjunction with other photographs, videos, screen casts, and/or recordings for publicity, commercial, or other business purposes. I understand that the term "photograph" as used herein encompasses both still photographs and motion picture footage.

I hereby release (producer) .... and/or (school) .... and any of its associated or affiliated companies, their directors, officers, agents, employees, customers, and appointed advertising agencies, and their directors, officers, agents, and employees from all claims of every kind on account of such use.

If student composer is under 18 or currently enrolled in high school:

I, ..., am the parent/legal guardian of the individual named above, I have read this release, and I approve of its terms.

Print Name of Composer: ....

Signature: .... Date: ....

Print Name of Parent: ....

Signature: .... Date: ....

Email of Adult Composer or Parent: ....

Phone of Adult Composer or Parent: ....

Aural Reporting

For this project, students create a report much as they would a research paper, but their reporting is done via audio or multimedia instead of the written word. This project is wide open as to the subject matter, scope, and length of the final product, which is why no extensions, modifications, or student assignment sheet are given. The project can be repeated in a single course or over a series of courses. This can be purely audio or a multimedia project using video or still pictures. Students can work in pairs or individually. It can even be a culminating project as part of a student's portfolio for graduation. If students are studying a particular point in history or a specific country or culture in another class, this project can be used as part of an interdisciplinary course of study. This can also be used as a vehicle for students to represent and present music of their own culture. Here are some topics to consider and stimulate the imagination:

My Favorite Style of Music
The Music I Created This Year
Get to Know Me: An Aural Collage
The Music of (pick any composers, era, or time period, any genre or culture)
The Distinctions of Contemporary Rock Music
The Evolution of Hip-Hop
The Differences between Techno and House Music
The Greatest Melodies in Hip-Hop
Use of the Melodic Bass Line in Contemporary Dance Music
Classical Music in the Remix
Classical Music in Commercials
The Music of Mickey Mouse

Keep the scope of the project in mind when choosing a topic. It can be as large or as small as the teacher likes, depending on the subject matter. In general, the more specific the topic, the less involved and shorter the project will be. For instance, a project that covers the topic "Top Hits of the Past Decade" will be longer than "Top Ten Hits of This Week." The class subject, requirements of the teacher, and weight of the project in the student's grade can also influence the length and content of a topic. If the topic is "Louis Armstrong during the Roaring Twenties," the expectations for a term project for high school students in a social studies class will be different from the expectations for a final project for college music majors in a jazz studies class.

Students are more likely to be engaged if they choose their topics, but the teacher should approve all topics. A written script is always a good idea and can be used as part of the grade for the project. As always, be careful when allowing students to use contemporary songs. A "radio mix" is when questionable or foul language are deleted, changed, or bleeped out to make the version acceptable according to the Federal Communications Commission (FCC) for radio play. Almost always, the original intent is still present, and what might be good for the FCC is not always good for your classroom. Advise students in advance that only lyrics that are "Rated G" are allowed and that the "radio mix" is not acceptable, and prescreen everything. College professors can use their discretion with these restrictions.

If students keep each music example to fewer than 30 seconds in length, it may be possible to post them on the Internet as podcasts or for them to be played on local radio as "news" shows. Check with your school's legal department for advice before posting any copyrighted material of any length on a website even if it is restricted to school employees or students. If students will be producing a series of podcasts, they can be encouraged to create theme music to be played at the beginnings and ends of their podcasts.

Skills Required:

Basic audio editing functions of the software.
Video and/or photo editing software (optional).

National Standards:

- Standard 4, Composing and arranging music within specified guidelines (optional).
- Standard 6, Listening to, analyzing, and describing music.
- Standard 7, Evaluating music and music performances.
- Standard 8, Understanding relationships between music, the other arts, and disciplines outside the arts.
- Standard 9, Understanding music in relation to history and culture.

Objectives:

Students will demonstrate their knowledge and skill in audio recording and editing by completing an audio or multimedia project on a specific topic.

Materials:

Podcast worksheet (lesson 26b).
Aural Reporting student assignment sheet (see below).

Procedure:

1. Develop an assignment sheet for the specific project. Consider:
    a. Time given to students to complete the project.
    b. Weight of the grade for this project in the scope of the class.

    c. Total length of the final product (i.e., a maximum of four minutes in length or a minimum of seven minutes and a maximum of twelve minutes).

    d. Time landmarks toward completion of the project (i.e., the topic will be due by Monday, May 15, a list of a minimum of five songs/pieces of music will be due the following Monday, May 22, the script will be due one week later, etc.)

    e. If working in groups, which student will be responsible for which specific aspect of the project.

2. Distribute the Aural Reporting student assignment sheet and the Podcast worksheet (lesson 26b) and review them with the students.

3. Explain all the expectations and limitations of the assignment.

4. Allow students time for research.

5. Schedule students for recording time if there is limited access to a recording booth or microphones.

6. Monitor students' progress throughout the project.

7. Check all aspects of the audio, including that the relative volume levels between spoken word and prerecorded music are even; the timing between audio clips; the length of audio clips; the use of plug-ins and sound effects; and so on.

8. Review the final product.

9. Have students load the project onto the school's website or their own website or post a podcast.

10. Incorporate time for the class to listen to and comment on students' work.

Music for Video

This is a project over several classes rather than a specific lesson. You'll need to spend some time explaining how to import a movie, how to eliminate or mute the original sound track, how to determine the basic tempo, how to beat map, and other techniques that might be specific to the software you use. Unfortunately, these techniques are different for each software program, and it is outside the scope of this book to provide these details. This is an instance where you will need to know some more advanced functions of the software to accomplish this project. Don't be afraid if you don't know these functions! Most of the currently available software for music creation makes all of this very easy, as long as you know exactly which buttons to press. A quick Internet search will probably reveal free instructional videos for you and your students that demonstrate how to do each function specific to your software.

Below is the basic outline for the project. If you can, invite a composer who writes for TV, movies, or commercials professionally to come and speak to your class. The composer can describe the composition, listen to students' music, and give them feedback.

A good first video is one that has scenes from outer space or under the ocean. These are great ways for students to have the freedom to compose in a rhythmically free environment without having to use a technique called beat mapping. Students can concentrate on the basic techniques of how to import video and how to mute or redact the prerecorded audio and other techniques of using the software for video.

In addition, many old cartoons have dance segments. Students can watch the feet of the character dancing and set the tempo by tapping a percussion part to the beat set by the dance steps. This new track can be used as the beat track or what is sometimes called beat mapping. A bit more advanced alternative is to use movie trailers. Give students a few choices of movie trailers that you have prescreened. Students can add the music, overdub the speaking, and add sound effects. Use all three of these types of videos, and you have a very full unit on music for video.

A few examples of video for this project are on the companion website.

Most software will accept .mov or Quick Time files. Check the software that you use for compatibility. Good sources for public domain video are available at www.archive.org and www.vintagetooncast.com. Many videos can be downloaded from iTunes. You can now legally download video from YouTube if the video has the appropriate Creative Commons license listed in the video information window. The Smithsonian has wonderful videos on many of their sites, including www.smithsonianchannel.com/. A good video capture tool is KeepVid.com, or your browser may have a plug-in that works well with Internet sites.

If a website does not allow you to download directly from it, you can use a screen capture tool to make a video of the screen. Screen capture tools can create single snapshots or capture high-definition video of the whole computer screen or part of it. These are available for all platforms of computers and include Camtasia, Screenflow, SnapzPro, or Jing. Many more are available, and prices range from free to hundreds of dollars.

> ## TIP
>
> Be careful when using video in the classroom. Some concepts, images, sounds, and language that once were acceptable might now be considered politically incorrect, offensive, or inappropriate. Be sure to prescreen your video. If you are only going to show or use the students' finished work in class and are not going to post on the Internet, otherwise distribute it, or sell the finished product, you can use almost any video regardless of copyright. This use of copyrighted material in the classroom can fall under the Fair Use terms of the current copyright law. Check with your district's legal team whenever you use copyrighted material in the classroom, and never post copyrighted material on the Internet, even if it's on a school website.
>
> The techniques used to capture video with a screen capture tool for this lesson can be used to capture any video that a teacher might want to show in the classroom. This way, you avoid having to worry about your district's firewall blocking you when you want to access video from the Internet in your classroom. Even if you prescreen video on a YouTube site, sometimes offensive material appears in the comments or side columns. Use a screen capture tool to get just the part you want your kids to see without worrying about what they shouldn't.

Skills Required:
Intermediate composition skills.

National Standards:
- Standard 4, Composing and arranging music within specified guidelines.
- Standard 8, Understanding relationships between music, the arts, and disciplines outside the arts.
- Standard 9, Understanding music in relation to history and culture.

Objectives:
Students will demonstrate a basic knowledge of syncing music to video or beat mapping by composing music to a short video clip.

Materials:
Music for Video student assignment sheet.
A movie clip approximately 30 seconds to one minute in length.
Sample movie files on the companion website.

Procedure:

1. Demonstrate some examples of videos with music.
2. Explain and demonstrate how to import a video clip into the software.
3. Explain and demonstrate how to choose and set the tempo.
4. If needed, explain and demonstrate how to beat map.
5. Demonstrate how to "spot" the video and place markers for "hits" or SFX.
6. Demonstrate some composition possibilities for a video.
7. Review the Music for Video student assignment sheet.
8. As students work individually, go around the room and encourage students to stay on task and within the guidelines and rules of the assignment.
9. Incorporate time for the class to listen to and comment on students' work.

Extensions:

1. Add sound effects.
2. Add voice-over.
3. Use videos from other classes in your school, for example a computer animation, film, or TV class.

Modifications:

1. Have students work in pairs or teams.
2. Use prerecorded music and sound effects, such as the built-in loops provided by the software, instead of composing new material.
3. Preload the video into the software for the students and distribute a file ready for them to use.

Music for Video

Assignment:
Create an original sound track to a prerecorded video.

Procedure:
1. Open a new file.
2. Save the file as "Video _ _" (your two initials).
3. Import a video clip into the file.
4. Set the metronome to the approximate tempo being reflected in the video.
5. Record a basic drum beat or other music to the video.
6. Align the beats to the video, using a beat map if available in the software, or automate the tempo to match the beat.
7. "Spot" the video and place markers for "hits" or sound effects (SFX).
8. Add melody, harmonies, and other music elements and/or sound effects (SFX) to complement the video and music concept.

APPENDIX

APPENDIX A Reading Rhythms with Rhythm States

Quarters, Eighths, Sixteenths With Rhythm States

Maine U - tah Mi - ssi - ssi - ppi

APPENDIX A Reading Rhythms with Rhythm States

Quarters, Eighths, Sixteenths Without Rhythm States

APPENDIX A Reading Rhythms with Rhythm States

Quarters, Eighths, Sixteenths Vertically

OVERHEAD 4

APPENDIX A Reading Rhythms with Rhythm States

Plus Triplets With Rhythm States

Maine   U - tah   Mi - ssi - ssi - ppi   Ar - kan - sas

APPENDIX A Reading Rhythms with Rhythm States

Plus Triplets Without Rhythm States

APPENDIX A Reading Rhythms with Rhythm States

Triplets Vertically

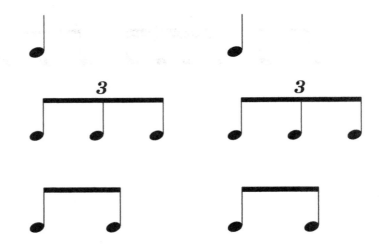

APPENDIX A Reading Rhythms with Rhythm States

Eighth-Sixteenth Combinations Vertically With Rhythm States

OVERHEAD 8

APPENDIX A Reading Rhythms with Rhythm States

Eighth-Sixteenth Combinations Vertically Without Rhythm States

APPENDIX A Reading Rhythms with Rhythm States

Eighth-Sixteenth Combinations Horizontally With Rhythm States

Maine   U - tah   Mi-ssi-ssi-ppi   U - ssi-ppi   Mi-ssi-tah

OVERHEAD 10

APPENDIX A Reading Rhythms with Rhythm States

Eighth-Sixteenth Combinations Horizontally Without Rhythm States

APPENDIX A Reading Rhythms with Rhythm States

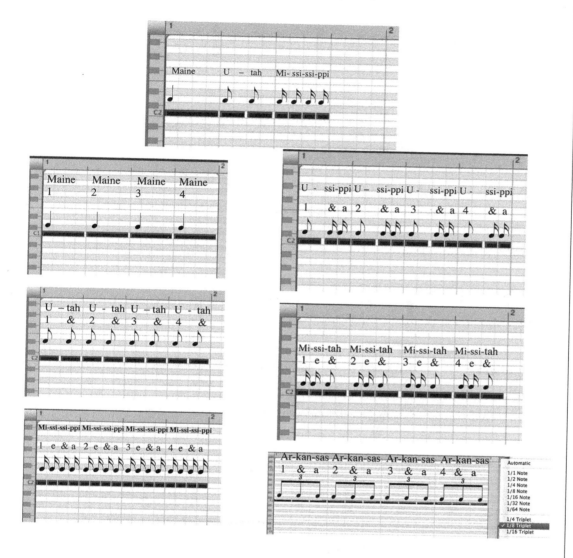

QUANTIZING CHART

APPENDIX A Reading Rhythms with Rhythm States

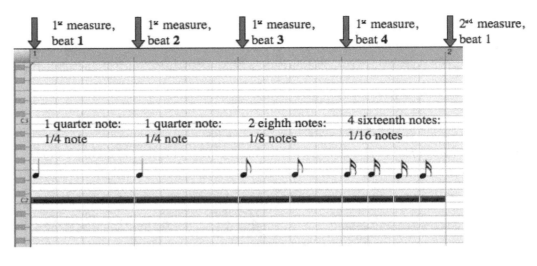

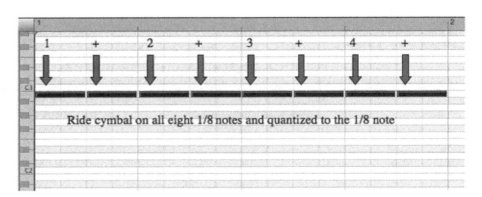

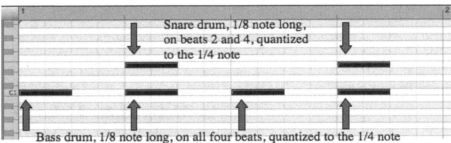

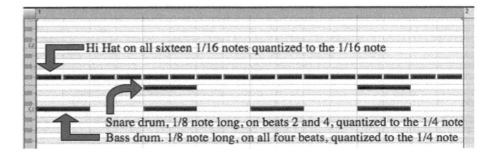

APPENDIX B Piano Supplement Material

About The Piano Supplemental Material

The Piano Supplemental Material is a collection of fingering charts and video demonstrations available on the companion website 🖥 of five-finger position, one-octave scales, two-octave scales, one-octave arpeggios, two-octave arpeggios, chords, chord inversions and I, IV, V chord progressions in a variety of keys. Each video is between 30 seconds and 1.5 minutes long and only contains demonstrations of the materials. They do not provide explanation or instruction. This is left to the teacher. The purpose of these materials is to provide students with the basic and essential materials of music at the piano. It is not intended to train students as pianist. Students learn the visual patterns at the piano keyboard and hear these patterns as they play. This strengthens their knowledge of music theory visually and aurally.

Each video demonstrates a topic, five-finger position, scales, arpeggios, etc. for a specific hand, right or left, in an exercise. There are two repetitions of the exercise on each video, the first with the fingerings being spoken as the exercise is played and then without. Teachers are encouraged to first instruct students on each topic, then allow students time to practice this topic using the fingering charts and to the video. If students play along to the video three times, they will perform six repetitions of the exercise and can accomplish this practice in a matter of minutes.

Students should set up a file in the software that they use to practice piano throughout the course. Set up the file with one track containing a basic piano sound and save the file as "Piano Practice__" (student's two initials). For the most part, students will play along to the videos using this file as a sound source. In this case, no metronome need be set and no recording need be done. As students become more adept at the exercise, they may not want to play to the video but play a bit faster. They can then use the metronome in the file set to about 70, play one note per click and increase their speed as they improve changing to two notes per click as appropriate. Teachers might consider having students record their work. I warn my students several days in advance that I am going to ask them to record their practice. Somehow they miraculously practice with greater focus and intension as the day for recording approaches! These recordings are good reference for student progress but I rarely use them for grades.

Try to balance instruction, practice and student composition time in each class session if at all possible. If the class session includes instruction on a new piano topic, I usually just assign the practice for that topic. For instance, when I introduce the C Major scale, I spend time on instruction, check for understanding and questions. I then ask students to play to the videos C Major One-Octave Scale Right Hand, C Major One-Octave Scale Left Hand three times each (six repetitions of the exercise in each hand). Students should start with the video that is their stronger hand, righty or lefty. The next class session, I might review and add the previously discussed material of five-finger position so their piano practice for the class session would be four videos, C Major Five Finger Position Right Hand, C Major Five Finger Position

Left Hand, C Major One-Octave Scale Right Hand, C Major One-Octave Scale Left Hand. The following session, I will announce what the Piano Practice for the day is, usually no more than four videos a day, and students can begin their practice as they come into the class.

A few minutes of piano practice a day goes a long way in reinforcing skills and helps students become more comfortable at the piano keyboard. I always find that each new topic somehow finds it's way into student music without even requiring it. Students learn chords and arpeggios and suddenly they appear in their compositions.

C MAJOR Scales & Chords

LEFT HAND

RIGHT HAND ★ = MIDDLE C

FIVE FINGER POSITION

FIVE FINGER POSITION

SCALES: 1 OCTAVE

SCALES: 1 OCTAVE

SCALES: 2 OCTAVES

SCALES: 2 OCTAVES

ARPEGGIOS: 1 OCTAVE

ARPEGGIOS: 1 OCTAVE

ARPEGGIOS: 2 OCTAVES

ARPEGGIOS: 2 OCTAVES

C MAJOR TRIAD (I ROOT POSITION)

C MAJOR TRIAD (I ROOT POSITION)

F MAJOR TRIAD (IV ROOT POSITION)

F MAJOR TRIAD (IV ROOT POSITION)

G MAJOR TRIAD (V ROOT POSITION)

G MAJOR TRIAD (V ROOT POSITION)

F MAJOR

F MAJOR Scales & Chords

LEFT HAND	RIGHT HAND
	 ★ = Middle C

Five Finger Position

Five Finger Position

Scales: 1 Octave

Scales: 1 Octave

Scales: 2 Octaves

Scales: 2 Octaves

Arpeggios: 1 Octave

Arpeggios: 1 Octave

Arpeggios: 2 Octaves

Arpeggios: 2 Octaves

F Major Triad (I Root Position)

F Major Triad (I Root Position)

B flat Major Triad (IV Root Position)

B flat Major Triad (IV Root Position)

C Major Triad (V Root Position)

C Major Triad (V Root Position)

G

G MAJOR Scales & Chords

LEFT HAND

FIVE FINGER POSITION

SCALES: 1 OCTAVE

SCALES: 2 OCTAVES

ARPEGGIOS: 1 OCTAVE

ARPEGGIOS: 2 OCTAVES

G MAJOR TRIAD (I ROOT POSITION)

C FLAT MAJOR TRIAD (IV ROOT POSITION)

D MAJOR TRIAD (V ROOT POSITION)

RIGHT HAND   ★ = MIDDLE C

FIVE FINGER POSITION

SCALES: 1 OCTAVE

SCALES: 2 OCTAVES

ARPEGGIOS: 1 OCTAVE

ARPEGGIOS: 2 OCTAVES

G MAJOR TRIAD (I ROOT POSITION)

C MAJOR TRIAD (IV ROOT POSITION)

D MAJOR TRIAD (V ROOT POSITION)

INVERSIONS

C MAJOR Inversions

LEFT HAND | **RIGHT HAND** | ★ = Middle C

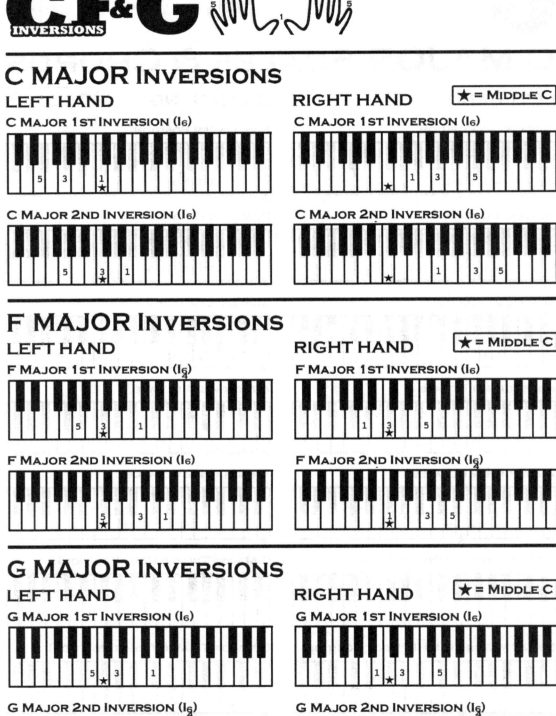

F MAJOR Inversions

LEFT HAND | **RIGHT HAND** | ★ = Middle C

G MAJOR Inversions

LEFT HAND | **RIGHT HAND** | ★ = Middle C

D MAJOR Scales & Chords

LEFT HAND

RIGHT HAND ★ = Middle C

FIVE FINGER POSITION

FIVE FINGER POSITION

SCALES: 1 OCTAVE

SCALES: 1 OCTAVE

SCALES: 2 OCTAVES

SCALES: 2 OCTAVES

ARPEGGIOS: 1 OCTAVE

ARPEGGIOS: 1 OCTAVE

ARPEGGIOS: 2 OCTAVES

ARPEGGIOS: 2 OCTAVES

D MAJOR TRIAD (I ROOT POSITION)

D MAJOR TRIAD (I ROOT POSITION)

G MAJOR TRIAD (IV ROOT POSITION)

G MAJOR TRIAD (IV ROOT POSITION)

A MAJOR TRIAD (V ROOT POSITION)

A MAJOR TRIAD (V ROOT POSITION)

C MAJOR PRACTICAL CHORD PROGRESSIONS

LEFT HAND **RIGHT HAND** ★ = MIDDLE C

C MAJOR ROOT POSITION (I)

F MAJOR 2ND INVERSION (IV$_4^6$)

G MAJOR 1ST INVERSION (V$_6$)

G MAJOR PRACTICAL CHORD PROGRESSIONS

LEFT HAND **RIGHT HAND** ★ = MIDDLE C

G MAJOR ROOT POSITION (I)

C MAJOR 2ND INVERSION (IV$_6$)

D MAJOR 1ST INVERSION (V$_6$)

A MAJOR Scales & Chords

LEFT HAND

★ = Middle C

RIGHT HAND

Five Finger Position
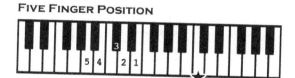

Five Finger Position

Scales: 1 Octave

Scales: 1 Octave

Scales: 2 Octaves

Scales: 2 Octaves

Arpeggios: 1 Octave

Arpeggios: 1 Octave

Arpeggios: 2 Octaves

Arpeggios: 2 Octaves

A Major Triad (I Root Position)

A Major Triad (I Root Position)

D Major Triad (IV Root Position)
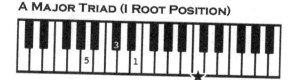

D Major Triad (IV Root Position)

E Major Triad (V Root Position)
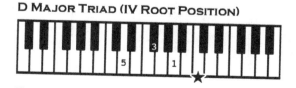

E Major Triad (V Root Position)

INSTRUMENT RANGE/EQ CHART

© 2001 Charles Houghton-Webb & BW Music
www.bwmusic.com

The black and white keys show the range of a standard concert piano.
Keys in light blue, from C0 to G#0 can be found on pianos such as
the Bösendorfer Model 290 "Imperial" Concert Grand.

N.B. The information contained herein is correct as far as can be ascertained, but its exactitude cannot be guaranteed.

This chart is used with permission by bwmusic.com

APPENDIX C Resources

Commercially Available Software

Abelton Live: www.ableton.com.

Apple: GarageBand, Logic: www.apple.com.

AudioMulch: www.audiomulch.com.

Avid (digidesign and M-Audio): ProTools, Sibelius, Scorch, Groovy: www.avid.com.

MakeMusic: Finale, SmartMusic: http://makemusic.com.

MOTU: AudioDesk, Digital Performer, MachFive: www.motu.com.

Sony: Acid, Sound Forge: www.sonycreativesoftware.com/acidsoftware.

Steinberg Products: Cubase, Sequel, Nuendo, Wavelab: www.steinberg.net/en/products.

Web 2.0 Software

Aviary: Myna, Roc: free audio recording, editing, and loops creator: http://advanced.aviary.com.

Audacity: free download audio recording and editing: http://audacity.sourceforge.net.

EAMIR: Keyboard Viewer, Mouse-Control, LazyGuy, padKontrol, GuitarEAMIR-o, DDR, and more: www.eamir.net.

Noteflight: free and paid notation online: www.noteflight.com.

MusicTechTeacher by Karen Garrett: free resources, lessons, online games and quizzes: www.musictechteacher.com.

MuseScore: free and paid notation online: http://musescore.org.

Sony: Acid Express: free limited version of Acid: www.acidplanet.com/downloads/xpress.

Soundation: online use http://soundation.com.

Music Theory/History and Other Resources

Ricci Adam: www.musictheory.net/index.html.

Dolmetsch: www.dolmetsch.com/ourresources.htm.

Toeria: http://teoria.com.

Musiccards.net: flash cards: http://musicards.net.

Printed Music

Petrucci Music Library: http://imslp.org/wiki/Main_Page.

Band Music PDF Library: www.bandmusicpdf.org.

Choral Music Public Domain Library: www.choralwiki.org/wiki.

Bibliography

Ainis, Jeffrey, William Russo, and David Stevenson. *Composing Music: A New Approach.* Chicago: University of Chicago Press, 1988.

Benward, Bruce, and Gary White. *Music in Theory and Practice.* 2 vols. Boston: McGraw Hill, 1998.

Burns, Amy. *Technology Integration for the Elementary Classroom.* Milwaukee: Hal Leonard, 2008.

Caltabiano, Ronald. "Melody." In *MUS231: Counterpoint.* San Francisco: San Francisco School of Music and Dance. Available at http://userwww.sfsu.edu/~rcalt/231/pdfs/231_all.pdf, accessed July 29, 2012.

Dennis, Robert. "Equalization by the Octave." *Recording Engineer's Quarterly,* April 2000. Available at www.recordingeq.com/EQ/req0400/OctaveEQ.htm, accessed July 29, 2012.

Fein, Michael, James Frankel, Robin Hodson, and Richard McCready. *Making Music with GarageBand and Mixcraft.* Boston: Cengage Technology, 2001.

Foreman, Greg, and Kyle Pace. *Integrating Technology with Music Instruction.* Van Nuys: Alfred, 2008.

Frankel, James. *The Teachers Guide to Music, Media, and Copyright Law.* New York: Hal Leonard Books, 2009.

Gibson, Bill. *The S.M.A.R.T. Guide to Mixing and Mastering Audio Recordings.* Boston: Thompson Course Technology, 2006.

Gibson, Bill. *Sound Advice on Compressors, Limiters, Expanders and Gates.* Vallejo: ProAudio Press, 2002.

Gibson, Bill. *Sound Advice on Equalizers, Reverbs and Delays.* Vallejo: ProAudio Press, 2002.

Gibson, David. *The Art of Mixing: A Visual Guide to Recording, Engineering, and Production.* Boston: Thompson Course Technology PTR, 2005.

Hewitt, Michael. *Composition for Computer Musicians.* Boston: Cengage Technology, 2009.

Hewitt, Michael. *Harmony for Computer Musicians.* Boston: Cengage Technology, 2009.

Hewitt, Michael. *Music Theory for Computer Musicians.* Boston: Cengage Technology, 2008.

Hodson, Robin. *ProTools in Music Education.* New York: Hal Leonard Books, 2011.

Hosken, Dan. *An Introduction to Music Technology.* New York: Routledge, 2011.

Hosken, Dan. *Music Technology and the Project Studio.* New York: Routledge, 2011.

Kornfeld, Jono. *Music Notation and Theory for Intelligent Beginners.* Rev. 2005. Available at www.jkornfeld.net/theory_text.htm, accessed July 29, 2012.

Lancaster, E. L., and Kenon D. Renfrow. *Alfred's Piano 101.* 2 vols. Van Nuys: Alfred, 1999.

Manzo, V. J. *Max/MSP/Jitter for Music: A Practical Guide to Developing Interactive Music Systems for Education and More.* New York: Oxford University Press, 2012.

Reimer, Bennett. "Music Education as Aesthetic Education: Past and Present." *Music Educators Journal* 75, no. 6 (February 1989): 22–28. Available at www.jstor.org/stable/10.2307/3398124.

Reimer, Bennett. "Music Education as Aesthetic Education: Toward the Future." *Music Educators Journal* 75, no. 7 (March 1989): 26–32. Available at www.jstor.org/stable/10.2307/3400308.

Rimsky-Korsakov, Nicolay. *Principles of Orchestration.* 1891. Reprint, Berlin, Garritan Interactive, April 2006. Available at www.northernsounds.com/forum/forumdisplay.php/77-Principles-of-Orchestration-On-line, accessed July 29, 2012.

Rudolph, Thomas E. *Teaching Music with Technology.* Chicago: GIA, 2004.

Paynter, John, *Music in the Secondary School Curriculum.* London: Cambridge University Press, 1982.

The Open University. *Composing with MIDI*. Available at www.open.edu/openlearn/science-maths-technology/engineering-and-technology/composing-midi, accessed July 29, 2012.

The Open University. *Music Technology Course*. Available at www3.open.ac.uk/study/undergraduate/course/ta212.htm, accessed July 29, 2012.

Thompson, Daniel M. *Understanding Audio: Getting the Most out of Your Project or Professional Recording Studio*. Boston: Berklee Press, 2005.

Wajler, Zig. *Mr. Zig's Literacy, Music and Technology Connection*. Van Nuys: Alfred, 2009.

Watson, Scott. *Using Technology to Unlock Musical Creativity*. New York: Oxford University Press, 2011.

White, Paul. *Basic Mixing Techniques*. London: SMT Sanctuary , 2000.

Interview with Sax. *Live at Tainted Blue: EQ Basics* 1.6 (video series). June 18, 2011. Video produced by WinkSound. Available at www.youtube.com/watch?v=88T_3_w2-4Y.

Index